Sir John A.

Sir John A.

An Anecdotal Life of John A. Macdonald

Edited by
Cynthia M. Smith with Jack McLeod

Toronto
OXFORD UNIVERSITY PRESS
1989

Oxford University Press, 70 Wynford Drive, Don Mills, Ontario, M3C 1J9

Toronto Oxford New York Delhi Bombay Calcutta Madras Karachi
Petaling Jaya Singapore Hong Kong Tokyo Nairobi Dar es Salaam
Cape Town Melbourne Auckland

and associated companies in
Berlin Ibadan

To D.C. and Margaret Thomas

CANADIAN CATALOGUING IN PUBLICATION DATA
Main entry under title:

Sir John A.: an anecdotal life of John A. Macdonald

Includes bibliographical references.
ISBN 0-19-540681-8

1. Macdonald, John A. (John Alexander), Sir,
1815-1891 – Anecdotes. 2. Canada – Politics and
government – 1867-1896 – Anecdotes.* 3. Canada –
Politics and government – 1841-1867 – Anecdotes.
4. Prime ministers – Canada – Anecdotes.   I. Smith,
Cynthia M.   II. McLeod, Jack, 1932-

FC521.M3S57 1989   971.05'092'4   C89-094795-3
75325   F1033.M3S57 1989

Selection copyright © Oxford University Press Canada
Introduction copyright © Cynthia M. Smith and Jack McLeod
OXFORD is a trademark of Oxford University Press
Printed and bound in Canada
by
T. H. Best Printing Company Limited

CONTENTS

INTRODUCTION

At the funeral of Canada's first and greatest prime minister, one of his loyal supporters was asked if he knew Sir John A. Macdonald. He replied, 'For thirty years I have known no other name.' Modern generations of Canadians must also know Sir John and his works if they are to understand the roots of this country's history and politics, for Macdonald's name and Canada were once almost synonymous. More than any other figure in our past, John A. created Canada, and he created it according to a carefully considered design.

Canada was to be British North America, conservative in its institutions, a monarchy within the parliamentary tradition, clearly separate from the United States, with a centralized federal system and an economy built on an east-west axis extending from the Atlantic to the Pacific. Macdonald's 'National Policy' of state-fostered economic growth and protectionism was in many ways the polar opposite of the 1989 Free Trade Agreement. Party philosophies often do change, but it is obvious that Brian Mulroney is not a Tory of Sir John's stamp. Probably John A. would not regard many contemporary Conservative policies as compatible with his principles.

To achieve his goals, Macdonald employed every possible stratagem and manoeuvre, plus some impossible tricks he invented himself. He was a political craftsman with no peer in the Dominion. Much of what he achieved can be attributed to the compelling power of his own rough-hewn personality. Today it is difficult to recall how immediate and personal politics was in the nineteenth century. No Canadian politician ever towered above public life and his party more completely than John A., or aroused more intense emotions. Accustomed as we now are to politics as media-packaged showbiz, to sleek politicians coached and cosmetized for television, reading speeches written by hucksters on the basis of ephemeral polls interpreted by professional 'spin-doctors', we find it hard to believe that in Macdonald's day a politician could be known so intimately by so many, warts and all, and could govern largely by the force of individual character, ideas, and guile.

Sir John Alexander Macdonald was a statesman and gifted political innovator, but also a rascal. This light-hearted wizard who drank and caroused managed to capture the imagination of Canadians as few men ever have or will. If his faults and foibles were extravagant, his accomplishments were extraordinary—and lasting. Enshrined in the history texts as the Father of Confederation, he is also cherished in Canadian political lore as our most lovable politician.

Master politicians, like others who rise to the top of their professions, are often narrow people with a single strength, but Macdonald was a complete man, functioning and flourishing on many levels of human experience: lawyer, husband, father, friend, politician, wit, raconteur, administrator, self-taught thinker, architect of a nation. The texture of his life was as rich and varied as his achievements. His colonial world was far from the centres of world power and culture, yet he created something vast and enduring from limited material.

Founding a new nation is always difficult, but Macdonald and the other Fathers of Confederation had less than, say, George Washington to build upon. Comparisons suggest that Sir John was much the greater and more interesting man. Washington worked from a founding Declaration and constitution drafted by the leading intellectuals of his society, and presided over a large population with a rich and growing economy; John A. began with scarcely four million scattered and impecunious people, jealous of their long-standing regional differences, and he had to invent a constitutional framework largely on his own. If a nation is defined as a group of people bound together by the ties of common language, common religion, shared beliefs and traditions, Canada was not a nation in any orthodox sense. But Macdonald made it one. In the shadow of the burgeoning giant to the south, faced with American claims of their 'Manifest Destiny' to overrun the continent, bedevilled by Fenian raids on the borders, and struggling with divisive forces of language, religion, and regionalism that threatened him at every turning, Macdonald somehow managed to create, expand, and consolidate a transcontinental political nation. More than any other man, he coaxed that nation into being, and he dominated its public life until its foundations were firm.

By today's standards he was a right-wing politician; he organized and led a party that was emphatically conservative, and founded the new nation on firm Tory principles. Canada in his time was not a republic or a complete democracy, but a constitutional monarchy. British North America was, in spite of all threats and pressures, not American. John A. was Canada's first major political and economic nationalist: his anti-revolutionary state, built upon a long tradition and a deeply felt past, aspired towards a bright, unique future.

Although John A. was a staunch defender of continuity and tradition, he was by no means a man of the privileged classes. He was, in fact, a poor immigrant, brought from Scotland to Kingston in Upper Canada in 1820, when he was five years old. His father, an unsuccessful merchant, was twice bankrupt and ended his life as a bank clerk. Young John Alexander received no privileges in his schooling; after five years of grammar school he was apprenticed to a lawyer at the age of fifteen, and was admitted to the bar at twenty-one. He read widely and deeply, becoming an educated man in spite of his modest circumstances. Although he was a director of several companies and speculated in real estate, he never acquired wealth through either business or politics. His career was always centred on public life, first as an alderman in Kingston from 1843 to 1846, and after 1844 as a member of the Legislature of the Province of Canada. Briefly occupying a cabinet post in 1847, he became a major figure in Liberal-Conservative administrations after 1854, and was joint Premier (with Étienne-Paschal Taché and later George-Étienne Cartier) from 1857 to 1862.

English and French Canada had been brought together by the Act of Union in 1841, but by 1864 political deadlock between Upper and Lower Canada had become vexatious. In the Reformers' view, voiced by Grit leader and Toronto *Globe* editor George Brown, the interests of Upper Canada were thwarted by the 'domination' of French Canadians. One potential solution was to adopt a federal system, possibly including all the colonies of British North America. When Brown offered a coalition to press this ambitious scheme, Macdonald and Cartier accepted.

Fortuitous circumstances helped. In September 1864 a conference had been called at Charlottetown, Prince Edward Island, to explore a proposed union of the Maritime colonies. John A., together with other representatives of Canada, attended and successfully urged the more extensive plan. The Quebec Conference that followed saw seventy-two resolutions passed to affirm agreements made at Charlottetown, and between December 1866 and February 1867, at the London Conference, these resolutions were translated into detailed legislation: the British North America Act, proclaimed on 1 July 1867.

Confederation had not been his idea originally, but with help from Cartier and A.T. Galt, Macdonald was the principal draughtsman of the constitution and took the lead in making Confederation a reality. For his skilful efforts and expert guidance of the negotiations, Queen Victoria award him the title of Knight Com-

mander of the Bath (KCB) and henceforth he was Sir John A. With the
proclamation of the BNA Act he was sworn in as Canada's first prime
minister.

Great as this achievement was, adding flesh and muscle to the
constitutional bone proved no easier a task. The North-West Territories were created with the purchase of Rupert's Land from the
Hudson's Bay Company, and Manitoba became the fifth province
of the Dominion in 1870. British Columbia was enticed to join in
1871 through the promise of a transcontinental railway. Prince
Edward Island entered the Confederation in 1873, and Sir John A.'s
government pressed on with construction of the Intercolonial Railway to link Quebec City with Halifax.

But the going was hard. Newfoundland decided to remain outside
the federation, and there were serious objections to the new nation
from New Brunswick and Nova Scotia. On the Red River in the
North West the Métis leader Louis Riel led a rebellion in 1870, and
it was clear that the Americans coveted the largely empty Territories. The organization and financing of a company to build the
railroad to the Pacific also proved troublesome.

Dealing with these and other problems taxed the prime minister's
skills. The burdens of day-to-day administration and the clamorous
demands for patronage tried his patience and drained his energies.
Much of his time was devoted to the building of a cohesive party—
for a government always needed a majority in parliament—and an
efficient party machine had to be created.

Unlike the Grit leader George Brown, John A. was not prickly,
and he could appreciate the French and get along with them. He
knew that his party had to be flexible, broad, and above all moderate
and non-doctrinaire, willing to negotiate with dissidents like Nova
Scotia's Joseph Howe and include them in the cabinet, willing to
listen to and accommodate the interests of Quebec. As early as 1856
John A. had written to an anglophone Montreal journalist: 'No man
in his senses can suppose that this country can for a century to come
be governed by a totally unfrenchified government. If a lower
Canada British desires to conquer he must "stoop to conquer". He
must make friends with the French. . . . Treat them as a nation and
they will act as a free people generally do—generously.'

A pan-Canadian party would have to be inclusive and pragmatic,
dealing with conditions and people as it found them. Aware of his
own human frailties, Sir John could understand and make use of the
frailties of others. He played the political game in the same manner,
cajoling here, rewarding loyalty there, tempting and jollying along
those who expected positions and preferments, or who merely
wished to bask in the glow of his approbation. He was capable of

passion and friendship, but also of manipulation, largely through his shrewdness, jocular ways, and extraordinary charm. A plain, House of Commons man, no great orator but always capable of playing on the susceptibilities of his listeners, always ready with a story or a quip to make his point, Sir John was a superb political orchestrator and party leader. Certainly there were those who feared and hated him, but there were more who loved him. Pierre Trudeau's phrase 'le style c'est l'homme lui-même' could well have been applied to Macdonald; his style was not that of the earnest and righteous politician, but of the canny, laughing Celtic Highlander who understood human nature and knew how to take risks. His manner and dress (particularly his waistcoats) could be flamboyant; there was a rumpled jauntiness about him, a devil-may-care air, a breath of smoky back rooms and a whiff of whisky. He revelled in feisty politics, and perhaps needed that bracing camaraderie as an antidote to the trials of office and the torments of a tragic personal life.

That he drank, and often over-indulged, is beyond question. In those days liquor flowed freely and cheaply in Canada, especially in public life; the bar in the parliamentary restaurant was a well-patronized institution. Public setbacks and political crises often prompted drinking bouts. But Macdonald had more reasons than most to seek liquid solace, for in his personal life he was scarred and disappointed. His first wife, Isabella, was an invalid who after a long decline died in 1857. He had a son by that marriage who survived, Hugh John, later a premier of Manitoba, but his first son died as a baby. After ten years as a widower, he married Susan Agnes Bernard in 1867, but their daughter Mary, born hydrocephalic, forever pulled at his heart. Thus his bouts with the bottle were understandable, and there was abundant evidence, as he himself said, that the voters preferred John A. drunk to George Brown sober.

During the summer of 1870 Macdonald was so desperately ill with painful gallstones that it was feared he might not live. His personal financial affairs were discovered to be strained, and a fund was raised by his supporters to provide his family with greater security. He rallied, and with Cartier conducted the intricate negotiations with Sir Hugh Allan's company to begin construction of the railroad to the Pacific. After winning the election of 1872 with an uncomfortably small majority, Sir John was rocked by accusations and damaging revelations of large contributions to his campaign fund from Allan. The Canadian Pacific Railway scandal of 1873 caused Macdonald to stumble, and to drink, before his government was defeated in the House in November. Many believed that his public life was finished.

A Liberal government was formed by Alexander Mackenzie, who carried the election of 1874. Economic depression and the Liberal reluctance to spend brought the railway project to a halt while Sir John licked his wounds and withdrew to the practice of law in Toronto. However, the party organization he had built, sustained by mass political picnics and the dream of a rail link to the west coast, proved as resilient as its leader. By 1876 John A. was advocating a 'readjustment' of the tariff, a policy that helped him vault back into power in the election of 1878. Once again in office, Macdonald elaborated the National Policy of high protective tariffs against the United States, railroad construction, and the encouragement of western immigration and settlement by which the Conservative government would create an east-west economy and offset the north-south pull.

But the Canadian Pacific Railway Company, heavily subsidized and protected by the state and re-organized to exclude American financial interests, faced enormous obstacles. Chartered in 1880, the new syndicate headed by George Stephen pushed the rails through the rock and muskeg of the Precambrian Shield, the vast emptiness of the prairies, and the formidable barrier of the Rocky Mountains. To fulfil his dream of westward expansion, Macdonald had to weather many political and financial storms and stake his career as well as his government's life on the completion of the CPR. The stakes were staggering. Daring—technical, financial, and political—was required before the line of steel could reach the Pacific in 1885. If it was 'private enterprise at public expense', he believed it necessary; like the creation of the CBC fifty years later, it was a question of 'the state or the United States'. There were those who believed that the railroad would bankrupt the country, who joked that Canada was not a nation but a railroad in search of a nation. Yet the bold concept was realized, and again the principal architect of the grand design was Sir John A. Macdonald. In the summer of 1886, when he and Lady Agnes travelled over the new line to Vancouver, John A. had every reason to rejoice in a triumph of nation-building far beyond the dreams of ordinary men.

The settlement of the west was now assured. A second Indian and Métis uprising led by Louis Riel was put down by troops transported by rail in 1885. This was not Sir John's finest hour. In his western policy 'Old Tomorrow' had postponed too much for too long. There is evidence to suggest that although he was himself the Superintendent of Indian Affairs, he neglected or misunderstood the fears and grievances of the Métis and native people. The hanging of Riel increased tensions between French- and English-speaking Canadians and weakened Conservative political support in Quebec. Nonetheless, the militia and the redcoats of the Royal North West Mounted Police imposed 'peace, order and good government' on a territory almost the size of western Europe, and with these vast plains secured to the Dominion, Sir John could turn his attention to other problems.

Not the least of these was the Liberal cry for tariff reduction and commercial reciprocity with the United States. Macdonald had easily defeated Edward Blake in the election of 1887, but the new Liberal leader, Wilfrid Laurier, posed a more serious challenge in 1891, particularly on the trade question. One last time the 'Old Chieftain' gathered his waning strength and his supporters, denouncing reciprocity with the US as 'veiled treason', a 'sellout' to the Americans. Appealing to the old Imperial spirit and wrapping himself in the Union Jack, emphasizing the themes of nationalism and loyalty, Sir John defiantly proclaimed: 'A British subject I was born, a British subject I hope to die.'

He won the 1891 election, but his energy had been sapped. When the voting results came in, he was in bed, grey and exhausted. Two months later he was dead.

The publication in 1988 of our *Oxford Book of Canadian Political Anecdotes* prompted many kind readers to suggest further collections, and we found that we had far more material on Sir John A. than on any other politician, material omitted from the first book for reasons of balance and space.

Immediately after Macdonald's death in 1891 the journalist E.B. Biggar put together *An Anecdotal Life of Sir John A. Macdonald*. It is a charming and lively work, the source of many an after-dinner speech, but it has been out of print for almost a hundred years. Consideration was given to a simple reprint of Biggar; however, that seemed inappropriate because of the important contributions to our knowledge of John A. by scholarly historians and popular writers in recent years. Biggar seemed too thin and dated, and we will have failed in our intention if we do not lead a new generation of readers not only to appreciate Macdonald the man, but to read more widely from the shelf of excellent books on Sir John now available. Our aim here is not to offer a formal history or a scholarly re-interpretation of his life, but to use the agreeable anecdotal method to present him to people, particularly young people, unfamiliar with his life and times, his wit and wisdom.

Foremost among the books on Macdonald, of course, is the magisterial biography by Donald G. Creighton, *John A. Macdonald* (Macmillan, 1952 and 1955).

No living Canadian historian writes with more grace, wit, or insight than P.B. Waite, whose *Macdonald: His Life and World* (McGraw-Hill Ryerson, 1975) is a delight, a short book in a good series on prime ministers written primarily for students; it is a shame that this work is not more widely known and more readily available. A handsome and wonderfully illustrated volume by Lena Newman, *The John A. Macdonald Album* (Tundra Books), was published in 1974 and is now, like Biggar, a collector's item but found in many libraries. Larger libraries will also contain earlier works by Sir John's personal secretary, Sir Joseph Pope, and Louise Reynolds' revealing study of Agnes Macdonald. J.K. Johnson has written and edited important material, particularly *Affectionately Yours: The Letters of John A. Macdonald and His Family* (Macmillan, 1969).

Some of the most useful writing interpreting John A. to the modern reader is found in D.C. Creighton's essays *Towards the Discovery of Canada* (Macmillan, 1972); sometimes it is difficult to keep clear which are John A.'s views and which are Creighton's, so closely did the two see eye to eye. Other excellent interpretive works focus on Sir John's political thought: T.W.L. MacDermot's 'The Political Ideas of John A. Macdonald' (*Canadian Historical Review* 14, no. 3 [September, 1933]) emphasizes the pragmatic and the anti-American elements, while Rod Preece's 'The Political Wisdom of Sir John A. Macdonald' (*Cannadian Journal of Political Science* 17, no. 3 [September 1984]) shows the similarity of Macdonald's political philosophy to that of Edmund Burke.

We are grateful to Richard Landon of the Thomas Fisher Rare Book Library, University of Toronto; Mark Lerman, Acting Archivist, ARCAT; the Archives of Ontario; the Jewish Historical Society of Western Canada; and the Ontario Legislative Library for making out-of-print material available to us, and to Marc Bosc, Senator John Godfrey, and Dr Colin Pearce for contributing illuminating material. We are very much obliged to the Oxford University Press and its staff, notably Richard Teleky and Sally Livingston, and most particularly Phyllis Wilson.

C.M.S.
J.T.M.

CHRONOLOGY

Macdonald born in Glasgow, Scotland	11 January 1815
Family immigrates to Kingston, Upper Canada	July 1820
Brother Jamie killed	Spring 1822
Commences study of law with George McKenzie, Kingston	1830
Opens Napanee branch of McKenzie firm	1832
Leaves McKenzie to take over practice of ailing cousin, L.P. Macpherson, in Hallowell, Ont.	Fall 1833
Begins practice of law in Kingston	24 August 1835
Admitted to the Bar of Upper Canada	6 February 1836
Gains notoriety in defence of rebel Nils von Schoultz	November 1838
Becomes a director of and solicitor for Commercial Bank of Midland District	June 1839
Union of Upper and Lower Canada	Summer 1840
Official announcement of Kingston as new capital of Canada	6 February 1841
Father dies	19 September 1841
Enters municipal politics as member of Kingston Town Council	28 March 1843
First marriage, to Scottish cousin Isabella Clark	1 September 1843
Transfer of capital of Canada to Montreal voted	3 November 1843
Elected to Legislative Assembly	15 October 1844
Maiden speech in Legislative Assembly	19 November 1844
Appointed Queen's Counsel	19 December 1846

Appointed member of Executive Council as Receiver General	11 May 1847
Son John Alexander born in New York City	2 August 1847
Re-elected as Kingston MLA	29 December 1847
Tory government resigns	4 March 1848
Infant son dies	21 September 1848
Passage of Rebellion Losses Bill	23 February 1849
Burning of the Parliament buildings at Montreal	25 April 1849
Opposes Annexation [to US] Manifesto of Montreal merchants	October 1849
Proposes formation of British American League, Kingston and Toronto	1850
Second son, Hugh John, born	13 March 1850
Re-elected as Kingston MLA	17 December 1851
Re-elected as Kingston MLA	July 1854
Joins coalition cabinet as Attorney General, Canada West	September 1854
Becomes Prime Minister of the Province of Canada	26 November 1857
Wife, Isabella, dies	28 December 1857
Ottawa chosen as capital by Queen Victoria	December 1857
Macdonald government resigns	29 July 1858
Brown government forms and is defeated in 'Double Shuffle'; Macdonald and Cartier return to power	August 1858
Outbreak of US Civil War	12 April 1861
Mother dies	24 October 1862
Political deadlock between Canada East (Quebec) and Canada West	1862-64
Macdonald-Brown Coalition formed with the goal of uniting the British North American provinces	30 June 1864
Charlottetown Conference	1-12 September 1864

Quebec Conference	10-27 October 1864
British government accepts Quebec Resolutions	3 December 1864
Macdonald visits London with George Brown	May 1865
Rise of (US) Fenian activity	Spring 1866
Fenian invasion of Canada at Ridgeway, Ont.	31 May-2 June 1866
Pro-Confederation government elected in New Brunswick	12 June 1866
London Conference	4-24 December 1866
Introduction of the British North America Bill at Westminster	12 February 1867
Marries Susan Agnes Bernard in London	16 February 1867
Appointed Knight Commander of the Bath	29 June 1867
Third reading of the BNA Bill	8 March 1867
Confederation; Macdonald becomes Prime Minister and Minister of Justice	1 July 1867
Murder of Thomas D'Arcy McGee	1868
Daughter Mary born	8 February 1868
Failure of Commercial Bank for Midland District (of which he was a director) and consequent financial setback	April 1869
Red River Rebellion	Winter 1869-Spring 1870
Manitoba joins Confederation	May 1870
Treaty of Washington negotiations	Fall-Winter 1870-71
Tories win election	1872
Pacific Scandal	1873
Macdonald government resigns	5 November 1873
Tories lose election	1874
In opposition	1874-78
Tories re-elected	17 September 1878
John A. beaten in Kingston but elected in Marquette, Man., and Victoria, BC	September 1878

EARLY LIFE

Born in Glasgow in January 1815 to a shiftless drifter with a penchant for the bottle and a strong mother of Highland ancestry, young John Alexander Macdonald came to Kingston in 1820 with his parents, his younger brother James, and his sisters Margaret and Louisa. His family were to remain in and around Kingston for the rest of their lives.

They settled at first with prosperous relatives, the Donald Macphersons; later, when father Hugh set up as a shopkeeper, the family lived over the store. Tragedy struck early when John A.'s younger brother Jamie died as the result of a blow to the head from a drunken manservant in whose care the young boys had been left while the parents went out for the evening. The failure of his father's first shop venture, followed by a move and yet another shop failure, led the family to Hay Bay, a little west of Kingston, in their fourth year in Canada. Hugh eventually became a miller at Stone Mills at Adolphus Reach on the Bay of Quinte and made a slight success of the operation. The dependable one, however, was Macdonald's mother, Helen, who remained an example to her surviving son, a strong helper in his tragic first marriage, and a force in his life until her death in 1862.

Young John A. was at first somewhat quiet and bookish, although capable of mischief. He attended various local schools until he was about ten, when the family scraped together the money for fees, board, and lodging at the Midland District Grammar School in Kingston, headed by a former Oxonian.

He left school at fifteen—a common school-leaving age for the times—and began articles in an established Kingston law firm headed by another Scot, George McKenzie. In 1830, after a year's training, he was examined by the Benchers at Osgoode Hall to see if he could begin the formal study of law, which normally took four terms. Meanwhile he continued in articles with his Kingston mentor, and in 1832, at the ripe age of seventeen, was sent by McKenzie to set up a branch law office at Napanee.

Although still a student at law, he used his years at Napanee to bury himself in books, develop friendships, and play a few pranks that would probably have landed him in a group home under the *Young Offenders Act* of today. *By the age of twenty-one, in 1836, he had been formally admitted to the Bar and taken over the prosperous, established practice of his deceased mentor McKenzie. In his first court case, in 1838, he gained notoriety by his defence of accused rebels including Nils von Schoultz, who had led an attack on Prescott.*

His firm was to remain in Kingston, mainly engaged in commercial law, until Macdonald set up another practice in Toronto in 1874. He acquired much real estate in the 1840s and became director of a number of companies. In 1843 he ran successfully for municipal office, and in 1844 was elected to the Legislative Assembly of the United Province of Canada for the first time.

John A.'s first major trauma came at the age of seven, when he witnessed the murder of his little brother by a drunken servant.

Before they moved to Hay Bay an accident occurred, if it can be called an accident, by which his younger son lost his life in a most distressing manner. Mr Macdonald had in his employ an old soldier by the name of Kennedy, who, unknown to his employer, was addicted to drink. Going out one evening, Mr and Mrs Macdonald left the two children, John and James, aged seven and five years respectively, to the care of this man, who, as soon as his master and mistress were out of sight, resolved upon spending the evening in his own fashion. Taking the two boys with him, he made his way to the nearest tavern, where, not content with drinking himself, he endeavoured to make the children follow his example. After a great deal of persuasion, he prevailed upon them to swallow some liquor. Going to the next drinking-place, he repeated his exploit. The children, however, not liking the beverage—it was gin—stoutly resisted, and John, taking his little brother by the hand, started for home. Kennedy ran after them, and in the pursuit the younger boy fell down. As he lay on the ground, the drunken soldier struck him with his cane. The blow, the fright, and the liquor combined were too much for a child of his tender years. He fell into convulsions, and shortly afterwards died.

Joseph Pope, *Memoirs of the Right Honourable Sir John Alexander Macdonald*, vol. 1 (1894), p. 5

John A.'s nephew reported that 'little Johnnie was very fond of playing soldier. He was always captain and his two sisters were the company. One day Louisa would not march properly, but went skipping about the room to his great indignation; so he picked up an old gun, and, pointing it at her, called out in wrathful tones, "Louie, if you don't be quiet, I'll shoot you!" She still kept playing about and he repeated the threat. His sister, Margaret, got very frightened and cried out, "Oh! Johnnie, Johnnie, put that gun down," which he did, most providentially, for it was afterwards ascertained to have been loaded.'

Lena Newman, *The John A. Macdonald Album* (1974), p. 24

The student at law was typical of his age in his inability to get out of bed in the morning.

At the age of fifteen, John went into the office of George McKenzie, where he remained until the death of the latter. Mr McKenzie was good enough to also take him to board. Mrs McKenzie was a kind-hearted soul, but was much worried by the difficulty of getting John out of bed in the morning, he was such a sleepy-head. So one day, finding she couldn't rouse him, she darkened his room so that not a ray of light could enter. After a time he awakened, but found all darkness. After vainly trying to go to sleep again, he got up, drew the curtains, and looked out of the window, when, to his astonishment, he saw the men returning from their work. He was so ashamed that a similar difficulty never occurred.

J. Pennington Macpherson, *Life of the Right Hon. Sir John A. Macdonald*, vol. 1 (1891), p. 81

'I had no boyhood,' I once heard him say. 'From the age of fifteen I began to earn my own living'; and, I suspect, more than his own living. His father, though not without parts, seems to have been unequal to the responsibilities of the head of a family, and much of the burden in consequence fell upon the young man. He once related an occurrence which gives an insight into the domestic arrangements of his early home—how, on returning from school one day, he found the door locked, and had to get in through the kitchen window; how he discovered the whole family ill in bed, and but indifferently provided for; how it devolved upon him to bake the bread; how he had not the requisite knowledge for the task; and how he overcame the difficulty by carrying his invalid sister downstairs on his back, and, laying her on a sofa before the kitchen fire, kneaded the dough under her supervision.

Joseph Pope, *Memoirs of the Right Honourable Sir John Alexander Macdonald*, vol. 1 (1894), p. 6

Although a law student, he was not above the pranks of the local Napanee teenagers.

One of the characters of the place was a burly and jolly-faced hotelkeeper named Bob Hopkins, who was very fond of fast horses, and never drove through the village but at a breakneck pace, which attracted everybody's attention. While Bob was down the village one night, John A. and the boys conceived the idea of checking his mad career homeward by building a rail fence across the road. This being done, the boys . . . lay off in the grass. . . . And they did not have to wait long till the buggy of Bob Hopkins was heard rattling up the street. Along came the horse at his usual impetuous pace, and dashed full tilt against the fence. There was a distant roar of laughter and a stampede, but the poor horse came out of the encounter maimed, the buggy was smashed, and Bob arose from the wreck a most astonished but, happily, uninjured man. The magistrate, a sort of Justice Shallow, heard of the case the next day, and felt that something must be done. Somebody must be punished, and so he caused the arrest, on suspicion, of a man who was not one of the party at all, and had not even heard of the affair. But there were some unexplained circumstances about his whereabouts on that evening, and the poor fellow was actually on the point of being convicted, when young Macdonald's sense of justice compelled him to go to the magistrate and confess that he was the ringleader, and that the accused was perfectly innocent. How the perpetrator managed to put the case so as to escape arrest himself is not known, but he afterwards, in telling the story, said the incident impressed him strongly with the doubtfulness of circumstantial evidence.

E.B. Biggar, *Anecdotal Life of Sir John Macdonald* (1891), p. 32

. . . he [Macdonald] and three or four chums were going home one summer night, when on Rear Street they observed the roadway covered with limestone to be used as a foundation for the street. Macdonald suggested that as it was yet early, —one o'clock—they would have time to build a pretty decent sized wall with the material.

'Where shall we build the wall?' was the query.

'Well,' said Macdonald, 'there is Jemmy Williamson's grocery story just across the street.'

'What's the matter with it?'

'It would not look amiss with a nice new stone front added to it.'

All agreed, and to work they went. For two hours they never worked so hard in their lives. At the end of that time they had completed a wall about seven feet high and eight feet long, completely closing up the shop door. They then gathered up small stones, and throwing a few at a time at the up-stairs windows, where the old gentleman slept, they awoke him, and raising the window, he inquired, 'Who's there? what's the matter?' Hearing nothing he closed the window, but the stones were again flung, and the window again went up. Hearing nothing he again retired. Presently, a light appeared in the room, and the conspirators guessed the old gentleman was making his way downstairs. They crowded close to the stone wall to hear how Jemmy would express his surprise.

They heard the door open, and the first exclamation was one of profound astonishment,—'My God! what is this I see? Has the house tumbled down since I went to bed? What does this thing mean? What sin have I committed that this horror should fall on me?'

Macdonald said they heard no more. They hurried home, reaching it before daylight.

Macdonald said he passed the store the next day, and the wall had vanished. 'And,' said Macdonald, 'were it not for the fact of the circumstance being mentioned in the papers, I should have been inclined to think it was all a dream.'

Ibid., pp. 46-7

As a teenaged law student, Macdonald lacked restraint in court.

In his first case, which was at Picton, Mr Macdonald and the opposing counsel became involved in an argument, which, waxing hotter and hotter, culminated in blows. They closed and fought in open court, to the scandal of the judge, who immediately instructed the crier [the clerk of the court] to enforce order. This crier was an old man, personally much attached to Mr Macdonald, in whom he took a lively interest. In pursuance of his duty, however, he was compelled to interfere. Moving towards the combatants, and circling round them, he shouted in stentorian tones, 'Order in the court, order in the court,' adding in a low, but intensely sympathetic voice as he passed near his protégé, 'Hit him, John!' I have heard Sir John Macdonald say that, in many a parliamentary encounter of after years, he has seemed to hear, above the excitement of the occasion, the voice of the old crier whispering in his ear the words of encouragement, 'Hit him, John!'

Joseph Pope, *Memoirs of the Right Honourable Sir John Alexander Macdonald*, vol. 1 (1894), pp. 8-9

John A. was always an avid reader.

Less than a month after his return to Kingston, he formed the idea of starting a literary association, and drew up a paper, the original of which, in his own handwriting, lies before me. It bears the signatures of John A. Macdonald, A. Campbell, T. Kirkpatrick, Henry Smith, and several other well-known Kingstonians. . . .

'The undersigned, convinced of the advantages to be gained by the formation of an association for the cultivation of literature—for the discussion (under proper restrictions) of the various subjects which ought to interest society—and for the formation of a library —do agree to unite themselves in such an association under the name of "The Cataraqui Club". The preparation of the rules for the association to be left to Messrs Forsyth, T. Kirkpatrick. S.F. Kirkpatrick. H. Smith. F.M. Hill, and J.A. Macdonald. Such rules to be reported at a meeting to be held in the library of Macdonald and Campbell on the first Monday after the close of the present assizes. —Court House, 11th April, 1848.'

Ibid., p. 61

His first platform for election to the Legislative Assembly was simple.

To the Free and Independent Electors of the Town of Kingston.

GENTLEMEN,—The approaching election calls upon me to redeem the pledge made in March last, in answer to the flattering requisition addressed to me by 225 electors, inviting me to become a candidate for the representation of this town.

A residence in Kingston since infancy has afforded every opportunity to *me* of knowing the wants and claims of our "Loyal Old Town"—and to *you* of ascertaining my political opinions and my qualifications for the office I now solicit at your hands.

I therefore, need scarcely state my firm belief, that the prosperity of Canada depends upon its permanent connection with the mother country, and that I shall resist to the utmost, any attempt (from whatever quarter it may come), which may tend to weaken that union.

The proposed measures for reducing the enormous expense of the public departments, for improving the system of common schools, and for opening and extending the advantages of our Collegiate Institutes, will receive my cordial support.

It is alike my duty and my interest to promote the prosperity of this city and the adjacent country. No exertion will be spared by me in forwarding the settlement of our rear townships, by the formation of public roads, in assisting and concentrating the trade of this port, and in such other local measures as will in any way conduce to your advantage.

I am deeply grateful for the confidence you have already reposed in me, and trusting that I have done nothing to forfeit it,

I have the honor to be,
Your obliged and
Faithful servant,
JOHN A. MACDONALD.

KINGSTON, *October* 5, 1844.

> J. Pennington Macpherson, *Life of Right Hon. Sir John A. Macdonald*, vol. 1 (1891), p. 93

MARRIAGE AND FAMILY LIFE I

Personal happiness seemed always to elude John A. Yet he was close to his mother and sisters, who proved the mainstays of his life prior to his second marriage. The most complete descriptions of his marriage to his cousin Isabella Clark are given by her nephew J. Pennington Macpherson, in a two-volume memoir begun in 1873 and published in 1891. It is from him that we learn that Isabella was pretty, gentle, and playful, and that John A. was smitten when they met. A chronic invalid from shortly after they married in 1843, Isabella nevertheless bore two healthy sons, the elder of whom died from convulsions suffered in a fall when a toddler. The family correspondence reveals a bleak home life but John and Isabella made the best of a bad situation. Their surviving second son, Hugh John, born in 1850, was farmed out, at first daily and eventually on a permanent basis, to relatives and friends as his father toiled in the political realm and his mother languished in bed, her senses often dulled by strong doses of opium. More than a century later, Dr James McSherry of Queen's University speculated in Queen's Quarterly *(Autumn 1988) that her illness was at first psychosomatic and, later, consumption, of which she died in 1857. Isabella's death freed John A. from the ties of parenthood, and when these were capably assumed by his mother and sisters he devoted himself to his political career, his legal practice, his convivial evenings in Mrs Grimason's Kingston tavern, and the occasional dalliance, for it would appear that women found him charming.*

J. Pennington Macpherson, nephew of Isabella Clark Macdonald, describes his warm relationship with his new uncle John A. and the newlyweds' first domicile.

This house was situated on Brock street, was large and commodious and contained all the comforts and conveniences then known to Canadian civilization. There was also a fine carriage and a pair of horses, 'Mohawk' and 'Charlie'. Here I spent some of the happiest days of my life, being allowed the honour of sitting beside the coachman if the carriage was taken out, or at other times, the almost equally enjoyable privilege of being my uncle's companion in his library. We seldom talked: he was deep in his books, while I had a corner to myself where were gathered together, for my special delectation, numerous illustrated books and such captivating tales as 'King Arthur and his knights of the round table', 'The Arabian nights entertainment', etc., etc. I have no doubt but that I was often troublesome, but I cannot recollect ever receiving from him one unkind word. On the contrary, I was always made happy by a warm greeting, a pleasant smile, an encouraging word, or an affectionate pat on the head. Often I used to meet him on the street, when going to or from school, and then it was his delight to indulge in the pleasant fiction that he was my debtor to an unknown amount, and proceed to liquidate this debt to the extent of the half-pence he might have in his pocket.

> J. Pennington Macpherson, *Life of The Right Hon. Sir John A. Macdonald*, vol. 1 (1891), p. v

Travelling south to await the birth of their first child, the Macdonalds were obliged by Isabella's ill health to go no farther than New York, where on 2 August 1847 she delivered a son. The baby, John Alexander, was sent to be cared for by his grandmother and aunt in Kingston while Isabella recuperated in New York. John A. wrote to his sister-in-law Margaret Greene:

New York, August 31, 1847

My dearest Sister—

. . . We have only heard once about Baby since he left us. He was then well. I presume he was quite well 4 hours ago, as we have a telegraph now to Kingston & any illness would at once be communicated to me. I shall write to Maria to send you a lock of his hair, which is at present exactly of the colour of his Mother's. His eyes are dark blue, *very large* & *nose* to match. When born his length was 1 foot 9 inches & was strong & healthy though thin, but as Maria told Dr Washington, that was not to be wondered at, seeing she had been living on *pills* [opium] so long. I shall remain here until Doctor declares Isabella convalescent. Our future course can only then be determined. With united love to Jane & yourself, I am my dear sister,

most affectionately yours
John A. Macdonald
J.K. Johnson, ed., *Affectionately Yours* (1969), pp. 52-3

Addiction to opiates was not unknown in nineteenth-century Canada.

Addicts experienced no difficulty in obtaining their drugs. . . . Not only did the drugstores sell the supplies cheaply and openly but all kinds of opiate-containing patent medicines were advertised. Thus the addict of the nineteenth century had unlimited sources of supply. He could buy paregoric, laudanum, tincture of opium, morphine, Winslow's Soothing Syrup, Godfrey's Cordial, McMunn's Elixir of Opium, or many other preparations. For a few cents a day he could keep himself loaded.

Alfred R. Lindesmith, *Addiction and Opiates* as quoted in Lena Newman, *The John A. Macdonald Album* (1974), p. 41

When Isabella returned to Kingston, the Macdonalds moved into a large house called Bellevue that had been built for a retired grocer —whence its nicknames along the lines of 'Tea Caddy Castle'. They enjoyed their new home, and in spite of her pain and daily use of opium, Isa seemed happy. John A. wrote to Margaret Greene:

Kingston, August 29, 1848

I made our final move to our new habitation, on Friday evening last, my dearest sister, and we are now trying to make ourselves comfortable in Pekoe Pagoda as we call it, until Jane gives us a better name. Isabella suffered a great deal from the journey, which though less than a mile exhausted her much. Fortunately Dr Hayward was here, and accompanied us on the way. After four days' rest, she now begins to feel the advantage of the complete quiet and seclusion of the house, which is completely surrounded with trees, and has a fresh breeze ever blowing on it from Lake Ontario. I regret to say that Isa suffers tic without much if any cessation, and is obliged to take opium daily. I still am sanguine as to the effect of a week's quiet on her system.

I have had a long and serious conversation respecting Isa's health and a day or two ago, with Dr Hayward, the gentleman, you may remember, who accompanied her from New York, and who when there conferred with Dr Johnston as to his treatment. Dr Johnston was of opinion that her left lung was affected, but to what extent he could not say. She has a slight cough, and occasional exhibitions (in small quantities) of blood on her handkerchief, from her lungs. Hayward says that these symptoms, the cough & the blood of course indicate something wrong, some cause of irritation. And yet she has none of the evidences on which a medical man could state there was any ulceration. There is no appearance of pus, or of any other matter, when she coughs. Her pulse is not feverish or accelerated, and she has never shown a hectic spot on her cheek. The Doctors agree that all that can be done is to use the necessary means to stop the hemorrage when it comes and to soothe the cough when troublesome, and that nature must do the rest. Thus stands the case at present. She is in God's hands and we must abide the result.

The nurse and child came out with us, & he is in good health. He sits by the hour now with his Mother, as contentedly as possible, and smiles & crows away from one end of the day to the other. He will be weaned in about a fortnight or three weeks, as the weather becomes cooler.

J.K. Johnson, ed., *Affectionately Yours* (1969), pp. 58-9

But the parents' reunion with their child was brief.

When at, perhaps, the most endearing age [13 months], just able to toddle about and to prattle a few words in his sweet infantile language, my mother came home one day and, in tearful words, told us of convulsions and approaching death. A day or two later we were taken to see and to bid a last sorrowful farewell to the little white-robed figure, lying so still and quiet in its tiny cot in a darkened room.

J. Pennington Macpherson, *Life of the Right Hon. Sir John A. Macdonald*, vol. 1 (1891), p. vi

In spite of his mother's drug addiction, Hugh John, the Macdonalds' second son, arrived safely on 13 March 1850. As John A. wrote to his sister Margaret, the baby was spared carrying the name of his dead brother by family remonstrations.

My dear Margaret

I received your kind and considerate letter of congratulation. We have got Jonnie back again almost his image. I don't think he is so pretty, but he is not so delicate. He was born fat & coarse. Isa was very anxious that he should get his *own* name again for she considers him almost the same being, but I think it right that the feelings of those we esteem should not be outraged by doing so. Mamma, Maria, Mrs Greene & many others have a prejudice against the renaming a child. What his name may be therefore we will leave to be settled until you come up. Mrs Greene & you will arrive about the same time & I will leave it to the female conclave.

I need not say that your presence is anxiously looked for. Mamma had one of her attacks on Friday, (Good Friday) and it still hangs about her to an unsafe extent. She seems lethargic, & not so free of speech as before, but I trust the active treatment she is under may set her up again. Meanwhile it is well to be always prepared for the worst news, and if any thing went wrong I would not hesitate to advise you of it at once by telegraph.

J.K. Johnson, ed., *Affectionately Yours* (1969), p. 71

J. Pennington Macpherson remembered his cousin as a toddler.

... from the hour of his arrival, this small atom of humanity was aware of the recurrence of birthdays, Christmas Day, and other important events, and was graciously pleased to testify his approval of the conduct of his youthful friends by presents of books, balls, fishing rods, and various other articles dear to the hearts of young boys. About the time that this wonderful possessor of supernatural powers had grown to such mature age as to be able to inform the world that his name was 'Hugh John Jin', I was sent away to a boarding-school at Cornwall.

J. Pennington Macpherson, *Life of the Right Hon. Sir John A. Macdonald*, vol. 1 (1891), p. vi

John A. was all too familiar with problems of daycare. Politics, his legal practice, and his chronically ill wife forced him to scramble to find daily care for his son.

Toronto, January 26, 1856

My Dearest Mother,

Isabella has been very ill since I wrote last. She was so low one day that the doctor sent for me to my office, thinking she was dying. She has rallied wonderfully again, and though still very weak and scarcely conscious, she is evidently on the mend. I sent Hugh every day to Mrs Cameron's to keep him out of the way, and not to interfere with Janet, who was constantly employed in looking after Isabella. Hugh is very well and in good spirits. He is quite a favourite at the houses which he visits. They are Cameron's, Vankoughnet's, David Macpherson's, and Lewis Moffatt's. At all these houses there are young people, well brought up, so that he has the advantage of a good companionship. He and I play beggar-my-neighbour every evening, and you can't fancy how delighted he is when he beats me. He knows the value of the cards as well as I do, and looks after his own interests sharply.

I get lots of invitations here. I was asked out for every day last week, but I declined, of course, on account of Isa's illness. Next week, or rather this week, it is the same thing. But I am obliged to refuse as I am getting ready for Parliament.

I trust, my dear mother, you are keeping well, and that Moll is all right again. Pray give my love to her and Loo, not forgetting the Professor.

Believe me, my dear mother,
Your affectionate son,
John A. Macdonald

Joseph Pope, Memoirs of the Right Honourable Sir John
Alexander Macdonald, vol. 1 (1894), p. 160

If he seldom saw the little boy, he was fond of him.

Toronto 17 Mar. [18]56

My dearest Mother,

. . . Hugh is, thank god, in prime health. He had a party of about sixteen, on his birthday & he has not yet got over his exertions or his stories of all their doings.

His teeth are coming out now without pain. He continually talks of Kingston however, Whenever he is asked whether he likes Kingston or Toronto best, he says always, 'I like Kingston best because my Grandmother lives there'. I was a good deal out of sorts for a time but I am now all right & hard at work. . . .

J.K. Johnson, ed., The Letters of Sir John A. Macdonald
1836-1857 (1968), p. 355

John A. always quietly regretted the death of his first son. Years later his attachment to the infant was discovered.

More than thirty years after the time of which I am now writing, Lady [Agnes] Macdonald was looking over some odds and ends at Earnscliffe, when she came upon a box of child's toys—a broken rattle, a small cart, and some animals, etc. Not knowing to whom they belonged, she took them to Sir John, who was lying on his bed. He looked at them at first carelessly, then thoughtfully, raised himself on his elbow, and took one up in his hands. 'Ah!' said he, 'those were little John A.'s.' He had kept beside him these mementos of his little boy all those years. Lady Macdonald replaced the box almost reverently where she had found it, and it is there today [1878].

Joseph Pope, Memoirs of the Right Honourable Sir John
Alexander Macdonald, vol. 1 (1894), p. 62

PRE-CONFEDERATION POLITICS, 1843-64

John A. entered politics at the municipal level in Kingston, serving as alderman from 1843 to 1846. In 1844, at the age of twenty-nine, he was elected to the Legislative Assembly of the Province of Canada.

Political life in the province was confused and confusing. Governments formed and fell and re-formed with remarkable rapidity. Somewhere near the middle were the Liberal-Conservatives, a loose association of the A.N. Morin-Sir Allan MacNab followers from the government of 1854. 'All my politics are Railroads', MacNab declared, underlining the importance he attached to economic development. John A. became the dominant force in several Liberal-Conservative administrations, holding office variously as Attorney-General (from 1854), Postmaster-General, Prime Minister (from 1857), and co-Prime Minister.

The opposition groups were three: the followers of George Brown, or 'Brownites'; the 'Clear Grits', who advocated full-blown democracy and universal manhood suffrage; and in Lower Canada the no less radical and democratic Parti Rouge. Shifting combinations and re-combinations of these groups and the loosely organized moderates made stable government almost impossible.

The alliance that John A. formed with George-Étienne Cartier united the moderates of the two Canadian races. The election of 1858 saw Macdonald and Cartier out and the Brown-Dorion Reform administration in, but only for two days. The 'double shuffle' manoeuvre allowed the former to regain their seats without another election, and until May 1862 John A. remained the linchpin of government in the Province of Canada. In March 1864 he became the Attorney General and de facto Prime Minister in the 'Great Coalition' that brought about Confederation in 1867.

Much of John A.'s early work in the House was typical of a backbencher.

He was a member of the committee on standing orders, and this was the only committee to which he was appointed. It is worth a passing remark, that there were then four McDonalds in the House, and his own name was spelt indiscriminately 'Mc' and 'Mac', then and for years afterwards. The first petition he presented was from Henry Smith, warden of the penitentiary at Kingston, asking for an increase of salary: and the second was on behalf of Bishop Phelan and others of the corporation of the College of Regiopolis at Kingston, asking for an act to enable them to hold real and personal property yielding an annual revenue of £5000. Was there in the third petition the suggestion of a forecast of the National Policy? It was from Alexander Smith and others, cordwainers (boot and shoe makers), asking that a duty be put upon boots and shoes imported from the United States.

E.B. Biggar, *Anecdotal Life of Sir John Macdonald* (1891), pp. 58-9

He introduced a bill to incorporate the 'Wolf Island, Kingston & Toronto Railroad Co.', and the following week moved the second reading of the 'Montreal & Lachine Railroad' bill. In the course of the discussion, Mr McDonald, of Glengarry, said he had brought in a bill that day for a road from Montreal to Kingston, which was to form part of a great chain of railroads from Montreal to Port Sarnia, and he feared this Montreal and Lachine road would be built on such an expensive scale that no company could buy it out at a profit. He, therefore, asked Mr J.A. Macdonald to postpone his bill. Mr John A. Macdonald did not see the matter in that light at all, and said these other roads referred to were got up for speculation, and were dependent upon English capitalists, while his was an all Canadian enterprise.

Ibid., p. 62

On an amendment to an act relating to the duties on leather, Mr Cayley called attention to a despatch received that year from Hon. W.E. Gladstone, saying that unless the duties on leather, imposed by this act, were reduced, it would not receive the Royal assent. . . . Mr Macdonald of Kingston, said a bill was passed last session, giving protection to the manufacturers of the colony, and the measure now before them was to make the legislation effectual. If the members did not make up their minds to carry it through, they must give up all they had fought for and all they had gained, and resolve to put our manufactures in competition with the convict labour of the American penitentiary. With respect to Mr Gladstone's despatch, whether the principle enunciated in it were right or wrong, we must be governed by it. The danger to our markets was not from British but from American manufacturers.

Ibid., pp. 62-3

The legislative debates, the newspaper articles and the stump speeches of this era bristle with personal abuse and shrieking adjectives in a way that our more polite and more lukewarm generation can scarcely conceive. 'Wretched trickster', 'imbecile poltroon', 'jackal', 'cunning coon', 'infamous traitor', were the common coin of political debate. A staff correspondent of the *Globe* thus pictured a man with whom that journal had once acted and whom it was to endorse again before two years had passed. 'Dr Rolph is a sleek-visaged man with cold grey eyes, treacherous mouth, and lips fashioned to deceive. . . . Dark, designing, cruel, malignant, traitorous are the depths revealed to a student. His manners are civil and insinuating. A cold distrustful sneer or grin plays habitually about his oily lips, while at times glance forth expressions indicative of polished ferocity of soul, revealing the hard and stony depths beneath. In short, he is a kind of highly polished human tiger.' Less laboured, but equally effective, were the remarks on the floor of the House made by one statesman, premier of Canada [Macdonald], to another statesman, later premier of Ontario [Oliver Mowat, his former law student], 'You damned pup, I'll slap your chops for you.' An intensely exciting incident occurred in February, 1856, when George Brown, accused by Macdonald of inconsistency, retorted in burning taunts against his rival, to be answered by astounding, and as it proved baseless, charges of having when Secretary of the Penitentiary Commission in 1848 falsified testimony, 'suborned convict witnesses' and 'obtained the pardon of murderers to induce false evidence'. In the same session a passage of epithets between Macdonald and Colonel Rankin, the member for Essex, led to fears that a challenge would follow; the Sergeant-at-Arms threatened to take both into custody, but they promised to take no further action. At the close of the session Macdonald sent a friend to tell Rankin that if he would venture to repeat outside of the House any of the injurious expressions used, he would issue a challenge, of course leaving Canada for the meeting, but thanks to diplomatic friends Rankin withdrew his charges, and the matter ended.

Oscar Douglas Skelton, The Life and Times of Sir Alexander
Tilloch Galt (1920), pp. 203-4

The burning of the Legislative building, 1849.

The Tory Government had fallen, and John A. Macdonald was now in opposition, when the Rebellion Losses bill came up. A commission had sat some years before to determine the losses suffered by those who helped to put down the rebellion, and since then great and increasing pressure had been brought to bear to compensate those who suffered on the side of the rebels, as well as the loyalists, when the Radical Administration now in power decided to include all who suffered loss, and passed the bill. There was a wild outcry from the loyalists, who looked upon it as putting a premium upon rebellion. Lord Elgin, who assented to the bill, was assailed, as he passed out of the Parliament building, with brickbats, bottles and with eggs, taken from the woman who kept the green grocer's stand under the portico of the building; and at night a great crowd, assembled by the agitators, gave three cheers for the Queen, and moved down to the Parliament buildings. Shattering the windows with stones, they burst into the chamber, where a committee of the House was sitting, and when the members fled in alarm through the lobbies, they mounted the Speaker's chair and principal seats in mock deliberation, and then proceeded to wreck the furniture. The symbol of majesty, the mace, was wrested from the Sergeant-at-Arms, and borne off in triumph. Amidst the crash of broken chandeliers, the cracking of seats, and the blasphemy and shouting of the rioters, the cry of fire was raised, and all rushed out. In a few minutes the building was wrapped in flames, and a library of 20,000 volumes, containing the most valuable records of the province, almost utterly destroyed. For this, the culminating act of the mob rule of Montreal, the city was punished by the removal forever of the seat of government.

John A. Macdonald took no part in the riots. He had protested in the debate against passing the bill, and had warned the Government that they were drawing down grave dangers, not alone upon their own heads, but upon the peace of the province; and to kill time and tire out the ministry, he kept the floor through the night, reading thirty of William Lyon MacKenzie's letters. But he took no part in the riot. A bosom friend, still living, says he was not in town that night, but others say he stood a silent spectator of a rueful scene, digesting no doubt some valuable thoughts on political agitation.

E.B. Biggar, *Anecdotal Life of Sir John Macdonald* (1891), pp. 67-8

George Brown, the former editor of the Globe, *was one of John A.'s most vigorous and outspoken opponents in the 1850s. In one debate,*

. . . . Mr Brown retorted that he was sorry Mr Macdonald should so much have changed his blast as to be blowing cold in 1855 against his hot of 1852.

To this Mr Macdonald replied: 'The breath of the hon. member for Lambton himself had not always been of the same temperature. During the late elections the *Globe* came out with the cry—"Down with Rolph and Malcolm Cameron. We can stand anything else— we can stand Toryism, we can stand Sir Allan McNab and John A. Macdonald, but we cannot stand Rolph. Corrupt may be Sir Allan McNab and steeped to the chin in Toryism, and John A. Macdonald may be following in his footsteps, a budding Tory at least—they are not bad fellows, however, for Tories—but put down Rolph and Cameron.'''

The expression, 'steeped to the chin in Toryism', was only a new rendering of a phrase which John A. Macdonald had coined the year before in the debate on the address to the throne, and which was in subsequent years to be turned into a byword against himself. He said: 'There may be Walpoles among them, but there are no Pitts; they are all *steeped to the lips in corruption*; they have no bond of union but the bond of common plunder.'

Ibid., p. 71

When in 1854 a bill was introduced to erect the town of Bytown into the city of Ottawa, quite a discussion arose on the change of name. Solicitor General Smith said 'a rose by any other name would smell as sweet', but Ottawa had a pleasanter sound than Bytown. Attorney-General Macdonald (John A.) said he would not like to oppose himself to the wishes of the people, but it was really absurd to call a town by the name of the river on which it is situated. How would it do to call Paris 'Seine' or London 'Thames'? Mr Brown here remarked: 'The Hon. gentleman seems to forget that there is a scheme now on foot to change the name of Hamilton to Ontario.' (Laughter.) Sir Allan McNab objected to the change, as it was a memorial of Colonel By, who had practically created the place. Mr Powell said he had thought of such words as By-zantium and By-copolis, but none seemed to suit as well as Ottawa.

Ibid., pp. 78-9

Macdonald became Prime Minister in 1857, with George-Étienne Cartier as his chief colleague.

The difficult question of establishing the capital in a fixed place, instead of shifting from place to place as had been done in the past years, had now to be settled, and local jealousies made it hard to do. The matter had been referred to the Queen, and on the recommendation of Mr Macdonald, Ottawa was selected as the permanent capital. This was announced at the meeting of Parliament in February, 1858, and the decision was immediately challenged by the Opposition. A resolution, declaring that Ottawa should not be the seat of government, was carried by 64 to 50. Believing that the Opposition would not form a ministry that would last, when other questions were considered, Mr Macdonald accepted a challenge thrown down on a motion by Mr Brown for adjournment, and that being carried, the Macdonald-Cartier Government promptly resigned. Sir Edmund Head, the Governor, sent for Mr Brown, and the Brown-Dorion Government was formed. The result proved the fore-knowledge of Mr Macdonald, for in two days a motion of want of confidence in the new government was carried, and they were forced to resign in turn, by the refusal of the Governor-General to grant a dissolution. The Independence of Parliament Act provided that a minister resigning one office and accepting another within one month would require re-election. Mr Macdonald was now sent for, and in order to avoid going to the country for re-election all the ministers took other offices than those held before the resignation, and then changed back to their old offices. This move, which was held to be a violation of the spirit of the act, became known as the 'double shuffle'. The *coup* made a sensation throughout the country, for in many districts the news of the resignation of the Macdonald Government had not arrived when they had actually returned to power. A Toronto paper cuttingly referred to the Brown-Dorion Government as 'A ministry of two days, a thing which was and is not, before either friend or foe can realize its existence.'

Ibid., pp. 77-8

In a letter to his wife on 28 August 1864, Brown made it clear that he and John A. did not always see eye-to-eye—this time on the construction of the parliament buildings at Ottawa.

'Do you know you were very near being stripped yesterday of your honours of Presidentess of the Council? Would not that have been a sad affair? It was in this way. The council was summoned for twelve and shortly after that we were all assembled by John A. We waited for him till one—till half past one—till two—and then Galt sent off to his house specially for him. Answer—will be here immediately. Waiting till half past two—no appearance, waited till three and shortly after, John A. entered bearing symptoms of having been on a spree. He was half drunk. Lunch is always on the side table and he soon applied himself to it—and before we had well entered on the important business before us he was quite drunk with potations of ale. After two hours and a half debate we closed the important discussions of three days on the constitutional changes and arranged finally all about our trip to Charlottetown and our course when there. John A. then declared he had an important matter to bring before us—the dispute with the Ottawa building contractors. You should know that the original *contract* for these buildings was $700,000—but when the Liberal party got into power they found that $1,200,000 had been spent—$550,000 was claimed to be owing —but the works were not with all this half finished! The government in consequence stopped the buildings and appointed commissioners to investigate the whole matter. They disclosed the most astounding folly and fraud in the business from beginning to end—and reported that instead of $550,000 being due the contractors they were already over paid, and there the matter has stood ever since—nearly three years.'

Now that Macdonald was back in power, Brown said, his friends, the contractors, were making a new attempt to secure their claim. 'I was quite willing to send this thing to arbitration—but determined that men only of the highest character and position should be entrusted with it.' Macdonald proposed to appoint three men, two of them unknown to Brown.

'I asked that the matter should be delayed until I made inquiries—John A. would not hear of delay and insisted loudly, fiercely, that the thing should be settled then and there. His old friends in the Cabinet saw of course that he was quite wrong—but they feared to offend him and pressed for a settlement. Matters came to point. He declared that if the thing was done then I would not sit in the council one moment longer. Mowat stood firmly by me and McDougall partly—moderately. Galt got alarmed and proposed a mode which in effect postponed the matter till Monday. I agreed to it and the council all but John A. adopted it. It was declared carried. Thereupon John A. burst out furiously declaring that his friends had deserted him and he would not hold office another day. The council adjourned in great confusion—John A's friends trying to appease him. . . . I don't imagine for a moment that . . . [these appointments] will be pressed. It will be utterly ruinous to John A. if the whole affair goes before the public. He will not think of it when he gets sober. To say the truth, were our visit to the Lower Provinces and to England once over, I would not care how soon a rupture came. The constitutional question would then be beyond all chance of failure—and I would be quit of company that is far from agreeable.'

J.M.S. Careless, 'George Brown and the Mother of Confederation',
Canadian Historical Association, Report (1960), pp. 67-8

The Orange Order, a Protestant fraternal society, was founded in Ireland in 1795 to commemorate the victory of King William of Orange at the Battle of the Boyne (1690). The order was introduced into Canada at Brockville in 1830 by Ogle R. Gowan, a prominent Tory politician. In 1844 the Orangemen controlled a powerful Tory vote and John A. Macdonald, ever pragmatic, joined the order. In 1853 trouble arose when the Conservatives became allied with the

French Catholic Tory 'blues'. The rift was healed in 1856, but thereafter the Orange vote was no longer solidly Tory.

Macdonald at times regretted his early affiliation with the Orange Order—particularly during the royal tour of 1860.

The Upper Canadian part of the tour could hardly have opened more auspiciously. Macdonald ought to have been completely satisfied. But he was not. As the train drove through the gathering darkness to Brockville, his worries and fear steadily deepened. All day he had known that at Brockville he would be given a last slim chance of averting what threatened to be a hideous contretemps. For days—ever since their visit to Montreal—he had seen it ominously approaching. He knew that he could not escape being involved. It concerned Kingston, which had been his faithful constituency since he had entered politics. It concerned the Orangemen, who under Gowan's leadership had gradually and largely become the zealous followers of the Conservative party. In Canada, the parades, banners, and insignia of the Orange Order were all perfectly legal; but in the United Kingdom they were not. The Duke of Newcastle, who accepted full responsibility for the actions of his royal charge [the Prince of Wales], decided that the Prince could not be permitted to compromise himself by acknowledging an illegal [in Britain] organization; and he therefore wrote a formal letter to the Governor, which Head forwarded to the mayors of Kingston and Toronto, warning all concerned that there must be no Orange banners or insignia along any route on which the Prince would pass. Most of the Orangemen, wisely advised by the new Grand Master, John Hillyard Cameron, grumblingly accepted this incredible veto. But some did not. And among these latter—to the discomfiture of Macdonald—were the Kingston Orangemen. A large and important body, nearly all stout Conservatives, they clamoured so long and so loudly to be permitted to parade under their Orange arch and in their Orange costumes that in the end the corporation of Kingston appointed a special delegation, which was to see the Duke and beg him to modify his decision. The delegation—the Mayor, Colonel Strange, Macdonald's old partner, Alexander Campbell, and two other Kingston worthies—reached Brockville some time before the Prince and his suite arrived.

It was eleven o'clock at night before the Duke was free to see the Kingstonians. They boarded the steamer apprehensively; Macdonald made the necessary introductions, and for two and a half hours the fruitless discussion lasted. The Mayor reminded the Duke that the Orange Order was entirely legal in Canada and that

its members could not be prevented from parading as they pleased;
and Macdonald argued that, since the favours extended to Roman
Catholics during the Prince's tour in Canada East had been widely
publicized, the Protestants of Canada West would be correspondingly quick to resent a slight offered to any part of their body. It was
all quite useless. The Duke remained adamant. And so, as it turned
out, did the Orangemen. On the afternoon of Tuesday, September
4, as the steamer drew close to Kingston harbour, the horrified
members of the Prince's suite could plainly perceive an Orange
arch, Orange banners, and a 'large concourse' of defiant Orangemen, 'occupying the street in great force so that the Prince
could not enter the Town without passing through the demonstration they had prepared'. The Mayor was hurriedly sent for and
informed that the Orangemen would be given until the following
morning to reconsider their scandalous conduct. The *Kingston*,
with offended dignity, remained all night in the harbour, in the
hope that a new day would bring repentance. But the new day had
barely dawned when the incorrigible Orangemen began to reassem-
ble. Once again, clad in their full regalia, they took up a position in
the immediate neighbourhood of the landing-place, from which
neither threats, remonstrances, nor supplications could move
them. The Duke was affable but firm. In such circumstances the
Prince could not be permitted to land and pay the town the expected
visit. The *Kingston*, which had remained in the harbour for twenty-
two embarrassing hours, now steamed away up the lake.

Macdonald was not on board. He had decided to stay with his
injured constituents. He had actually abandoned the royal tour in
mid-career!

Donald Creighton, *John A. Macdonald: The Young Politician*
(1956), pp. 301-3

WOMEN

*John A. always enjoyed the company of women and was very popu-
lar with them. Even during his tragic first marriage, there is some
evidence to suggest that flirtations existed, and between marriages,
as the eligible bachelor Prime Minister, he was the pursued as well
as the pursuer. He seemed to have a particular attraction for widows. In addition to a possible romance with a Peterborough widow,
he enjoyed a long, loyal friendship with a Kingston widow and*

tavernkeeper, a loyal Tory supporter who was said to control one hundred votes.

A lively bachelor, the young John A. had a way with women.

As a youth he was quiet in manner, but full of fun and mischief, quick at repartee and unable to resist a joke. One evening, at a large party, he forgot an engagement to dance a quadrille immediately after supper, and appeared to claim his partner when it was too late. She was very indignant she had lost her dance, and would not forgive. He tried to appease her in every way, but finding it of no avail, to her horror and dismay flung himself at her feet, and with eyes twinkling with merriment, but in the most heartbroken tones cried out, 'Remember! oh remember! the fascinations of the turkey.' This was too much, and the ridiculousness of the situation, together with the laughter of the bystanders, brought about a speedy reconciliation.

> J. Pennington Macpherson, *Life of the Right Hon. Sir John A. Macdonald*, vol. 1 (1891), p. 81

On a trip to the British Isles in 1842 (during which he first met Isabella), he did not lack for other female companions, as he wrote home to his mother.

In one of Scott's novels he speaks of the unrivalled scenery of Windsor, and certainly the prospect from the Terrace opened to my eyes a view which I could not before conceive. I saw it under favourable auspices. The day was clear, the weather warm, and I had a very pretty girl, Margaret Wanklyn, on my arm, to whom the scene was also new, so we were very agreeably engaged in comparing our impressions. Our ideas sympathized wonderfully. The engraving of Windsor Castle from the Albion is a very correct one, but gives an inadequate idea of the extent and magnificence of the most splendid royal residence in the world. Theatricals I have seen again and again, together with a countless number of exhibitions of all sorts and sizes. At every one of these places I have purchased a catalogue *raisonné*, or descriptive account of the exhibition. These I will bring with me—even to the very play-bills—so that you will have every opportunity of tracing my progress thro' the capital.

I have formed acquaintances and dined with two or three lawyers here, by whose assistance I have seen all the great guns of the law. Indeed, I have been lucky in all my sightseeing. The first time I went into the House of Lords they were sitting as a Court of Appeal, and there I saw the four great law lords, Lyndhurst, Brougham, Campbell, and Cottenham. At Guildhall I saw Lord Denman and Sir Nicholas Tindal presiding over jury trials; and when I went to the House of Commons, I heard speeches from Peel, Goulburn, Lord John Russell, Lord Stanley, O'Connell, Duncombe, Wakley, Sir James Graham, and most of the leaders in Parliament. I go to-day to the Tower and the Tunnel . . .

Your affectionate son,
John A. Macdonald

Joseph Pope, *Memoirs of the Right Honourable Sir John Alexander Macdonald*, vol. 1 (1894), p. 14

En route to Savannah, where Isabella was to winter, he enjoyed the companionship of some Philadelphia women, among them one in particular—to the chagrin of his invalid wife.

Philadelphia 3 Nov. 1845

My dearest Sister.

Isabella was very tired all Friday, as you may imagine, but hoped everything from her nights rest. Unfortunately her rest was disturbed, and on Saturday morning she was unrefreshed. During the day she was visited by your friend Mrs Biddle, and exerted herself too much, so that in the evening she was a good deal exhausted, and was threatened with tic so that she had recourse to opium. It rained all night and all Sunday, and she felt out of sorts & uncomfortable all day. She slept a good deal during the afternoon but not much during the night. This morning the weather was unsettled & damp, and Madame Isa still felt uncomfortable, so we have stayed over. Tomorrow we hope to leave here without fail. She has had a good day today, has walked a good deal & eaten pretty well, and if she only has a good night, will be bright as need be tomorrow.

I was asked to Mrs Biddle's on Friday evening but did not like to leave Isabella. On Saturday evening however, I was seduced from my allegiance to my Petticoat Government by Mr Robinson who took me to a conversazione of the Wistar Club and Dr Randolph's, where I met all the Science & *Belles Lettres* of Philadelphia. I was much gratified by the feast of Reason, but I say it with shame & confusion of face that my supper of terrapins and champagne lingers more pleasingly on my recollection, than all the 'wise saws and modern instances' that were uttered by the *savans* [sic]. Like the apostles my spirit was willing but my flesh was weak & required those creature comforts. It rained so tremendously yesterday that I was prevented from going to church, and as they say in Galway, 'I made me Sowl' at home. Today after a saunter thro this city of marble steps, broad brims & scrubbing brushes, I called on Mrs

Biddle whom I found at home. I like her self possessed English manner very much. She is a ladylike & intelligent person and I regret having had so small an opportunity of knowing her. Mr Biddle I was not fortunate enough to meet, but his son Thos called & him I saw. . . .

I forgot to tell you that Mrs Robinson, a sweet pretty woman called on Saturday, & I went to find her out to day, but the directory was vague & I was stupid, & so I did not see her again, much to Isabellas delight, who says she does not like my taking so much to your lady friends. By the way, sister there is a latin proverb 'Noscitur a Sociis' which may be translated for the benefit of the country members, 'birds of a feather flock together'. I always considered you *a Charming Woman*, but I did not calculate for all your friends being so. From those I have seen, I have only to say, that you will confer a great favor on me by sitting down & writing me letters of credence to *every one* of your Yankee lady friends, and it will go hard but I deliver most of them. . . .

> With Love to Jane I remain D^r
> sister
> Yours most truly
> John A. Macdonald

ps. I say like Jeanie Deans in her letter to Reuben [Bullen] 'Excuse spellin' & ritin' as I hae an ill pen'.

> J.K. Johnson, ed., *The Letters of Sir John A. Macdonald*
> *1836-1857* (1968), pp. 20-2

The bill that Lena Newman mentions here was dated 1 September 1857—only a few months before Isabella Macdonald's death in December.

That John A. was a gallant beau is shown by a bill for a lady's riding whip, purchased in London for seven pounds fifteen shillings. There is no record of who was given such an expensive riding accessory.

> Lena Newman, *The John A. Macdonald Album* (1974), p. 51

He was a particular favourite of two widows. One, Mrs E.M. Hall, widow of his friend Judge Hall of Peterborough, was clearly fond of him.

My loved John,

I hope I shall have a letter from you today, my darling, as if not I shall not be able to hear for another week as intending to leave here for Buckhorn tomorrow . . . where I only intend to stay a week. So you will have no letter for that time. If that is a privation to you, what must I feel—a fortnight without hearing from you. I cannot bear to think of it.

Mrs Boucher and I spent yesterday evening with the Kirkpatricks. A lady who was there made a set at me to find out if I was to be married in the spring. I told her my mother advised me when setting out in life to 'believe nothing I heard, and only half what I see' and I wished my friends would do the same. She then tried Mrs Boucher, who told her she would not believe it till told by the parties themselves . . . that she had been asked the question at least fifty times since I came up, and when saying that I knew nothing about it, she was met by the question 'What! Have you not asked her?' 'Certainly not!' was her reply.

The horses are ready. I must stop. . . .

Goodbye my own darling,
Love your loving Lizzie

Ibid., p. 51

The other was Mrs Eliza Grimason, an avid Tory. She was the widowed tenant of Grimason House on Princess Street, Kingston, a building John A. had bought from her husband in 1856, although Grimason owed money on it at the time of the sale and it was owned by a Mr Rourke. When he died in 1867 Macdonald did not press the widow for the remaining money. Business was good and Mrs Grimason managed well, in the end becoming independently wealthy. Both were married when they met; the nature of the relationship is unclear, but they are buried in adjacent plots in the Cataraqui cemetery, and Mrs Grimason was given the family cradle by Sir John. Doubtless her tavern afforded him a welcome break from a dreary domestic environment. It is reported by Lena Newman that he kept two rooms in the hotel for his personal use (The John A. Macdonald Album, 1974). Certainly theirs was a close and loyal friendship, later tolerated by his second wife Agnes.

. . . when she spoke of him the pronouns He and Him were alone sufficient to designate by way of distinction the one from all other beings to whom a pronoun in the masculine gender could apply. She had a kind, honest face, was sincere in her friendships as in her dislikes, and though without education to speak of, had sterling good sense and much natural intelligence. Through her devotion to Sir John she acquired quite an acquaintance with 'practical politics',

and there were few prominent members of Parliament whose leading traits she did not know. . . . She became so absorbed in that one
personality that, in spite of her keen sense of what was becoming in
a woman, she would be drawn to his meetings when often she would
be the only female present. More than once on election night, when
the returns were brought in, she would appear at Sir John's committee room, and walk up among the men to the head of the table and,
giving Sir John a kiss, retire without a remark to anyone. When a
political picnic was held near Kingston, Mrs Grimason's van was
always at the disposal of Sir John and his party, and in former days
she always made one of the party. One beautiful trait in this remarkable old lady was, that she never presumed upon the fact that
she was favoured with the affection of Sir John. It was only on rare
occasions, such as the laying of the corner stone of the dry dock, or
the supreme moment of his triumph at an election, that she came
within the veil, as it were, and stole a kiss. At any other time she
would let him come and go in Kingston without obtruding herself
into his presence, although he might playfully take her to task for
neglecting to call; and in an election contest she might never go near
to take up his time, but would work for votes with all the soul that
was in her.

> E.B. Biggar, *Anecdotal Life of Sir John Macdonald* (1891),
> pp. 237-8

[Mrs Grimason] often longed to go to the Capital and see her deity
on the throne of his glory, or, as she expressed it, to see Sir John 'take
his seat', and at last, some years ago, at the opening of Parliament
she made the venture. It was the event of her life, and it is no
exaggeration to say that both Sir John and Lady Macdonald were
proud and glad to see her. . . . After the sitting was over, she was
shown all the sights of the Parliament Buildings, and the wife of the
Speaker took her to his rooms and had luncheon. When here Mr
Mulock, of Toronto, the Liberal member, happened in, and was
introduced to her. She thought it strange that an enemy should be
admitted to these sacred precincts, and after manifesting her nervousness and restraint for a few minutes, she determined to tear off
the mask, and as she turned a sidelong glance upon him, asked:
'Excuse me, Mr Mulock, may I ask your politics?' Mr Mulock, who
had heard of Mrs Grimason before, . . . hesitated and presently
admitted, in the apologetic way of one whose crimes have just been
unearthed for the first time, that he was a Reformer. Mrs Grimason's comment on the confession was not soothing to the ears of
the criminal who made it, and Mr Mulock pleaded: 'That's rather
hard, isn't it, Mrs Grimason?' Mrs Grimason did not assuage the

wretch's fears by any soft remark: 'You live in Kingston, I believe, Mrs Grimason. You may know an uncle of mine there, Mr — —?' 'And now I think less of ye thin before,' quickly retorted Mrs Grimason, 'for your uncle is a good Conservative'; and after making more remarks on people who disgrace the political traditions of their family, she added with dreadful emphasis, 'I hate them damn Grits!' Sir John dropped into the room just in time to hear this last imprecation, and taking in the situation, laughed till the tears came down.

Ibid., pp. 238-9

Mrs Grimason's language was quaint.

Lady Macdonald took her [Mrs Grimason] down to Earnscliffe, and she never tired of telling of the kindness that was shown her. In her good rich brogue she would describe her visit: 'They have a lovely place all their own, down there by the Rye-do. The house has a lovely slate roof like they have in England, and beautiful grounds, and everything in style, an' a man to wait on the dure. Lady Macdonald kapes her own cow and hins, and they make their own butter, man dear. They have two fine cows and six servants. Lady Macdonald showed me over the house, and in the fine big library there was my picture up beside o' His, just where He sits. After showin' me through the house, she says: "There now, haven't I made him very comfortable?" She's a very plain woman is Lady Macdonald—not good lookin'—but oh, she's the fine eddication, and that's where she gets the best of thim. Why, I heard her talkin' Frinch to the carpenter workin' about the house. It's her fine eddication that makes her so nice, and she takes such good care o' Him. And if I went back there today she would make as much of me as if I was the richest woman in the counthry. His library is beautiful, and it's covered over with books to the tip top of the wall. While I was there, the man brought in his letters from the mail, — as thrue as I tell ye there was the full of that of thim' (holding out her apron). As for her sentiments concerning Sir John, words were too weak to express her worship. 'There's not a man like him in the livin' earth,' was her sincere and simple estimate.

Ibid., pp. 239-40

On extending the franchise to women John A.'s ideas were liberal.

'I believe that is coming as certainly as came the gradual enfranchisement of woman from being the slave of man until she attained her present position as almost the equal of man. I believe that time is coming, though perhaps we are not, any more than the United States and England, quite educated up to it. I believe the time will come, and I shall be very proud and very glad to see it, when the final step towards giving women full enfranchisement is carried in Canada.'

Commons Debates (1885), p. 1134

CONFEDERATION

In the late 1850s and early 1860s, the unsettled politics of the United Province of Canada saw four short-lived governments enter and leave office. Stability was achieved when Canada West's Grit leader, George Brown, proposed a coalition government to pursue his goal of a Confederation of all British North America. John A., not previously a champion of the scheme, accepted, and the Great Coalition was formed in June 1864.

In the Atlantic colonies proposals for a Maritime Union had made little headway, and Canadian representatives participating in the Charlottetown Conference in September 1864 swept the board with the grand design of a union a mare usque ad mare. The Quebec Conference followed a month later, and spelled out in the form of seventy-two Resolutions the fundamental decisions taken at Charlottetown. Although Newfoundland and PEI stayed out, and opposition to Confederation was strong in Nova Scotia and New Brunswick, Britain and the Colonial Secretary pressed hard for the scheme, and at the London Conference between December 1866 and February 1867 it was translated into law: the British North America Act, proclaimed on 1 July 1867.

Certainly Confederation was the product of politicians of all stripes from five colonies, and certainly the idea did not originate with Macdonald. To Brown's original concept were added the financial expertise of A.T. Galt and Cartier's insistence on minimum essential guarantees of provincial rights. However, it was John A. who took hold of the scheme and pushed it forward, contributing most of the practical ideas that shaped and created the constitutional settlement. In recognition of his efforts the Imperial government created him Sir John A. Macdonald, KCB, and he became Canada's first prime minister.

While John A. lived at Quebec in the days before Confederation, he boarded almost constantly with Mrs McHugh, La Chevrotière street, and after in Ann street. It was in Mrs McHugh's house that he and Messrs Cartier and McGee first talked over the details of the Confederation scheme. At the time of the Confederation conference [1865] he had a room at a Mr Cheshire's house. On the day preceding his speech here, he had shut himself up all day. Cheshire considering this rather unusual, listened at the door and frequently heard the solitary voice of his lodger. As he knew no one else was in the room, he commented on the proceeding thus to one of John A.'s friends who came to inquire after him: 'I thocht the mon was surely daft, for he's been all day alone in his room talkin' till the cat.' It was supposed that John A. had been rehearsing his speech.

E.B. Biggar, *Anecdotal Life of Sir John Macdonald* (1891), p. 225

Macdonald was . . . . an adroit and a responsible chairman. Sir Frederick Rogers, the Permanent Under-Secretary of the Colonial Office—our equivalent is a deputy-minister—watched Macdonald with admiration as he steered some of the delicate compromises through the London Conference, with Cartier and Hector Langevin very conscious of their own need for security on critical points, and the Nova Scotian and New Brunswick delegates sometimes jealous of Quebec. 'He stated and argued the case with cool, ready fluency, while at the same time you saw that every word was measured, and that while he was making for a point ahead, he was never for a moment unconscious of the rocks among which he had to steer.'

P.B. Waite, *Macdonald: His Life and World* (1975), p. 63

Toronto, 23rd June, 1864.

My dear Macdonald

Allow me to congratulate you upon the successful issue of your negotiations with Brown. It is a great and patriotic achievement—putting an end to the bitter party animosities and intense personal antipathies that have characterized public life in Canada for so many years; effecting this too, by the only honourable and enduring means, the removal of the cause, the settlement of the disturbing sectional questions. Yourself, Galt, and Brown and (as Brown justly says in his speech) especially Taché and Cartier, deserve the thanks and gratitude of the country for making in the interest of the country what must have been to all of you a great sacrifice of personal feeling.

I am quite sure that in what you have done you will have the approval of every man whose interests are not antagonistic to those of the country. It must also be no small satisfaction to you, and especially to Galt, that the movers of the unhandsome and unfair attack upon him have been so utterly discomfited. I notice you said in the House that the Intercolonial had not been named in the discussions with Brown. Naming it would have been very superfluous. Without it there can be no federation. It is the keystone, the very foundation stone. The early carrying out of this enterprise seems at last probable. It must now be placed on a broad and safe basis. I beg of you to take care that the control is kept in the proper hands and that no opening or opportunity is left for [name indecipherable] scheming.

I wrote you about a fortnight ago but you have had something else to do than answer private letters.

I remain my dear Macdonald

Yours very faithfully,
D.L. Macpherson

Joseph Pope, *Correspondence of Sir John Macdonald* (1921), p. 12

In 1865, en route from Charlottetown to Quebec, Macdonald addressed the Confederation delegates.

At the dinner in Halifax . . . . Mr Macdonald, in the course of his speech, said: 'The question of Colonial Union is one of such magnitude that it dwarfs every other question on this portion of the continent. It absorbs every other idea as far as I am concerned. For twenty long years I have been dragging myself through the dreary waste of colonial politics. I thought there was no end—nothing worthy of ambition; but now I see something that is well worthy to be weighed against all I have suffered in the cause of my little country. There may be obstructions; local differences may arise, disputes may occur, local jealousies may intervene, but it matters not—the wheel is now revolving, and we are only the fly on the wheel; we cannot delay it. The union of the colonies of British America under one sovereign is a fixed fact.'

He then pointed out that though the constitution of the United States was as perfect as human wisdom could make it, yet being the work of men it had its defects, and one of these was that each state was an individual sovereign power. We could avoid this danger by forming one strong central government, having all rights of sovereignty except those delegated to the local government.

E.B. Biggar, *Anecdotal Life of Sir John Macdonald* (1891), pp. 182-3

Macdonald wrote to his sister Louisa from the London conference in 1866.

London Dec. 27, 1866

My dear Louisa

. . . . For fear that an alarming story may reach you, I may as well tell it you as it occurred. Cartier, Galt & myself returned from Lord Carnarvon's place in the country late at night. I went to bed but commenced reading the newspapers of the day, after my usual fashion. I fell asleep & was awakened by intense heat. I found my bed, bed clothes & curtains all on fire.

I didn't lose my presence of mind, pulled down the curtains with my hands, extinguished them with the water in my room. The pillow was burnt under my head and bolster as well. All the bed clothes were blazing. I dragged them all off on the floor & knowing the action of feathers on flame, I ripped open bolster and pillows and poured an avalanche of feathers on the blazing mass, & then stamped out the fire with my hands & feet. Lest the hair mattress might be burning internally I then went to Cartier's bedroom, & with his assistance carried all the water in three adjoining rooms into mine, & finally extinguished all appearance of fire. We made no alarm & only Cartier, Galt & myself knew of the accident. After it was all over, it was then discovered that I had been on fire. My shirt was burnt on my back & my hair, forehead & hands scorched. Had I not worn a very thick flannel shirt under my nightshirt, I would have been burnt to death, as it was my escape was miraculous.

It was found that my right shoulder blade was much scorched, so I got it dressed and thought no more of it. In a day or two, however, I found that it would not do and have been under the Doctor's hands for a week. The wound at one time took an ugly look. I was kept in bcd for three days & have not left the House these eight days. I shall take a drive today, if the doctor allows it when he calls to look at my back. So much for that story. I had a merry Xmas alone in my own room and my dinner of tea & toast & drank all your healths in bohea though you didn't deserve it. I was to have gone to Evan Macpherson's to dinner, if I did not go down to William Clark, but I could do neither. The town is quite empty and I have no news to tell.

I shall know tomorrow whether I can have anything like a holiday, before the British Parliament meets.

Love to Hugh, Magt & the Parson & believe me,

affectionately yours
John A. Macdonald

I got all kinds of praises for the presence of mind and admonitions agt reading in bed. I still read however. . . .

J.A.MD.

J.K. Johnson, ed., *Affectionately Yours* (1969), pp. 102-3

Derby Day at Epsom Downs provided some lighter moments.

The last day of May was Derby Day. Business was suspended. Everybody was out of town. The Canadians made up a party of eleven, with Russell of *The Times*, Grant, and Brydges of the Grand Trunk, and D'Arcy McGee, the Canadian Minister of Agriculture, who had also arrived in London. They set out for Epsom at nine o'clock, in two stout carriages with postillions, and with a huge basket of food and wines from Fortnum and Mason's tucked away inside. The road was jammed with an unending stream of vehicles. They took hours to cover the sixteen miles to the Downs; and it was twelve o'clock before they had established their carriage in a good position and were washing away the dust of the journey with sherry and seltzer water. The crowd thickened every minute. Macdonald and Galt walked about for a bit, with Russell as their guide, and when they turned back could scarcely discover their own carriages in the dense mass of vehicles. Somebody suggested a pool at a guinea a draw. Galt—he was always a person to whom things happened— drew the favourite, the French horse, Gladiateur. Macdonald drew the field.

'You are a lucky fellow,' said Macdonald.

Galt gazed at his ticket doubtfully. He would have gazed doubtfully at any ticket he could possibly have drawn. 'I do not know about that,' he said slowly. 'There are fourteen horses running, and it is a great chance if one of them does not come in ahead.'

'Well,' said Macdonald, 'I will swop and give you a guinea to boot.'

They swopped and then it was time for Macdonald and Galt to go. Russell, who knew everybody, had got the pair an invitation to the pavilion and stand, just opposite the royal party, which was provided by Todd Heatly, the wine merchant, for his race-going patrons and friends. Inside the pavilion there was turtle soup, 'and all the delicacies and substantials of the season', and a brimming fountain of champagne. Outside, on the stand, was an uninter-rupted and magnificent view of the entire course. There were a dozen false breaks, and then, just at two minutes to four, the horses were off at last and streaming up the hill. Wild Charley, Christmas Carol, Eltham, Broomielaw, and Oppressor were out in front; and somewhere in the ruck, almost unnoticed at first, were the blue and red sleeves of the 'Frenchman', with Harry Grimshaw up, carrying Macdonald's guineas as a part of his enormous baggage of metal. It was the crowd, rather than the race, that fascinated Macdonald. As the horses pounded round Tattenham Corner, the enormous black mass of spectators turned as one man; and—it was like a flash of lightning—a multitude of white staring faces rushed in a second into view. Now the horses were into the straight. Broomielaw was still going very fast; but soon 'those light back ribs could do no more'. The two 'magpie jackets', Eltham and Christmas Carol, shot out together; but deep on the inside was a stealing blur of blue and red that swept into a lead, 'and nothing else was in it'. Macdonald could have dropped his handkerchief on Gladiateur's head, as the horse passed the post, a winner by two lengths. Then it was all over; and the crowd, shouting, pushing, gesticulating, and fighting, poured out onto the course.

'The Road', the creeping cavalcade back from Epsom to London, was a licensed saturnalia of horse-play and broad good humour. The Canadians buttoned up their greatcoats tightly, crammed their hats down on their heads, and armed themselves with peas, pea-shooters, pincushions of bran and little bags of flour. Macdonald, greatly daring, even bought a bag of peas for the 'old chap', George Brown; and Brown, for a few wild, uncovenanting hours, developed an unexpected zeal for the pea-shooter. Galt thought himself lucky to be in the same carriage with Macdonald and Russell, who were 'past masters at the art of chaffing'. Macdonald kept up a constant raillery with the strangers on every side; and once, when they were blocked for an hour at a railway bridge, Russell got up on his seat and addressed the crowd in an eloquent extempore election speech. Assaulted in turn with cheers, jeers, peas, flour, and uproarious abuse, their carriage maintained its reputation for originality and high spirits all the way to London. It took them five hours to reach the capital. They were tired out when they walked into the Westminster Palace Hotel, and white as millers with dust and pelted flour.

Donald Creighton, John A. Macdonald: The Young Politician
(1956), pp. 413-15

The creation of a first cabinet was difficult.

This left only four members, all Conservatives, to Quebec. But the trouble then arose that Cartier insisted three of these had to be French-Canadians, Cartier, Chapais, and Langevin, which necessitated the dropping of either Galt or McGee. That this was a difficulty long foreseen is evident from a letter McGee had written Macdonald from Paris:

> 71 Champs Elysees, Paris,
> April 9th, 1867.
>
> My dear Macdonald,
> . . . You observe in your last that my own 'political future is at stake.' I feel the whole force of that remark, and will not lose a day in returning, that I possibly can. As to Montreal West, I do not fear any issue which I may have to meet there, with any one; but the other two seats in that city can only be secured by actual co-operation of those I can influence, as was shown to Cartier's and Rose's satisfaction last time, and time before. Whatever I can do westward, will be, as it always has been, at your service. Ever since we have acted together, I recognize no other leader in Parliament or the country; and I only ask in return, that you will protect my position in my absence—till I am able to mount guard over it myself. I certainly have no desire to embarrass future arrangements, which will naturally be under your direction, but in a Confederation Government, founded upon principles which I have always zealously advocated, I will, if in Parliament, give way neither to Galt, nor to a third Frenchman, 'nor any other man.'

When Cartier insisted on the three French-Canadians, McGee's position, which had been previously secured to him by a letter from Macdonald, became, nevertheless, strategically the weak one. Galt represented a geographical and local minority—the English-speaking Protestants of Quebec. This minority could be represented in the Cabinet only in the Quebec section. The Irish Catholics, on the other hand, were found in all the provinces, so it was not essential a Quebec man should represent them.

During one solid week of deadlock, Macdonald arranged and rearranged all his various factors, the limited number possible, with the certain men who had to be included, as well as the sectional, party, and religious requirements. Then he diplomatically allowed his lieutenants to understand that the problem appeared beyond his power of solution, and that he would have to allow George Brown to form the first Dominion Cabinet.

At this crisis Tupper brought forward a proposal. He would be willing to step out and make way for an Irish Catholic Conservative from Nova Scotia, E.F. Kenny, if McGee would do likewise and thus allow one man to take the place of them both. This met no opposition in the party's council. The Conservative leaders had been irritated by McGee's May-Day manifesto, and his unpopularity created by the Fenian excitement together with the Irish quarrel in Montreal made many of them feel it would be better if he were only a private member in their ranks. Also, there was no doubt that personal jealousy and long-nursed political animosity dulled the conscience of one or two when it came to be a question of weighing McGee's just deserts.

Cartier undertook to put the matter to McGee personally. He spent two long mornings with him and eventually emerged with McGee's consent to withdraw and with Macdonald's letter of appointment to him safely in his keeping.

> Isabel Skelton, *The Life of Thomas D'Arcy McGee* (1925), pp. 530-1

1 July 1867.

By nine o'clock, the public buildings and many large houses were illuminated all across Canada. And in Toronto the Queen's Park and the grounds of the private houses surrounding it were transformed by hundreds of Chinese lanterns hung through the trees. When the true darkness had at last fallen, the firework displays began; and simultaneously throughout the four provinces, the night was assaulted by minute explosions of coloured lights, as the roman candles popped away, and the rockets raced up into the sky. In the cities and large towns, the spectacle always concluded with elaborate set pieces. The Montrealers arranged an intricate design with emblems representing the three uniting provinces—a beaver for Canada, a mayflower for Nova Scotia, and a pine for New Brunswick. At Toronto the words 'God Save the Queen' were surrounded by a twined wreath of roses, thistles, shamrocks, and *fleur-de-lys*; and at Hamilton, while the last set pieces were blazing, four huge bonfires were kindled on the crest of the mountain. In Ottawa, long before this, Monck and Macdonald and the other ministers had quitted the Privy Council chamber; and Parliament Hill was crowded once again with people who had come to watch the last spectacle of the day. The parliament buildings were illuminated. They stood out boldly against the sky; and far behind them, hidden in darkness, were the ridges of the Laurentians, stretching away, mile after mile, towards the north-west.

> Donald Creighton, *John A. Macdonald: The Young Politician* (1956), pp. 480-1

John A.'s second wife, Susan Agnes Bernard, was the sister of his secretary Hewitt Bernard. When he first saw her in 1856 in a Toronto hotel, where she was dining with her brother Richard, he recorded that she was . . . . 'very tall, very much [like her brother] and . . . . had fine eyes'. It was not until four years later that they were to meet. It is likely that they got to know one another in Quebec, where Agnes and her mother had moved after living in first Barrie and later Toronto. Jamaican-born, Agnes had come to Canada from England with her mother and brothers after her father's death. Her father, a Jamaican lawyer, landowner, and politician, had lost his money when his western properties were burned after the freeing of the slaves in 1834. Although Agnes once described herself as a 'poor creole without a shilling', she was in fact intelligent, well tutored, cultured, lively, spirited, and sociable; she had a part-time career as a journalist, and made a warm and convivial home for her husband. An Anglican with a deeply pious, self-analytical, disciplined side to her, she became an abstainer 'as an example' to her bibulous husband. She was a frequent observer of proceedings in the House, where she was seen to stamp her foot in anger on at least one occasion. Her attempts to influence her husband politically were of no avail, as her correspondence ruefully shows. She is known for her adventurous trip of over five hundred miles through the Rockies sitting, mostly alone, on the cowcatcher of the CPR train, a journey that met with much attention when she described it in one of her frequent articles in **Murray's Magazine** (London, Eng.). No mean journalist, she also contributed to the Ladies Home Journal and her articles there reveal a shrewd mind. She loved to travel all over Canada and to her adored England, and in later years shuttled back and forth between England and Italy, restlessly trying to assuage the pain of her husband's death. That these two so disparate people, twenty years apart in age, loved each other was apparent.

The Macdonalds were also bound by tragedy, for their only child, Mary Theodora Margaret, was born hydrocephalic, at a time when that condition meant almost certain retardation. Biographers vary on the degree to which Mary was affected. She never walked, and from the words and letters attributed to her, it seems that her speech was difficult to understand. But she expressed a touching awareness of everything going on around her and of her own limitations. Like many mentally handicapped children, she was gentle *and appealing, and her friends and companions, lovingly provided by her parents, adored her. Her stepbrother Hugh John—always at a distance from this second family through age and later estrangement from his father (over his first marriage to a Roman Catholic widow)—once shrewdly observed that if Mary had been provided with companions her own age or older, rather than the younger ones her parents selected, she might have been stimulated to advance further; it is difficult to say. She outlived her parents and died in the care of her beloved custodian in England in 1933.*

Hugh John, farmed out from an early age to be raised by relatives and friends, became a lawyer like his father. After a brief period with his father's firm in Toronto, he moved to Winnipeg, where he established a successful law practice, entered politics and eventually became the Premier of Manitoba. Like his father, he was left a widower at an early age, and his second marriage was to a family friend. He had a child by each marriage: his daughter Daisy was raised a Roman Catholic in accord with her mother's wishes; his son, an Anglican like himself.

John A. Macdonald and Susan Agnes Bernard were married in London on 16 February 1867.

... the Canadian delegates went in a body to see their chairman married. The ceremony took place in St George's Church, Hanover Square, long known as the wedding altar of England's noted men. By a happy coincidence, Bishop Fulford, the Metropolitan Bishop of Canada, happened to be in London, and was selected to tie the knot. The weather was heavy and overcast—but that is the almost certain lot of a bride in London. The wedding party consisted of between seventy and ninety guests, among whom were some of the wives of British Cabinet Ministers, with Sir Richard Mayne (head of the Metropolitan Police of London), his son, and his daughter who was to have married Colonel Bernard on the same occasion. Lord Carnarvon's son was one of the groomsmen, while among the four bridesmaids were Miss Emma Tupper, daughter of Sir Charles; Miss Jessie McDougall, daughter of the Honourable William McDougall; and Miss Joanna Archibald, daughter of Sir Adams Archibald, all these ladies being daughters of delegates. The bridesmaids were attired in the fashion of that day; two of them in blue and two in pink, with pink crepe bonnets and long tulle veils. The bride wore white satin with the usual wreath of orange blossoms and a veil of Brussels lace. Among the many wedding presents a correspondent of the *Globe* noted a complete set in opaque enamel and amethyst and carbuncle, the gift of the delegates. After the ceremony a grand wedding-breakfast was given at the Westminster Palace Hotel. Governor (Sir Francis) Hincks proposed the bride's health in a speech, and John A., in reply, made one of the many witty speeches which have never been reported. He alluded to the plan of confederation, whereby all the provinces of Canada were united under one female sovereign, and that perfection of the idea of union had so occupied his mind that he had sought to apply it to himself. Before sitting down he made his bride and his assembled colleagues promises of future happiness in their union, which were certainly as well fulfilled as humanity could demand.

E.B. Biggar, *Anecdotal Life of Sir John Macdonald* (1891), pp. 102-3

A month later, the newlyweds were presented at court.

48, Dover Street, London, March 21, 1867.

My Dear Louisa,

Thanks for Margaret's and your kind letters. . . . You will have seen by the papers that she and I were at Court, and kissed hands. Now, you must understand that this was not a general levee or drawing-room where every one goes, but a special Court at which only those specially summoned appear. This took place at 3. In the morning at half-past twelve, I and four others, as a special honour, had private audiences of Her Majesty. We went in separately. I went in first, as head of the Conference. There were only in the room the Queen, Princess Louise, and Lord Carnarvon, the Colonial Secretary. On entering, the Queen put out her hand, on which I knelt and kissed it. On rising she said, 'I am very glad to see you on this mission.' I bowed. 'I hope all things are going well with you.' I said I was happy to inform Her Majesty that all things had been prosperous with us, and by the aid of Lord Carnarvon our measure had made great progress and there had been no delays. H.M. said, 'It is a very important measure, and you have all exhibited so much loyalty.' I replied, 'We have desired in this measure to declare in the most solemn and emphatic manner our resolve to be under the Sovereignty of Your Majesty and your family for ever.' And so ended the audience. She had kind words for all those who followed me, Cartier, Galt, Tupper, and Tilley. Lord Monck is to return to Canada as Governor General, and has, but this is *entre nous*, charged me with the formation of the first Government as Premier. We have been quite lions here. My wife likes it from its novelty to her, but it rather bores me, as I have seen it all before. . . .

Your affectionate brother,

John A. Macdonald.

Joseph Pope, *Memoirs of the Right Honourable Sir John Alexander Macdonald*, vol. 1 (1894), pp. 318-19

Their family life was simple and agreeable. (Lady Rose was the wife of John A.'s friend Sir John Rose.)

[Macdonald's] appetite was small and easily satisfied. On rising he took a cup of tea in his bedroom. His *dejeuner* consisted of a minute portion of fish, game, or often a marrow bone, of which he was very fond; toast and butter without salt. Occasionally, when he saw anybody at breakfast with an appetite like his own, he would tell them of Lady Rose's remark to him on a like occasion, that 'only innocent people ate breakfast'.

He generally managed to devote at least two hours a day to his departmental duties. His afternoons were spent in Council, which generally rose in time for him to dine at half-past seven. The half-hour before dinner was given up to his invalid daughter, whom he loved with all the warmth of his affectionate nature. His first words on entering the house frequently were, 'Where is my little girl?' He would sit down beside her, and talk over the events of the day. Such conversations, brimful as they were of light *badinage*, in which they both excelled, were delightful to listen to. Sometimes he joined in a game with her, or read to her some story in which she was interested. His dinner was simple in character, a single dish and a glass of claret often sufficing for his moderate wants. His leisure evenings were generally spent in the library, looking over the newspapers, or playing a game of 'patience' of which he was very fond, and in the mysteries of which he was always ready to instruct any of his little daughter's friends who displayed curiosity to know what he was doing. Most of the time in which I knew him, he played 'patience' several times a day. Often before going to Council, when his carriage was at the door, he would sit down at the table sacred to this amusement, and play a game, which he said had the same soothing effect upon him as a cigar upon a smoker.

Ibid., vol. 2, p. 269

Macdonald on his own hearth was extremely gracious and kind to his wife; but let Lady Macdonald tell: 'My lord and master who in his private capacity simply lives to please and gratify me ... is absolutely tyrannical in his public life as far as I am concerned. When I pressed on him on an appointment Sir John looked very benign, very gracious, very pleasant—but—*answered not one word!* He never does.'

P.B. Waite, 'Sir John A. Macdonald: The Man', *Dalhousie Review* 47, no. 2 (Summer 1967), p. 150

Agnes's Victorian earnestness is evident in her diary.

January 7 and 8 [1868]. As for Sir John, the doctor tells me he is working himself terribly. He is so precious to us all that we are perhaps oversolicitous, but his constant attention to close business seems to overlap. I have brought it before my Heavenly Father in my prayers, and I know all will be well. . . . I am trying to disentangle my life, and make my thoughts arrange themselves. In reading I have given up novels . . . all those which are frivolous. . . . And then I have given up wine—that is for example's sake! And because I think it is necessary. I dislike all games of cards but 'Patience', which we read 'Albert the Good' was fond of. I hope to be able to take a right stand about Balls and to set my face against theatricals.

Quoted in Lena Newman, *The John A. Macdonald Album* (1974), p. 88

Sir John was concerned that his own investments in real estate and those of his wife should not be perceived to be in conflict of interest.

When the city of Vancouver was in its infancy, or, rather, before there was any city there at all, Lady Macdonald one day expressed the wish to purchase two lots on what is now the town site, and asked Sir John's permission to do so.

Said she, 'I don't want any money; I have three or four hundred dollars of my own, and the Colonel' (her brother) 'will give me three or four hundred more.'

'No, my dear,' he replied, 'you had better not!'

'Why?' said Lady Macdonald.

'Well, if you were to buy any lots out there, the first thing I should know would be that a post-office or a customhouse was put on them without my knowing anything about it, and I should have it thrown at me in Parliament that you had been paid for them ten cents more than they were worth.'

So the lots were never bought.

Joseph Pope, *Memoirs of the Right Honourable Sir John Alexander Macdonald*, vol. 2 (1894), p. 253

The New Year's levee:

January 2, 1871. What a bustling day! All the fires blazing and crackling; all the house in its best order; all the servants important and in a hurry, and I, in my best black velveteen gown, receiving New Year visitors. The house was thronged from noon till dinnertime with men of all ages, sorts, and sizes. Some 130 in all. Some merely shook hands and bowed, exchanged a few commonplaces about the weather; but the larger part lunched at a continually replenished table in the dining-room and wished me and mine all happiness for the New Year between mouthfuls of hot oyster soup or sips of sherry. Sir John spoiled everything by having ordered a Council. I had set my heart on having him with me, and lo! he went away before one single caller had rung the bell. I never enjoy anything much at which he does not assist and his pleasant easy manners make all go on well. He only came in at dinner-time, all covered with snow.

> Quoted in Lena Newman, *The John A. Macdonald Album* (1974), p. 90

Mary's birth was at once a joy and a tragedy.

On May 1, 1869, Agnes admitted to her diary the greatest sorrow a mother can ever know: that her child would never develop normally.

> The day has been stamped with the world's greatest seal—it is graven, I think, with the word 'disappointment'. Perhaps yesterday was one of the saddest times of my life—let it pass—let it die—only teach me, Heavenly Father to see the lesson it was destined to teach, and while I learn it to do so cheerfully. . . .

For both parents, the sorrow was intense. Agnes did not, could not, express her thoughts even on the pages of her diary, and, for some six months, she did not write a word there. When she did write again, in November, she was in a thoughtfully sad mood:

> What has happened with me since this day last year when I sat writing —as I sit now—in my big Diary? Wonderfully little—and yet wonderfully much. Outwardly all is nearly the same except that my darling child's smile brightens my home—but in my heart I feel that much is totally different. I ought to be wiser for I have suffered keenly in mind since I last wrote here. Only One who knows all our hearts can tell how keenly and painfully or how for long weeks and months all was gloom and disappointment.
>
> Louise Reynolds, *Agnes: The Biography of Lady Macdonald* (1979), pp. 60-1

Other aspects of Mary's development—or lack of it—are less clear, partly because no one seems to have retained records, partly because both her parents, well in advance of their time, were determined to treat her as much as possible as a child of ordinary physical and mental capabilities. In 1873, when she was four-and-a-half, John A. sent her a charming note at Rivière du Loup . . . . Depressed or not, harried by politics or not, he made it appear as if his only thought was about his little girl's return from the cottage.

> My dearest Mary
> You must know that your kind Mama and I are very anxious to see you and Granny again. We have just put a new carpet in your room and got everything ready for you.
>   The garden looks lovely just now . . . there are some fine melons. . . . You must pick them for dinner and feed the chickens with the rind. You remember that Mama cut my hair and made me look like a cropped donkey. It has grown quite long again. When you come home you must not pull it too hard.
>   I intend to have some new stories for you when you come in the morning into Papa's bed and cuddle him up. . . .
>   . . . and so goodbye my pet and come home soon to your loving papa.
>
>   John A.
>   Ibid., pp. 78-9

By 1877 it was Mary's turn to write to John A. In a letter which is marked as verbatim dictation, the little eight-year-old said:

>   Toronto, October 12, 1877
> My Dear Father
> I hope you are quite well. Your wife Agnes sends her love. She did not tell me to say so but I am sure she would if she knew it.
>   . . . Dear Father, when are you coming back? I hope you will be back very soon. . . . The house seems so dull and lonely without you and I miss my evening stories very much. . . .
>   Your affectionate Baboo and daughter.
>   Mary Macdonald
> Oh! What a scrimmage I've made. I forgot to say anything about my old hen. Sarah is well and chirpy as ever. That's all.

This letter and many like it raise the question of how much verbal communication Mary ever attained. The notation of 'verbatim dictation' suggests that, unlike many hydrocephalics, she did learn to speak rather well. Yet, as late as 1906, her mother wrote she could not 'speak more than a few words and those very badly'. Clearly, she did learn to communicate with at least those close to her, but when and to what extent may never be known.

                                                                     Ibid., p. 79

Her parents continued to hope and seek help.

Ottawa Oct. 3, 1880

My dear Louisa

... I have been rewarded by success and am in good health and spirits. I found Agnes *very* well and Mary much improved. Agnes and she will go to New York next month for medical treatment as to Mary's walking. Always my dear Louisa,

most affectionately yours,
John A. Macdonald
J.K. Johnson, ed., *Affectionately Yours* (1969), p. 143

In Mary's teens, it must have been particularly difficult to accept the fact that she could join in her friends' fun only from her wheelchair. John A., especially, tried to soften the blows. One time, as the guests were preparing to leave at the end of a dance which Mary had given, he quietly persuaded them to stay a little longer. 'When they resumed the dance, he leaned over his child's chair and said, "You see, Mary, they want a little more of your society and a little dancing by the way".'

If John A. occasionally over-compensated by indulging his little 'Baboo', as he sometimes called Mary, it was left up to Agnes to be the disciplinarian, and she wrote of this to Louisa in 1887: 'I have tried to teach Mary what my mother tried to teach me, that she must do, or have done, what is best for her and for others and not grumble & she has perfect faith in our plans for her.'

Whether because of her mother's teachings or not, Mary seems to have inspired quite genuine love in almost everyone who came in contact with her. Her half-brother, Hugh, summed it up nicely in a letter to the Professor [Williamson—his uncle] in 1889: 'She is a gentle amiable girl and no one who sees much of her can help being fond of her.'

Hugh, who had firm convictions about Mary's condition, preceded this remark with some shrewd insights into her development during these years of late adolescence. During the summer of 1888, he had spent some time with his father, Agnes and Mary and concluded that:

> [Mary's] mind was developing and that she was becoming more of a woman and less of a child than she had heretofore been, although in many respects she was still very childish. This, however, is accounted for by the fact that both my father and mother generally treat her as a child and that her companions, when not people well advanced in life, are as a rule much younger than herself.
>
> Louise Reynolds, *Agnes: The Biography of Lady Macdonald* (1979), pp. 124-5

During John A.'s years in opposition, the family lived in Toronto.

*Agnes, typically, tried to be a good stepmother to Hugh but felt
uncomfortable.*

For much of 1874 and early 1875, John A. travelled back and forth
between Ottawa and Toronto. . . . For nearly a year after the move,
they rented a pleasant, roomy house, set in spacious grounds in a
quiet neighbourhood on Sherbourne Street, from their friend, T.C.
Patteson, of the *Mail*. John A., however, had his eye on . . . an
impressive residence . . . at 63 St George Street; he finally bought it
in the spring of 1876. It was a new building, but even so it required
alterations to adapt it to the Macdonalds' special needs, and Agnes
spent the spring supervising the work of carpenters and painters. In
early May she organized yet another move, but once they were
settled, the family found that the house was ideal.

One important factor in the Macdonalds' decision to move to
Toronto had been a desire to be closer to Hugh John. Father and son
had seen each other only at intervals since Isabella's death, and John
A. often felt that the role of 'visiting parent' was a highly unsatisfactory one. His second marriage had not really improved the situation. Hugh was already seventeen at the time, only fourteen years
younger than Agnes, who, for years past, had had little contact with
young people. Not since her days in Barrie had she lived close to
youth, and Hugh John was no mere youth—he was her step-son. In
those first days of feeling her way into a totally new life, she had
been unsure how to approach the young man when he visited during
school holidays. Certainly, she had welcomed him warmly, even if
she had not been sure how to react: 'So glad to see the dear old boy. I
love him if only for his likeness to my husband.'

During that visit, she had even tried giving a little party for him,
but, for the new hostess, the entertaining of teenagers had proved
no easier then than it is now. The party, she thought, 'was very
stupid. I could do nothing to promote gaiety myself. . . . Sir John
was charming, however, and we could never have done without
him.'

Later, her step-son became 'Hughie' to her, but her uncertainty
still showed up in her diary, uncertainty as to whether or not her
feelings were more of concern than of 'motherly' love: 'Hughie is
here—our good, steady going dear old Hugh, one cannot help respecting and loving him. John's both fond and proud of him but the
boy has been brought up necessarily much away from his father.'

Ibid., pp. 82-3

They returned to Ottawa in 1878, and in 1882 bought a new home.

Their friend Thomas Reynolds had died two years previously and his house, Earnscliffe, which had been their favourite Ottawa home, became available. In 1882, they bought it. Many years later, Agnes admitted that she had

> begged Sir John very hard before he would buy it. He was always thinking of me and a possible future without him and did not want to diminish his savings, by putting it into property.
>
> But I did want him to have a really nice comfortable home & *coaxed hard* & had the great satisfaction of knowing that he thoroughly liked & enjoyed the place. . . . It was a very wise purchase, made a delightful home for us.
>
> Ibid., p. 96

Sir John was the honorary patron of the Oshkosh Toboggan Club.

. . . tobogganing and skating had not lost their appeal for the residents of Ottawa. Successive Governors-General entertained their guests in this manner, and the Stanleys, who had succeeded the Lansdownes a few months earlier, were no exception. They were, possibly, trying too hard to fit into Canadian society, John A. confided in a letter to George Stephen: '[They] are working hard to make themselves popular and are succeeding but *entre nous* are making themselves far too cheap & therein causing disadvantageous comparisons to be drawn by our upper classes between them and the Lansdownes.'

Whether or not the Stanleys were cheapening themselves, they would have had to put on quite a show to match the one their predecessors had staged one December. It was of such magnificence that Agnes had to write about it for *Murray's Magazine*.

> An annual midnight fête at Government House about Christmas time is particularly attractive, if the weather be fine and the cold not extreme. Then the little valley and the dark sleeping woods around flush crimson in the glare of two enormous bonfires, near which the 'music' sits with circled stands on the snow. Engine headlights, placed at intervals, pour their white shafts of dazzle far and wide. Thousands of Chinese lanterns glow in the air, and suspended on wires, in double rows encircle each crowded rink, outline also both slide and stairway, and dance in vistas under the purple night sky. Great is the fun and merriment, for all the world is there. Those who themselves take no active part in the sports sit in a much-windowed building overlooking the grounds, and watch the swift gleam of many shining skates, or the flight of descending tobogans [sic] as they dart—a flash of light and colour—across the snowy landscape, for sometimes the foremost sitter holds aloft a blazing torch which throws a line of fire over her red and blue companions. Presently rockets, Roman candles, and

lights orange, green and blue, dazzle through the air, and as they fade out, a belt of dark wood is seen spanned with a contrivance in gas jets wishing all there present . . . a Merry Christmas and a Happy New Year.

Ibid., pp. 127-8

Saturday night dinner parties during the session had been a long Earnscliffe tradition. Agnes held Saturday afternoon teas too. Sara Jeannette Duncan went to one of the latter in May 1888. A large good-natured mastiff was sunning himself in front of the door. The hall was large and old-fashioned and at the end was the drawing room, sunlit and comfortable, which looked out on the Ottawa River through pines and birches. At five o'clock tea was brought in, and occasionally Macdonald himself would leave affairs of state and come to chat with Agnes' visitors, 'in the jocund fashion that brings, with his name, so ready a smile to the lips of his friends. I am bound to say,' Sara Duncan went on, 'that not many Liberal foes are to be seen within the portals of Earnscliffe.' That would be Agnes' doing, more than Sir John's. In party matters she was more Conservative than the Prime Minister. If there were the usual tea party, Saturday afternoon, May 23, 1891, Macdonald did not come. He had a cabinet meeting, and came home for the dinner party at seven o'clock. He was in tremendous form that night at dinner. When Joseph Pope left Earnscliffe at ten o'clock, he really felt that the vigorous Macdonald of 1887 had been restored to them.

P.B. Waite, Macdonald: His Life and World (1975), pp. 211-13

While John A. was not generally considered to be religious, this newspaper sketch reveals another side of his character.

'I knew that Sir John Macdonald had religious convictions. Several years ago, when the United Empire Club was in existence, he came in there one night—I think it was Sunday night. Mr Manning and a party of solid old Tories were at one end of the parlour. James E. Smith was there also, Jack Beatty, Col. Arthurs and several others I can't now remember. The entry of Sir John caused some little excitement, and there were hearty hand-shakings and exchanges of compliments. The visitor had just come from the Metropolitan or some other church, where he had heard Rev. John Potts preach. A sort of incredulous little laugh went round among a few, when Sir John said that he had been at church. . . . As he leaned easily on the back of a chair, he began to speak to those seated around him of the Beatitudes. One by one he told them over, commenting on each, and showing by the deep reverence of his manner that he had a high conception of the majestic mind that wrought them. He spoke for about ten minutes, perhaps more, with an attractive earnestness that had its effect upon all who heard him. And when he had ended he gravely wished his company "good evening!" and departed. There was silence in that room for five minutes after he went out. . . .

'When he was travelling through the country on the parlour car Jamaica during the last campaign up near London, or on the Western Division somewhere, that I do not remember very well, a stick of timber protruding from a passing train struck the Jamaica and smashed one end of it. When the train arrived in the city the next night, I went down to see what damage had been done, for it had been noised abroad that an attempt had been made to wreck the train. The coloured porter answered my summons at the door, and he showed me into one of the compartments fitted up as a parlour. Sir John Macdonald sat in an easy chair reading the Bible. He was alone in the car, with the exception of the porter, the other ministers having gone elsewhere, and he was about going to bed. He looked very lonely sitting there in the dim light. He was reading David's Psalms, that have been a comfort to the weary for many hundreds of years. My stay was brief, for it was only to congratulate him on his escape from injury. As I passed out I put a question to the porter. It was prying into private affairs, but I could not help it. The porter's reply was "Yes, sir; he always reads the Book before going to bed." I had formed a different opinion of him. I had judged him by his reputation, until I knew his character. . . .'

E.B. Biggar, Anecdotal Life of Sir John Macdonald (1891), pp. 267-8

PARLIAMENT: PROCEDURES, STAFF, INSTITUTIONS

No book on this era would be complete without a glimpse into the world of the House, its institutions, and its staff in the early years after Confederation. The years before Macdonald's death saw the first committees, the formation of a parliamentary library, and the development of Hansard (which Macdonald seldom read because it took so long to produce, and the earlier newspaper Hansard was so partisan). Whereas today political neutrality is a requirement for a

*parliamentary staff position, in those years the choice of the House
staff was dominated by partisan politics.*

*On occasion there were serious breaches in House procedure, occa-
sioned, undoubtedly, by the ready availability of parliamentary
saloons. Once Macdonald's sharp-eyed secretary averted a fiscal
and procedural disaster as the speech to prorogue the session was in
progress.*

I remember one unusual parliamentary experience. It occurred during the prorogation ceremony of 1884. I was on hand as usual,
moving about behind the Throne. The bills passed during the session were assented to in the customary manner, and the Governor-
General had just unrolled and was beginning to read his speech,
when I realized that the royal assent . . . had not been given to the
Supply Bill. There was not a moment to be lost. Withdrawing the
curtains which hung at the side of the Throne, about which the
Ministers stood grouped, I pulled Sir John's coat tail. He turned
sharply round, evidently resenting the intrusion, when I whispered
in his ear that the Supply Bill had not been assented to. Like a flash
he took in the situation, and stopped the proceedings. The omission
was speedily repaired, and the reading of the speech resumed. Had I
not acted quickly . . . it would have been necessary to issue a fresh
Proclamation summoning Parliament anew for the express purpose
of enabling the Governor-General to accept in the Queen's name,
from Her Majesty's faithful commoners, the supplies necessary to
the carrying on of the public service.

> Maurice Pope, ed., *Public Servant: The Memoirs of Sir Joseph
> Pope*, (1960), p. 46

John A.'s opinion on the introduction of closure:

The session of 1885 was marked by the hitherto unparalleled
obstruction offered by the Liberal Opposition to the passage of a
Franchise Act for the Dominion. Up to this time the provincial
franchises had been in use for the Dominion House of Commons,
but Sir John Macdonald had long felt that the Parliament of Canada
should fix the electoral qualifications for its own body. The Opposition resisted this change, and their obstruction reached such a pitch
that the Government of the day seriously contemplated . . . intro-
ducing the closure. Sir John, however, opposed this policy, which he
regarded as an interference with the freedom of debate. While
admitting that the closure might eventually become a necessity, he
declared that he would prefer its introduction by a Liberal rather

than by a Conservative Government. He considered that on purely party grounds its adoption would be a tactical mistake.

Ibid., p. 51

His views on precedence and rank:

The following letter, addressed by Sir John Macdonald to the Governor General on the subject of proposed changes in the table of precedence . . . in force in Canada, discloses his views on certain questions of interest in official circles:

Earnscliffe, Ottawa, April 15, 1886.

Dear Lord Lansdowne,

Sir Alexander Campbell has seen the members of Council about the question of precedence.

They are all agreed that the Dominion has outgrown the position in which the General commanding at Halifax should represent Her Majesty in case of the Governor General's temporary absence, and unite in thinking that the Governor General should be empowered, in the event of leave of absence, to appoint, under his seal-at-arms, the Chief Justice or other judge of the Supreme Court as Administrator.

It might also be provided that, in the event of the Governor General's sudden decease, the Chief Justice, if within the Dominion, or, in his absence, the senior judge, should assume the Administration until a successor is appointed.

You will observe from the proposed table of precedence that a change is made, giving to members of the Cabinet precedence over Lieutenant Governors of provinces. Personally, I have no opinion in the matter, and should be well satisfied to leave things as they are, giving the Lieutenant Governor the *pas*. My colleagues, however, are unanimous the other way. . . .

My colleagues think that whatever position may be given to Lieutenant Governors of Provinces, the following words should be added: 'At Ottawa, and elsewhere out of their own provinces; but, within his own province, each to take precedence of every one, save the Governor General and the members of his Cabinet.'

Believe me, dear Lord Lansdowne,

Yours very faithfully,
John A. Macdonald.

Joseph Pope, Memoirs of the Right Honourable Sir John Alexander Macdonald, vol. 2 (1894), pp. 240-2

Early Speakers of the House were clearly partisan and often argued in debates, although they were certainly not supposed to. John A. posed little difficulty for the Speakers of his own choice, but during his years in opposition he was known to try to control the Speaker.

The convention of alternating Speakers between French and Eng-
lish did not begin until 1879 when J.G. Blanchet was appointed.

The manner in which the Speaker was chosen militated against his
having a strong hold over the Commons, and particularly over the
majority, for he was invariably selected by the Government, sometimes without having been forewarned himself, and normally without the rank and file supporters of the Government having been
consulted. Six individuals held the speakership in Macdonald's day,
and most of them were men who might legitimately have aspired to
a cabinet post. . . .

The first several Speakers, while in the Chair, continued to look
after patronage in their constituencies as though they were ordinary
members. [T.W.] Anglin was so zealous in this regard that the
[Liberal] Prime Minister reprimanded him sharply in 1875: 'It is
impossible,' Alexander Mackenzie wrote, 'that, in the public interest, I can force inexperienced men upon the Railway Manager, and I
can scarcely help thinking that you are somewhat unreasonable in
expecting that I should do so.' At least three of the first six Speakers
aspired to a cabinet post after their terms in the Chair. . . .

At least three of the early Speakers felt somewhat unfulfilled in
the Chair. [James] Cockburn threatened to resign the speakership in
1870 in order to participate freely in the debates over an issue on
which he felt strongly. In 1871, noting that 'I have got through the
Speaker's duties this session with éclat and have had praises on all
sides,' he asked Macdonald to send him out as first Lieutenant-
Governor of British Columbia. [G.A.] Kirkpatrick advised Macdonald in 1885, 'I do not think I can sit in the Chair another
session. . . . Premonitory symptoms tell me I must take more exercise.' Anglin, a forthright and talkative individual, when testifying
in 1877 before the Committee of Privileges and Elections about the
contracts he held with the Crown, said he 'had always regarded the
Speakership as a most irksome and unpleasant position'. With his
habits, he said, accustomed as he was to taking an active part in the
business of the House, he felt that the occupancy of the Chair would
be for him a particularly unpleasant position. Anglin undoubtedly
did find the speakership irksome at times. The Chair was no place
for a devout Catholic during the heated debates in 1874 over Louis
Riel, for instance, and an alert Press Gallery reporter noted Anglin's
agitation. And quite apart from the Riel debates, the reporter observed, Anglin 'talks too much. . . . He explains, expostulates, nay
even argues from his seat.' Cockburn, on the other hand, though 'a
little man, low voiced, retiring and apparently timid, [whose] rul-

ings were by no means infallible . . . [with] no prestige about him to awe the House,' had done well from 1867 to 1874.

. . . Not once between 1867 and 1891 was a Speaker's ruling even formally challenged, let alone reversed; on rare occasions a potential challenge was averted when a Speaker changed his mind. The right to challenge a Speaker's ruling was fully recognized, and often referred to, but the simple fact that the Speaker was from the first a partisan appointee meant that the support of the majority for any ruling he might make could virtually be taken for granted. Speakers checked members on both sides of the House impartially, and both Liberal and Conservative leaders were called to order by their own appointees. Kirkpatrick on one occasion, against his will, stayed away from a public demonstration in honour of his party chieftain, remembering, as he told Sir John, 'Your admonition to me "to assume a virtue even if I have it not".'

Norman Ward, 'The Formative Years of the House of Commons,
1867-91', Canadian Journal of Economics and Political Science
18 (1952), pp. 435-7

Not the least of the Speaker's problems was John A., who on several occasions tested the former's ability to maintain order.

. . . Speakers and deputies alike commonly had the greatest difficulty in discharging one of their most important functions, the maintaining of order. The temper of the old House was not conducive to continued calm, and a tolerant view was taken of the rules. No one had a greater affection for the Commons than Macdonald but Macdonald, unrebuked by the Chair, more than once threw into debate remarks such as: 'The honourable member— honourable by courtesy only after tonight . . .' or 'Well then, in a parliamentary sense I do not believe it, but in the other sense, I do.' Macdonald sharply challenged the only Liberal Speaker he had to put up with: 'Do you decide, Mr Speaker, that you are to be the judge of the manner in which an honourable member is to address the House? Never was there a Speaker in any House of Commons who made such a misrepresentation of British institutions.' Macdonald on occasion called his own Speakers to order: 'Really, Mr Speaker, there must be some order kept, and you were evidently not listening when the honourable gentleman . . . was clearly out of order.'

Ibid., p. 438

When the first Deputy Speaker was chosen in 1885, the creation of the office caused some controversy.

When the deputy speakership was created in 1885, the Government accepted an amendment, moved by a French-speaking Manitoban, that required the Deputy 'to possess a full and practical knowledge of the language which is not that of the Speaker'. The Speaker at the time was Kirkpatrick, from Ontario; and his first Deputy Speaker was Malachy Daly, an Irish Catholic from Halifax who, Sir John A. Macdonald admitted, could not speak the French as well as his own language—'[but] I am sure will be quite competent'. The second Deputy Speaker, chosen when Ouimet had the Chair, was from Ontario. For years the Liberal Opposition scouted the idea that a Deputy Speaker was necessary at all, arguing that the real purpose in establishing the office was to provide the Government with one more salaried post for political patronage, and that the practice that had prevailed to 1885, whereby the Speaker selected a deputy from the floor of the House any time he needed one, was both adequate and inexpensive.

Ibid.

The staff of the House:

The Speaker, to assist him in managing the affairs of the House, had after 1868 a statutory group of assistants drawn entirely from the cabinet, and which always included the Prime Minister. The relevant statute, a singularly incoherent document, read:

> The Speaker of the House of Commons for the time being, and any four members of Her Majesty's Privy Council for Canada, for the time being, who may be appointed by the Governor in Council as Commissioners under this Act, (they and each of them being also Members of the House of Commons,) and the names and offices of whom and their appointment as Commissioners shall be communicated by message from the Governor to the House of Commons in the first week of each Session of Parliament, shall be, and they are hereby nominated, constituted and appointed Commissioners for the purposes of this Act, and any three of the said Commissioners whereof the Speaker of the House of Commons for the time being shall be one, shall be and they are hereby authorized to carry this Act into execution.

The Act then went on to empower the Clerk of the House and the Sergeant-at-Arms to prepare annual estimates for their separate departments; but 'such estimates shall be submitted to the Speaker for his approval and shall be subject to such alterations as the Speaker shall consider proper'. Whatever the statute was intended to do (and its purpose is certainly not clear from the text), in practice the internal affairs of the House of Commons, in so far as such matters as personnel, size of establishment, and rates of pay were concerned, were in the sole control of the executive branch of the government.

Ibid., pp. 439-40

Of the first three Clerks of the House, two were men of long experience in the old colonial Assembly, W.B. Lindsay and A. Patrick; and J.G. Bourinot's distinguished writings are still useful. Alpheus Todd, who was Parliamentary Librarian until his death in 1884, was no less eminent than Bourinot as a scholar and an authority on the constitution. Letters to Sir John A. Macdonald from all these men make clear that, however non-partisan they were officially, they were privately in sympathy with the Conservatives, and not only were helpful when consulted, but frequently volunteered advice.

Ibid., p. 440

John A. took a concerned interest in the Library of Parliament.

The Library of Parliament, which is today . . . the only surviving relic of early parliamentary days in Canada, can fairly be said to have been as useful to members as were the Commons' staff and the Hansard. Sir John A. Macdonald had high hopes for the Library. He said in 1868: 'The Library could not be considered merely as a legislative but as a national institution, which should take some such position here as that of the British Museum . . . and must be made open to all students or readers desiring reference to scarce and valuable stores of information.' Macdonald continued to voice these hopes from time to time for the remainder of his life, but he was not blind to what the Library really was. In 1882 he said: 'It is too large for a parliamentary library, and too small and confined for a public and general library. . . . I fear, from the casual glance which I take occasionally in the Library—and this is not very often at present—that there is an enormous quantity of trash and rot . . . which ought not to be in any decent library.'

Macdonald's opinion was well founded, and for two reasons. The Library, in some mysterious way, early shared the fate of the Commons' restaurant and became in every sense a public institution, though presumably one attracting a class of trade different from that of the saloon. The general public seems to have been more interested in light and frivolous reading than in philosophy and history, and Alpheus Todd was a co-operative librarian. An able scholar devoid of business instincts, Todd early solved the vexing problem of buying books outside his own field by the simple device of letting somebody else do it for him, and the person so elected was an English bookseller. The books, Macdonald said, 'are shovelled over here instead of being carefully selected.'. . .

. . . The librarian's post lay vacant for more than a year after Todd's death, and then the Government introduced the curious two-headed system which still prevails. Ostensibly, the Government's purpose in 1885 was to establish a national library with two librarians in charge, one a General Librarian 'to look after the Library as a whole, as a scientific and literary institution', the other a Parliamentary Librarian to 'apply himself specifically to parliamentary precedents'. The Opposition's view was that the Library of Parliament had fallen prey to the Government's inability to make up its mind whether to appoint a French or an English-speaking successor to Todd, and Richard Cartwright predicted that 'within a short number of years . . . we will have two Librarians, two heads of a Department, and two staffs.' . . .

The perceptive Nicholas Flood Davin, who had an active interest in books, wrote Macdonald a remarkable letter in 1884, urging him to get the best man he could for the vacant librarianship. Davin said in part: 'At the present the Library as a reference library is by no means in first rate condition, and in those departments of literature with which I am familiar there are serious gaps. How can a man who is not a literary man and who has only read a little repair defects which only a well-read man could perceive? . . . Remember, if the politicians are the immediate donors of power, you will be dependent on literary men for the way posterity will regard you.'

Ibid., pp. 446-8

The first general librarian of parliament, A.D. DeCelles, a former journalist and editor of La Minerve *(1872-78), forecast the need for what today is known as the research branch as early as 1885.*

. . . in 1885 he wrote a memorandum for Macdonald, suggesting 'a class of men who could be safely consulted. . . . During the recess these officers would have ample time for study, especially if admission to the Library were more restricted than it is at present.'

Ibid., p. 447

The standards for those employed at the lower levels of the House staff were questionable.

The use of patronage for manning the lower echelons of the House of Commons staff resulted in the employment of some people of remarkable incapacity. The group of cabinet ministers which assisted Mr Speaker in the management of the House (the group was variously called the Commission of Internal Economy, the Board of Internal Economy, and the Internal Economy Commission) caused an investigation to be made of the House of Commons staff in 1884. The investigators, who were organized as a quasi-commission of three members, one of whom was [J.G.] Bourinot, were to examine the problem of regulations which then existed. The quasi-commission reported in favour of adopting civil service rules, and the Commission of Internal Economy promptly produced a schedule classifying the employees of the House of Commons. The report of the quasi-commission was not overly critical of the permanent staff, many of whom were drawn for the session from the regular government departments; but of the sessional employees, a multitude of whom appear to have swarmed around Parliament Hill at times, the report said that they were 'too often selected without regard to qualifications or habits. . . .

The pressures to which the Speaker and the Prime Minister were subjected on account of House patronage were phenomenal. As long as the legislative staff was not under any civil service rules, citizens who were too old for the regular departments, or otherwise incapacitated, sought employment in the House of Commons. (The most interesting of these by far was a man who, ordered to take six months' rest by his doctors because of congestion of the brain, asked Macdonald if there were not in the Government's gift some position he could fill.) . . .

Former speaker Anglin provided a coda: 'I experienced a similar pressure for some years,' he said, thus exonerating the Conservatives on any charge that they had enjoyed a monopoly when it came to abusing the House. He told how he had once investigated the activities of some [sessional] clerks who had aroused his suspicions; he found them disporting themselves about the streets, having done nothing for several weeks but draw their pay, and he fired them all.

Ibid., pp. 441-2

It was not until 1878 that the office of Auditor General was created.

. . . before that the auditing was in the hands of the Department of Finance, whose minister would presumably have been responsible for any irregularities unearthed by the audit. After 1878, the Government was scrupulously careful to observe the independence of the Auditor General, but his office was chronically short-staffed. The Auditor General informed the Prime Minister in 1881 that, 'the ordinary work is in arrears and there are certain duties of great

importance and requiring much labour and thought which have not
been begun. An accountant from the audit office testified before the
Public Accounts Committee as late as 1891 that 'we are short-
handed, and are therefore not able to make the system even all
along.'

Ibid., p. 449

The problem of Hansard:

After several false starts, the House's initial solution . . . consisted
of hiring a private contractor to provide a record, and appointing a
committee to keep an eye on the contractor, while every member of
parliament reserved the right to complain endlessly about the record, the contractor, and the committee. Naturally the private
contractor (commonly a gifted shorthand reporter who hired three
or four more stenographers to assist him, often recruiting them
from the Press Gallery) wanted to enlarge his profits by minimizing
his costs. The result was that the daily edition of the Hansard, from
which members had expected much, sometimes was days and even
weeks late; in 1878 a leading Liberal said that he had received his
daily editions of the 1877 session in August, several months after
Parliament had been prorogued. The French version was often
weeks and even months behind the English. Members objected
frequently to the inaccuracy of the record, and while there was
general agreement that on the whole the Hansard was not bad, there
was equally general agreement that it was not good. The private
contractors were not entirely to blame, for members used to hold up
proofs of their utterances for prolonged periods, occasionally edit-
ing them out of recognition. Responsible parliamentarians like
Blake and Langevin remained sceptical about the Hansard for years
after its establishment, and Alexander Mackenzie and Sir John A.
Macdonald both testified that they did not read it.

Ibid., p. 445

On a motion of Mr Macdonnell (Inverness), that the Hansard reports should be discontinued on account of the cost ($18,562),
amendments were moved, one by Mr Jones, that the reports be
made verbatim.

Sir John in the course of his speech upon the subject said—'It is
well known that objection was made a good many years ago by some
members to the reports in the *Times*, and they demanded that the
reports be taken "verbatim et literatim". The *Times* took them at
their word, and for two or three weeks published their speeches

verb. et lit. until they had to go on their knees and beg that the practice be discontinued. It might suit some who speak with peculiar verbal accuracy, and round off their sentences, as if they had been prepared. Some have that happy faculty. I for one have it not, and I should be very sorry to have my speeches reported "verbatim et literatim". To do away with the reports altogether would be a retrograde step. We all know the regrets expressed by every literary man, every statesman and every historian that the speeches made by great men in the days of old were lost forever. . . . Even in Canada how deeply interesting would be a Hansard showing the debates in the old province of Upper Canada or Lower Canada, giving the discussions of 1791-2. If we had *that*, it would be the most interesting volume in the world to any Canadian. We could learn the chief subjects of interest, the style of speaking and the manner of thought, not only of the leaders, but of the great body of the representatives of the people in those early days. And we are in a great measure without a colonial history. We have no means of tracing out the very groundwork of all our legislation, the motives and impulses of those petty municipal questions which were the chief subjects of interest in those early days, and which have expanded into the large subjects that are now engaging the people of Canada.'

E.B. Biggar, Anecdotal Life of Sir John Macdonald (1891),
pp. 177-8

By today's standards, members' 'perks' were meagre indeed.

Lacking an office and clerical assistance, the members of the House of Commons had one real piece of equipment, the boxes of stationery awarded them every session of Parliament. The boxes were large, and contained such necessities as paper, envelopes, pens and pencils, pocket-knives, pen-knives, paper-knives, glue, scissors, red tape, wallets, pocket-books, and card-cases. The members did not stint themselves and by the end of three or four sessions, one of them said frankly in 1890, each had enough of these things to do for himself, his children, and his grandchildren. But the giving of boxes (to which travelling trunks were added) was, as a cabinet minister asserted, one of the ancient usages of Parliament: 'It began a long time ago, has been well taken care of and nursed with a great deal of tenderness. Would it not be too bad to remove it all at once?' Besides, a Liberal Whip added, while there might be a certain embarrassment involved in having one's home encumbered with shoddy stuff received in Ottawa, 'every member ought to be thankful he has something to point to, to show that he has been a member of parliament during his life.'

Norman Ward, 'The Formative Years of the House of Commons, 1867-91', *Canadian Journal of Economics and Political Science* 18 (1952), pp. 443-4

Early committees were not unlike those of today.

... standing committees sometimes worked intensively, and sometimes not at all, and their reports were often able, and often inept. Special committees were granted when the Government was not opposed, and occasionally the Government itself sought a special committee to investigate a matter on which it was unprepared, or unwilling, to declare a policy. One unique characteristic of the early Public Accounts Committee was that its work was often less investigatory than inquisitorial. A member of the Opposition, usually a lawyer, would prepare a case against some public servant, politician, or contractor, and procedure in hearings was frequently more reminiscent of a courtroom than of a legislative committee. The committees were weakest when Sir John A. Macdonald was strongest.

Ibid., pp. 449-50

On the need for a Senate John A. was very clear.

Among constitutional questions few possessed for Sir John Macdonald greater interest than the bicameral system. . . . His view of the necessity for a second chamber may be expressed briefly by the story told of Washington, which Sir John was fond of relating. It is said that on his return from France Jefferson called Washington to account for having agreed to a second chamber.

'Of what use is the Senate?' he said, as he stood before the fire with a cup of tea in his hand, pouring the tea into his saucer as he spoke.

'You have answered your own question,' replied Washington.

'What do you mean?'

'Why did you pour that tea into your saucer?'

'To cool it,' quoth Jefferson.

'Even so,' said Washington, 'the Senate is the saucer into which we pour legislation to cool.'

This illustration, Sir John used to say, was perfect.

Joseph Pope, *Memoirs of the Right Honourable Sir John Alexander Macdonald*, vol. 2 (1894), p. 233

On the Senate's role, however, his ideas changed. Although originally he had favoured the concept of an elected Senate, he came to support a nominative system.

To his mind the chief among the objections to a Senate chosen by the popular vote, was the ever-present danger of its members claiming the right to deal with money Bills, and the consequent possibility of disputes with the House of Commons. The proposal that the provincial legislature, whose members are elected for purely local purposes, should choose the senators to legislate on matters of general concern was also objectionable, being opposed to the spirit of the constitution, which confined the local assemblies to a strictly limited sphere of action. He held that the system unanimously agreed to at the Quebec Conference had worked well, and should be undisturbed. A senatorship, in his opinion, was an important and dignified office, and a worthy object of ambition to any Canadian.

Ibid., p. 236

Despite his normally vigorous support of partisan appointments, John A. was decidedly non-partisan in his choice of judges. Excellence was his watchword—which explains why many of his major appointments crossed party lines.

In 1868, the retirement of Mr Draper from the Chief Justiceship of Upper Canada, called for a general reorganization of the Bench. To aid him in effecting the best possible arrangement, Sir John sought the opinion, among others, of Mr Edward Blake, the eldest son of the late Chancellor, already eminent both in his profession and in politics. Mr Blake was, at that time, leader of the Opposition in the Ontario Legislature, and one of Sir John's most formidable opponents in the House of Commons. Yet this fact never seems to have weighed for a moment with the latter in considering how best he could add to the strength of the courts. Thus, he writes to the Chancellor whom he proposed should succeed Mr Draper, as Chief Justice of Ontario:

'I am a good deal puzzled about the Court of Chancery.... If, however, Blake would take that Chancellorship, I think that, for the good of the Court, I ought to appoint him.'

And again:

'I waited for you at Toronto as long as I could, but I was due here on Saturday. I saw Blake before I left, and had a confidential talk with him. I told him exactly how matters stood—that you expressed a desire to stay where you were, but that I was to see you again on the subject. I said that I had no right to ask whether he would accept the Chancellorship, without offering it to him, but, under the circumstances, would ask him to give me some idea whether he could take it.'

To Mr Blake he subsequently wrote:

Ottawa, November 9, 1868.

My Dear Blake,

After I had the pleasure of seeing you in Toronto, I waited a day for Vankoughnet, but, as he did not arrive, I was obliged to return here. I wrote him on the subject of his change in full, and he at last decided to remain where he now is. On public grounds I regret this much, as with your help we could have made a good court of Equity, and the Common Law Bench could have been strengthened by Vankoughnet's accession to it. However, it cannot be helped. I have done everything in my power to keep up the efficiency of the Bench, but have been thus far thwarted. . . .

Yours very faithfully,
John A. Macdonald.

On the death of Mr Vankoughnet, in the following year, Sir John at once offered the Chancellorship to Mr Blake. An intimate friend, to whom he had confided his intention, having expressed a fear that the appointment of so many 'Grits' in succession to high office— 'Howland, McDougall, Gwynne and now Blake'—would demoralize the Conservative party, was thus answered:

'As you are aware, my only object in making judicial appointments is the efficiency of the Bench. . . . I am not insensible to the fact that Blake's politics render his appointment difficult. It is an unfortunate as well as a singular coincidence that the members of the Equity Bar are very nearly all Grits. But what can be done? Besides, I feel to a certain extent committed to Blake. Had Vankoughnet decided upon accepting the Chief Justiceship last year, Blake would have had the offer of the Chancellorship beyond a doubt. I told him confidentially that I would make him the offer, if the vacancy occurred. I do not think that anything has happened since then to warrant me in changing my course.'

Ibid., pp. 74-5

To those candidates he considered inappropriate, his approach was tactful.

Macdonald is always credited with having exercised discretion in his appointments to the bench. How he looked on it, and how he could gently turn aside an unwelcome candidate comes out in the following:

Ottawa, 26 Dec., 1882.

My dear Landry

I have your letter on the subject of a vacancy on the bench of your province. . . . It certainly never occurred to me that you would be an aspirant for the position. You are so important to the administration and to the party that I have looked forward to your career being a political one. . . . I cannot help thinking that it would be a great mistake for a young man like you, in the full vigor of health . . . to shelve yourself on the bench. . . . Ten years hence, after a successful political career, will be time to set yourself aside and make yourself in effect a legal monk. . . .

A.R.M. Lower, 'Sir John A. Macdonald', *Dalhousie Review* 19 (1939-40), p. 87

He had little interest in a position on the bench for himself.

When the Supreme Court was established at Ottawa a friend advised him to take the chief justiceship, and retire into the comparative quiet of that position and take life easy. He ridiculed the idea, and said he would rather be a dead premier than a live chief justice.

E.B. Biggar, *Anecdotal Life of Sir John Macdonald* (1891), pp. 251-2

PARLIAMENTARY LIFE

Parliamentary life under our first Prime Minister was a good deal more boisterous than it is today. Macdonald was not so much an orator as he was a House of Commons man, effectively presenting his arguments for the House's deliberation and spicing those arguments with wit and anecdote. Whereas D'Arcy McGee and Edward Blake were orators capable of grandiloquent flights, and Blake in particular could speak for hours on end, John A. could command the attention and respect of the House with shorter speeches that seldom strayed from the point to hand, playing on his knowledge of human nature and the appeal of plain speaking.

His style, like everything belonging to him, was peculiarly his own. Mr [Hector] Fabre thus admirably portrays his lighter moods:

An actor Sir John undoubtedly is. Graceful and pleasant in bearing, quick and ready in word and action, he acts his speeches as much as he delivers them; he acts with voice, head, and gesture. The inflections he gives to his voice awaken his dormant energy: he warms to his work, the hand ever in motion gives as it were a fresh impetus to every shaft as it falls from his lips and imparts to it a twofold force of irony.

Sir John is, indeed, given to lashing himself, particularly in his opening sentences: but the process seldom fails in its effect: his energies
are aroused, the flame bursts and the adversary is scorched. Sir John
excels in reply; he is, above all, brilliant in retort. He is languid at
times in stating his case, and rather gropes through his opening
sentences; but when he is stung in the fight, and has to give back a
blow, he is himself at once, and his keen incisive words, piercing the
flesh like a highly tempered blade, never fail to draw blood. Yet he is
too clever and too well versed in the knowledge of mankind to be
cruel: his executions are always amusing: they extort a smile even
from his gloomiest victims themselves.

> Joseph Pope, *Memoirs of The Right Honourable Sir John*
> *Alexander Macdonald*, vol. 2 (1894), p. 285

In the words of J.S. Willison, an ideological opponent who had long
observed him:

Sir John Macdonald was neither a popular orator nor a parliamentary debater of the first order. He was, however, a profound student
of character. He had humour, adaptiveness, and readiness. He could
break the force of an attack with a story or an epigram. He had that
mysterious quality of personal magnetism which gives to its fortunate possessors a strange and mighty power over their kind. During
the last four or five years of his life, his seat in Parliament was often
vacant. He nursed his strength and avoided so far as possible the
worry and fatigue of late night sittings. It was his habit to sit with
his legs crossed and his head thrown back, with a jaunty air and an
alert look, except now and then when some keen debater across the
floor was pressing him hard, dealing square, strong blows at 'the old
man and the old policy', with perhaps a touch of bitterness in the
words, and a keen knowledge of the old man's ways revealed in the
method of attack. At such time he would move uneasily as the
enemy pressed him close, toss his head, bite his lips, glance angrily
back upon his followers, throw some taunt to his opponents, and at
last come to his feet and retort upon the adversary. In later years he
rarely lost his complete self-control. In his angriest mood he was
deliberate, and seemed as he faced his opponents to be coolly and
craftily seeking for the weak spots in the indictment. He did not
always meet argument with argument. He had little eloquence. He
had no loftiness of speech. He never sought to cover the whole
ground of an opponent's attack. That elaboration of argument and
exhaustive mastery of detail which distinguished the speeches of
Mr Blake is generally lacking in the speeches of Sir John Macdonald.
In Parliament he rarely spoke to convince or win the Opposition.
His aim there was to touch the party loyalty and rouse the party

enthusiasm of his supporters. He would often turn his back upon the Liberals and address himself directly to the Ministerialists. He would strike some happy thought, some sentence full of keen sarcasm or genial ridicule, and with a shrewd look and smiling face and jaunty air, would drop the sentence with a shrug of the shoulders and a half-contemptuous gesture that always tickled his followers, and often exasperated his opponents. There he would stand with his back to the Speaker, while the Opposition chafed at the cool but skilful exaggeration of their position, and the Conservatives cheered with delight, and wagged their heads and shrugged their shoulders with sympathy with the old man's bantering humour.

He would pass one of Mr Blake's most powerful arraignments of his policy with a shrug and a story that perhaps had grown old in his service. He would meet one of Sir Richard Cartwright's most scathing exposures of the tendencies and results of his rule and methods with a smile for his followers and a jocular reminder for his opponents that the country had heard these arguments, and he was still in office. His relations with Mr Laurier were always cordial. He seemed to appreciate the courtesy of the brilliant young Liberal leader, as he respected the firmness with which he stood upon his rights, and the tenacity with which he held to his programme. With Mr Mills he had most cordial relations, and yet no man could more readily disturb his equanimity and touch his temper. Mr Mills' courage, his pertinacity, his baffling questions, his calculated, persistent, roundabout methods of getting at the truth sometimes greatly aggravated the Conservative leader. He hated to be forced into a corner. He hated to make any confession or to be driven from any position. Mr Davies, too, when he came out from behind his desk and flung his keen and vigorous eloquence into the face of the First Minister, often stirred his anger and sometimes roused his resentment. Mr Lister could likewise move him out of his usual smiling humour; and though Mr Paterson did not often drive the old man to anger, he was one of the few Liberals who could reach his political conscience.

Sir John Macdonald was fond of applause. He delighted in a bit of flattery from an opponent. He knew, as few men have known, how to use the social influence to political advantage. The man who came to Parliament with unsettled opinions, who wanted social notice, who wanted something for his constituency, was likely soon to find himself at the wheels of the old man's chariot. The young member was always noticed. The waverer was strengthened, and the wounded were healed. His appeals to party loyalty were always effective. His followers never failed to laugh when he joked. They always cheered his appeals. They always warmed into enthusiasm when he pointed to his majority in the House and in the country, and to the record of his achievements. The Conservatives in Parliament and in the constituencies loved Sir John Macdonald, and few men who had ever followed him could withstand his personal appeal. He had won great victories for his party, he had led them to triumph again and again, and they were grateful and loyal to the end, and mourned for him as for one taken out from their very households. Many Liberals, too, while they quarreled with his methods and were uncompromisingly hostile to his whole system of government, rather liked his cheerful audacity, and were not quite without a feeling of admiration for his strong and picturesque personality. He knew men to the core, and he could play upon their passions and prejudices as the master player upon the instrument that he loves. He was fertile in expedients, bold in the use of means, a master at the board by his very fondness for the great game he played. He was a favourite with journalists. He deemed no man beneath his notice. He never forgot that popularity was power. It may be that he was a supreme opportunist in face of forces which he could not control, or which he desired to control for his own political purposes. But in this sense Gladstone and Peel and even Cromwell were opportunists. It is only those whom Stevenson would call the 'faithful failures' of politics that are willing to go down into history as the champions of lost causes, and to forego temporary advantage in hope of reaction or in expectation of the applause of posterity.

But Sir John Macdonald was more than an opportunist. He had clear and definite ideals. He could face a popular clamour with signal courage. He seldom forgot that in order to promote the true interests of the Confederation it was essential to maintain good relations between the two races which comprise the bulk of the Canadian population, to resist the destructive tendencies of racialism, to respect even the prejudices of minorities, and to maintain loyally the guarantees of the Constitution. It is true that he often profited by racial and sectarian movements, but he was always their master, or at least seldom their servant, and in the end he moderated the temper, or baffled the purposes of the extremists. It was here that he did his best work, and his example of patient conciliation and resolute toleration was of inestimable value to the country in its formative period and must stand always as a beacon light to Canadian statesmen. He was jealous for the dignity of Parliament, for the integrity of the Bench, for the commercial credit of the country, for the legislative independence and self-governing rights of Canada.

J.S. Willison, *Sir Wilfrid Laurier and the Liberal Party* (1908), pp. 19-26

A summons to the Bar of the House (as opposed to the saloon) was a disciplinary measure.

Calling citizens to the Bar was commonly practised, and a wide variety of people ranging from minor election officials to the Prime Minister appeared in the custody of the Sergeant-at-Arms. Sir John A. Macdonald missed in 1873 a meeting of an election committee at which attendance was compulsory. When summoned before the House, he had a colleague produce a medical certificate saying that his doctor had advised him to take things easy; the certificate was signed by the Nova Scotian Conservative, Dr Charles Tupper.

Norman Ward, 'The Formative Years of the House of Commons 1867-91', *The Canadian Journal of Economics and Political Science* 18 (1952), p. 434

A meeting of a Committee of the Whole House in the 1860s was far from sedate.

Some half a dozen or a dozen Members gather around the Clerk's table, and the clauses of the bill are passed one by one in rapid succession, while the rest of the Members, who have not escaped to the saloon, amuse themselves in various ways, somewhat after the manner of irrepressible school boys in the absence of the teacher. Some few, more staid and sober than the rest, settle down in their seats in the hope that they may be allowed to pen a letter or perchance read an article in their local paper. Unfortunate man! Vain hope! A huge paper ball, thrown from some skilful hand in the rear, scatters pen, ink, and paper in rude confusion over the desk, while a seat cushion or a formidable blue book from another quarter comes thundering down upon the worthy Member's head, sending his ideas in a hurly burly race after his writing material, and arousing within him the spirit of retaliation. And thus the sport commences. Paper balls, blue books, bills, private and public, cushions, hats and caps of all styles, are brought into requisition, and are sent whirling through the room in every direction.

New Brunswick Freeman (1868)

A debate in 1870 was prompted by the third reading of a bill concerning the Canadian Central Railway.

Mr Ferguson commenced a long speech against the Bill with the evident purpose of talking out the hour allowed for private bills. In the course of his remarks, made amid continued interruptions, which the hon. member took no notice of, he exhibited a map of the proposed route, and was about to refer to it when

Hon. *Sir George-E. Cartier* rose to a point of order. He said it was out of order to produce any printed document in the House.

Mr *Ferguson* said he did not hear distinctly the observations of the Minister of Militia, and asked him to repeat them.

Hon. *Sir George-E. Cartier*, amid great laughter, repeated his objections in French.

Hon. *Mr Macdonald* (Cornwall) immediately rose, and, to the astonishment of the House, proceeded amid roars of merriment to speak in the Gaelic language.

Hon. *Sir George-E. Cartier*, again, and essaying to speak in Latin, managed, with the help of Sir John A. Macdonald, to make himself understood to the extent of saying that he had risen to call to order that most learned man, the member for Simcoe. He then said he would speak in Greek. He then, amid a multitude of noises and much laughter, proceeded to jumble together a dozen of Greek words having no connection with each other, and finishing with the words *arqureoro boioio*, a scrap from Homer, meaning 'of the silver bow'.

Hon. *Mr Le Vesconte*, in Spanish, said it was time the discussion should cease.

Hon. *Sir John A. Macdonald* was of the opinion of the last speaker.

Hon. *Mr Abbott* objected to a discussion of serious matters being carried on in that House in the Choctaw language. (Hear, hear.) The hour for private Bills having elapsed the discussion was postponed.

Commons Debates, 22 April 1870 (contributed by Marc Bosc)

In 1877 there was a motion to introduce prayers into the House of Commons. The Liberal Prime Minister of the time, Sir Alexander Mackenzie, a man of unbending rectitude, was inclined to support the motion but could foresee problems. Macdonald, as Leader of the Opposition, made his objections clear.

'Were this assembly composed entirely of Protestants, although of various denominations,' he [Macdonald] said, 'I fancy no practical difficulty would arise.' But the presence of large numbers of Roman Catholics in the Commons, he thought, added a serious complication. 'They form so large and important a body,' he averred somewhat tactlessly, 'that their feelings and even their prejudices should be respected.' He felt that the 'very praiseworthy object of the mover of the resolution would be thwarted if by its adoption the feelings of our Catholic friends were wounded, and they were caused to abstain from entering the House during prayer.'

The obvious immediate step was the appointment of a committee to look into the whole business.

Norman Ward, 'Prayers in the Commons', *Dalhousie Review* 32, no. 2 (Summer 1952), pp. 140-1

A special committee was duly created, on the motion of John A., in which all possible prejudices, objections, and queries were raised, exposing all the usual Protestant-Catholic, French-English conflicts. Even the timing of the prayer, beginning or end of the day, was brought into question. The language of the prayer became an issue more because of the relative inability of the Speaker to cope in French than any refusal to consider both languages. The status of the reader was questioned—Speaker or Clerk—and it was decided that it should be the Speaker. The final recommendation was that prayers were to be printed in both languages in the House records at the beginning of each session and read at the beginning of each day by the Speaker in his native language.

One immediate result of passing interest was that members of parliament began to use the Speaker's facility in reading prayers as a measure of his fitness for his task, and soon after 1877 we find a Speaker being lauded in extravagant terms for the fine sonorous tones in which he read prayers. 'We thought', a perceptive member assured the Speaker, 'that we would hear the rustling of divinity, the fluttering of angelic wings, and the odour of violets and orange flowers in our passages and corridors . . . and we trust that when the period arrives, which comes to Speakers as well as to meaner organisms, when you will be exalted into the political arcana—we hope then when you will be transferred to another sphere, you will pass your time studying patiently, parliamentary problems and curious constitutional questions so that you may enjoy the utmost happiness consistent with the state of things here below. And I am sure I shall express the opinion of every member in saying we trust that when that time arrives, you will have so comforted yourself that we will be able to join in saying: ''Well done good and faithful Speaker, enter thou into the new governorship, the collectorship, or the judgeship prepared for you.'' '

Ibid., p. 143

The saloon was an integral part of parliamentary life.

The only popular part of the old House was the saloon in the basement, and even it had its critics. The saloon was under the legislative chamber, and reached by a door which led directly down to it from a point in the chamber on Mr Speaker's left. (There is no evidence, however, that opposition members, because of its convenience, used it more than government supporters.) The saloon was ostensibly the House of Commons' restaurant, and a logical extension of the bicameral (or perhaps tricameral) principle had put a similar institution under the Senate. Both these restaurants seemed like saloons because liquor was sold in them, and for an interesting set of reasons. As was explained in its sessions more than once, the Commons had to have a restaurant; the prevailing and genuine belief in *laissez faire* meant that it could not go into business and run its own restaurant; no Ottawa hotelier could then run a restaurant at a profit without a bar; therefore either the restaurant had to have a bar, or some philanthropist had to be found who would operate it at a loss. No such philanthropist was even sought.

. . . Certainly, newspapers were not slow to mention the close correlation that seemed to exist between sundry unrestrained debates and the saloon. The *Globe* said in 1881: 'If it were not for the fatal facility with which members obtain intoxicating liquor within a few steps of their chamber, the brawls and scenes which have disgraced not only this but previous Parliaments would never had been witnessed.' The *Week* commented in 1884: 'The politicians of the House of Commons shut up their own bar in deference to the Temperance Vote, and then run across the building to refresh themselves at the bar of the Senate.'

. . . 'On Friday,' a correspondent reported to his paper in 1870, the House of Commons enjoyed 'what appears to have become a recognized institution: its annual saturnalia.' After explaining that the excitement occurred during a standing vote in committee, the yeas lining up on one side, the nays on the other, he went on:

> The fun consists in members dragging or carrying other members who are opposed to them to their side of the House, with the purpose of securing their votes against their wishes. The thing is carried on good-humouredly, but there is a great deal of pulling, hauling and scuffling, especially between the front ranks of the opposite sides. Mr Mackenzie, on this, as on all similar occasions that I have witnessed, selected Sir George E. Cartier for his prize. It is no impugnment of Mr Mackenzie's courage that he should select a small-sized man for the contest, for Sir George kicks and struggles with an energy and determination worthy of a Goliath. . . . The contest waxed warm, and members could be seen rolling and struggling for mastery on the floor —please let this be taken literally—and potent debaters for once

yielded to mere muscular power. An excitable Irishman in the gallery, new to Parliamentary usages, was with difficulty restrained from joining in the sport. He gave a Donnybrook shout, threw off his coat, and made an attempt to slip down into the House; but cooler heads interfered.

However accurate that quotation may be as a description of a particular debate, it is wholly truthful in the general picture it conveys of the House of Commons on fete days. The throwing of books, papers, and on at least one occasion, firecrackers; the pro-longed mimicking of cats, roosters, and bagpipes; the singing of songs; and even dancing in the aisles; all these occurred infrequently enough that they attracted attention when they did happen, but they attracted attention with surprising frequency.

. . . A veteran politician, commenting on the early House of Com-mons, has told me in a letter dated April 10, 1952: 'I do know that Sir Wilfrid once told me that in the old days when he first entered the House it was quite an ordinary thing for at least fifty percent of the members to be more or less under the influence of liquor when the House adjourned around midnight.'

These statements about the saloon (the last one excepted) were made at a time when a resolution closing the place was theoretically in force. Mr Speaker said in 1874, when invited to padlock the bar, that 'he would do all he could, with the limited means at his com-mand, to enforce the order of the House.' But the co-operation of the restaurateur in the basement and of members of Parliament was not readily obtained, so the bar remained open though officially closed. In any event, closing the Commons' bar, as long as the Senate's was open, merely caused an annoying overcrowding in the latter and, as Sir John A. Macdonald once said, made the fortune of the man at one end of the building at the expense of the man at the other. Other members averred that experience showed that the determined parliamentary bacchant either neglected his duties to go downtown, or brought his own refreshments; and neither of these practices was an improvement on having him on hand in the official restaurant whence he could at least answer the division bells.

Norman Ward, 'The Formative Years of the House of Commons, 1867-91', *The Canadian Journal of Economics and Political Science* (1952), pp. 432-4

Three weeks before passing the Canada Temperance Act in 1878, the House treated itself to one last binge.

It had started during a long debate on the Letellier affair, a debate that Alexander Mackenzie, the prime minister, wanted to end, but with a provincial election campaign on in Quebec, Conservatives wanted to prolong. The Conservatives could not be turned off. Sir John Macdonald started drinking in the evening and by 7:30 in the morning, after a final tumbler of whisky, was quietly stowed away by the Conservative whip in the rooms of the deputy Sergeant-at-Arms. Several other Conservatives had not the sense to get themselves out of the way. William McDougall, MP for Trois Rivières, spent two hours talking and was barely able to stand during it; Lt Col. C.J. Campbell, JP, MP for Victoria, Cape Breton, known as 'Tupper's Goose', was worse, getting onto the floor in front of the Speaker, with his hat on, flourishing a stick round his head, stamping his feet on the floor, declaring his utter independence of Governments, Parliaments, and Speakers, or any one else, daring the Government, or any member of it to fight, and all at the top of his voice. He was taken away by friends before the Sergeant-at-Arms intervened. James Domville, President of the Maritime Bank, MP for Kings, NB, following a colleague at 8 in the morning, rose to be greeted with shouts of ribald laughter from friends and foes. 'Button up your pants' 'Shame' . . .

> P.B. Waite, 'Sir Oliver Mowat's Canada: Reflections on an Un-Victorian Society', *Oliver Mowat's Ontario*, ed. Donald Swainson (1972), p. 21

Physical violence was not unknown in the Commons.

Canadian society in late Victorian times was still rough and ready. There was a school of hard knocks because there was a world of hard knocks. Duels had been fought within the memory of most of the members of the House of Commons. Macdonald challenged a man in 1856, when Attorney General! In this respect Parliament was only a reflection of society. In the tense session of 1878, there occurred—among many other incidents—the Cheval-Bunster row on March 29. Guillaume Cheval, MP for Rouville, had been playing music—a Jew's harp was a favourite instrument in the Commons— while Arthur Bunster, representing Vancouver Island, had been speaking. Bunster was a thick-set Irishman who had taken a remarkably short time to become the ass of the House. He challenged Cheval to a fight. Cheval went, of course; a gentleman could not do otherwise, and still retain his self-respect; he found Bunster with a knife—mainly for effect, apparently. There was a fight all right, in which Cheval got struck (not, it seems, by the knife), and Bunster got a black eye. There is conflicting evidence whether Macdonald tried to stop the fight, or tried to stop it being stopped.

> Ibid., pp. 24-5

Puns, however dreadful, were an accepted part of parliamentary life in the late nineteenth century. Macdonald had a regrettable fondness for them.

Mr Bunster, referring to a previous speaker's denunciation of beer, said he was sorry to see the hon. member for North York down on his own country's beverage. How does he know but he was suckled on it as an infant?

Sir John—'It is generally at the end of life, rather than the beginning, that men want their bier.'

E.B. Biggar, *Anecdotal Life of Sir John Macdonald* (1891), p. 122

On occasion even visitors to the Commons got into the fray. To observe this brawling, fractious forum of democracy must have been an enlightening, even frightening, experience. From all reports, language as well as behaviour was exceedingly unparliamentary.

The correspondent of the *Canadian Illustrated News* wrote in 1878: 'If the debates go on as they have begun, we may expect to see a cheap edition of the Hansard brought out . . . for the special benefit of cabmen and omnibus drivers . . . whose vocabulary of abuse and retort would be greatly enlarged by a careful study of that interesting publication.' Even visitors had an opportunity to participate, for it was the practice for years (as it still is in at least one provincial assembly) to seat distinguished guests on the floor of the House. In 1880, a leading Conservative from Toronto, seated near the Liberals in the Commons, remarked to Mr Huntington, MP, who was speaking, 'You are a cheat and a swindler.' Ejected by the Sergeant-at-Arms, the guest returned and repeated his opinion. Ejected once more, he returned by a different door, still carrying his message. And when permanently ousted at last, he sent a note in to Mr Huntington, reiterating his charge. The guest ultimately appeared at the Bar (as distinguished from *the bar*) of the House, and offered an apology to the House, although not, curiously enough, to Mr Huntington. Attempts on the part of the Liberals to get a better apology were resisted by the Conservative majority, partly on the grounds that no reflection had been cast on Mr Huntington in his capacity as a member of Parliament.

Norman Ward, 'The Formative Years of the House of Commons, 1867-91', *Canadian Journal of Economics and Political Science* 18 (1952), p. 444

Donald Smith (later Lord Strathcona) fought keenly with the Conservative front bench. The sniping erupted into a frenzy when the session of 1878 was prorogued.

The hour for prorogation arrived. All over the Chamber were evidences of early flitting, in open desks and torn and scattered papers, whilst the Members waited for Black Rod to appear. Donald A. Smith entered the House somewhat abruptly, and scarcely reached his seat before beginning to address the Speaker. He started to complain about an uncalled-for reflection about his personal honour in a speech made the day before by Sir John A. Macdonald, a report of which had appeared in the newspaper which he proposed to read to the House. In one moment the House was in an uproar! Together with shouts for order, could be heard, 'Treachery', 'Liar', and other terms still more unparliamentary. The sound of the guns could be faintly heard, which announced that His Excellency had arrived at the Senate, and was awaiting his 'Faithful Commons', but His Excellency's 'Faithful Commons' was quite otherwise engaged. Sir John A. Macdonald, Dr Tupper, Dr Sproule, Mackenzie Bowell, John Rochester, and many others, were yelling themselves hoarse, and shaking their fists at Donald A. He waited quietly for a chance to continue. . . .

Black Rod knocked. The Speaker tried to make himself heard. In vain! Both Liberals and Conservatives were determined to fight it out and to be recorded in Hansard. The Speaker resumed his seat. Outside, impatiently waited an indignant Black Rod. While in the House, communications between erstwhile friends, confidential and intimate, never intended for the public ear, were announced as from the house-tops. A shout in Dr Tupper's stentorian tones, 'You asked me to get you made a Privy Councillor', what piece of secret history was this? The Sergeant-at-Arms endeavoured to notify the Speaker that His Excellency's messenger waited. His efforts were in vain. Black Rod knocked, and knocked again. He might as well have knocked at the portals of the tomb. Finally the Speaker motioned to the door. Black Rod entered. He bowed, as usual. His lips moved, but no sound reached the frantic House. The Speaker stood up and evidently made an announcement. He was not heard—the 'Faithful Commons' continued to shout at one another, with unabated fury! Finally, with what dignity he could muster, the Speaker stepped down from the dais, the Sergeant-at-Arms shouldered the mace, and preceded by Black Rod, they slowly made their way to the lobby leading to the Senate. The Cabinet followed, and then as excited a mob as ever disgraced a House of Commons. . . .

It was a shuffling and slightly dishevelled crowd that finally reached the Senate Chamber, but once inside those dignified precincts the excitement quickly subsided.

W.T.R. Preston, *My Generation of Politics and Politicians* (1927), pp. 112-14

DRINKING STORIES

John A. often drank too much, of that there is no doubt. The more important question is to put his use and abuse of alcohol into the perspective of his society. In his own day and ever since, innumerable stories have circulated about John A. and the bottle. Many of these yarns are as charming as they are vivid; they tend to be the best known and most frequently quoted parts of the Macdonald legend. But there is always a danger of leaving the distorted impression of a lovable drunk or a sozzled clown with a penchant for puns. No such person could have achieved what John A. did.

On the other hand, it would be no less wrong to neglect or downplay the topic of drink. The demon rum was ubiquitous in nineteenth-century Canada; whisky was twenty-five to fifty cents a gallon and in respectable households was commonly kept in a bucket, like water, with a cup beside it. Drink was the elixir of life in many an election campaign, and drunken revelries were not unusual in the House of Commons (see pp. 67-70 above).

His loyal secretary was discreet in talking about Sir John's drinking problem.

Ottawa, 13th December, 1900

Dear Mr Goldwin Smith,

In 'Bystander's' ever delightful comments on current events I read in this week's issue of the Sun that my 'misplaced delicacy' has led me to conceal Sir John Macdonald's intemperate habits and thus to spoil the good story which you relate.

It had not occurred to me that I concealed this failing in writing his life. On the contrary (Vol. I, p. 325), I avow it in words which seem to me sufficiently clear to prevent any misunderstanding on the subject. In the lifetime of his wife and children it would be difficult for me to be more outspoken, particularly as the weakness we are discussing was merely a tradition during my association with him. Again, how do I spoil the story? I tell it almost in the words you employ and, if I do not explicitly fasten it on Sir John, I do not deny it as his.

Pardon my troubling you with this note, but I am so completely a captive to your charm of style that your slightest censure is no light matter. Among the many obligations I am under to Sir John Macdonald, not the least is that to him I owe the honour of dining at your table and of enjoying your conversation of men and things.

Believe me,

Yours faithfully,

Joseph Pope

Maurice Pope, ed., *Public Servant: The Memoirs of Sir Joseph Pope* (1960), p. 130

I may mention here a good story, . . . which was told of Sir John, not by him. Without reaching for its truth, I give it for what it is worth. It is related that, many years ago, Sir John was present at a public dinner, at which he was expected to deliver a rather important speech. In the conviviality of the occasion he forgot about the more serious part of the duty of the evening, and when at a late hour he rose, his speech was by no means so luminous or effective as it might have been. The reporter, knowing that it would not do to print his notes as they stood, called on Sir John next day, and told him that he was not quite sure of having secured an accurate report. Sir John received him kindly, and invited him to read over his notes. He had not got far when he interrupted him: 'That is not what I said.' There was a pause, and Sir John continued, 'Let me repeat my remarks.' He then walked up and down the room, and delivered a most impressive speech in the hearing of the delighted reporter, who took down every word as it fell from his lips. Having profusely thanked Sir John for his courtesy, he was taking his leave, when he was recalled to receive this admonition: 'Young man, allow me to give you this word of advice. Never again attempt to report a public speaker when you are drunk.'

Joseph Pope, *Memoirs of the Right Honourable Sir John Alexander Macdonald*, vol. 2 (1894), p. 273

There is an authenticated story of Macdonald in the early sixties. He was Attorney-General for Upper Canada, and lived in lodgings in Quebec. He had been absent from duty for a week; public business was delayed, and the Governor-General became impatient. He sent his aide-de-camp, young Lord Bury, to find the absent Minister.

Pushing his way past the old housekeeper, Lord Bury penetrated to the bedroom where Macdonald was sitting in bed, reading a novel with a decanter of sherry on the table beside him. 'Mr Macdonald, the Governor-General told me to say to you that if you don't sober up and get back to business, he will not be answerable for the consequences.' Macdonald's countenance reflected the anger he felt at the intrusion: 'Are you here in your official capacity, or as a private individual?' 'What difference does that make?' asked Lord Bury. 'Just this,' snapped the statesman, 'if you are here in your official capacity, you can go back to Sir Edmund Head, give him my compliments, and tell him to go to h---; if you are simply a private individual, you can go yourself.' In after years Lord Bury often told the story but with more of affection than of censure for Sir John Macdonald.

Sir John Willison, *Reminiscences Political and Personal* (1919), p. 180

Sir John's reputation as a *raconteur* was widely established and justly deserved. He had an inexhaustible fund of anecdotes, which he was wont to draw on at his party dinners with marvellous effect. I shall relate only one which he generally kept for those of his friends who were rigid total abstainers.

Many years ago there resided in what is now the county of Elgin a gentleman of the name of Colonel Talbot, who belonged to the family of Lord Talbot de Malahide. Colonel Talbot had obtained from the Crown a large grant of land in the early days of the province, and had settled on it. He was a gentleman of the old school. One day Sir James Alexander, who was at the time engaged in collecting materials for a history of Canada, passed near by Port Talbot, and called on the Colonel, who received him hospitably, and pressed him to remain to dinner. Shortly after sitting down, the host turned to Sir James and said, 'Do you drink sherry or claret?' 'Neither, thank you,' replied Sir James. The Colonel looked keenly at his guest, but said nothing, evidently making up his mind that he had some reason for not taking wine at the moment. When the cloth was removed and the decanters were placed on the table, he said again to him, 'What wine do you drink, Sir James?' The latter replied, 'Thank you, I never drink wine.' 'The devil you don't,' replied Colonel Talbot, reaching his hand for the bell-rope; 'Order Sir James Alexander's horse,' he said to the servant, and he then and there turned his guest out of his house.

Joseph Pope, *Memoirs of the Right Honourable Sir John Alexander Macdonald*, vol. 2 (1894), pp. 270-1

His drinking had serious repercussions during the CPR scandal of 1873.

Within a fortnight . . . [Alexander] Campbell was looking gloomy
again. . . . The trouble was that the Premier, for the first time in
anyone's memory, was manifestly incapable of pulling himself together to deal with a crisis. Instead of rising to defend himself and
his government while one after another of his MPs defected, Macdonald slumped white and shaky in his seat, 'showing to everyone',
as Lord Dufferin wrote, 'as his colleague and doctor, Tupper, admitted to me, that he was quite tipsy.' Nor did it help that when, on the
night of November 3, Macdonald at last rose to the occasion with a
fitfully brilliant five-hour oration, he fortified himself with tumbler after tumbler of gin-and-water, supplied, by previous arrangement, by the Minister of Fisheries. On Wednesday, November 5, as
the last of his 'loose fish' slithered away, Macdonald rose in the
House to announce his resignation. 'The Opposition', Lady Dufferin reported to her husband, 'directly crossed the House to their
new desks.' Later that evening, in the Commons smoking room, as
the Liberal member George Ross recounted, he and his fellow back-
benchers sang, 'Sir John is dead and gone forever', to the tune of 'My
Darling Clementine'.

Two days later, while clearing out his office, a dejected and
bitterly angry Campbell beckoned in [E.A.] Meredith to say good-
bye. 'He said that had Sir J. kept straight during the last fortnight,
the Ministry would not have been defeated.' After Macdonald's
restoration in 1878, Campbell again served his chief as Minister of
Justice and as Postmaster General, but he never regained his respect
for his old mentor.

Sandra Gwyn, The Private Capital (1984), p. 131

[Alexander] Mackenzie . . . had a happy habit of writing letters to his
family and friends while sitting at his desk in the Commons and not
otherwise occupied. They are remarkably perceptive letters . . . and
here is a sample, written on 12 April 1878, to George Brown, the
editor of the Toronto *Globe*:

> My Dear Brown,
> . . . I gave John A. and his party two whole days for the Quebec
> business, but I insisted on a vote at 2 last night. This was resisted and
> speaking against time has been going on since. John A. got very drunk
> early last evening and early this morning they had to get him stowed
> away somewhere. McDougall of Three Rivers is also very drunk and
> kept the floor off and on for nearly two hours uttering utter nonsense
> and just able to stand.
>   Campbell of Cape Breton was in a shocking state. He got on the
> floor in front of the Speaker with his hat on and a stick in his hand
> which he flourished round his head daring the Gov't or any member

to fight him yelling at the highest pitch of his voice. Plum Caron and others were also drunk but did not so seriously expose themselves. I suppose Dymond will write some description of the scene but I think the Globe should in plain language characterize this drunken brawl in the House of Commons. I am glad to say that not one person on our side tasted any liquor though there was the usual noises in putting down men like Plum who tried to force themselves on the House. I never saw such a scene with whiskey before.

Macdonald and his friends have been doing their very utmost to delay the business all through, and on several occasions drunken scenes occurred with him and others. About six this morning he drank a tumbler full of sherry and at eight Mills saw him drink a tumbler full of whisky. The last dose laid him out and his friends hid him somewhere. . . .

Yours very truly,
A. Mackenzie

. . . The *Globe*, as it happened, took Mackenzie's advice and printed a story about the duelling scene in the House, closely following Mackenzie's own words; several papers who quoted the *Globe's* story were arraigned for libel, though nothing much came of it.

Norman Ward, Her Majesty's Mice (1977), pp. 127-8

At one time . . . more especially the period between the death of his first wife and his second marriage, he frequently gave way to drink, sometimes absenting himself from work for days at a time, and paying little heed to the quality of the liquor he drank, or the standing of the place at which he got it. But even at such times his mind retained its seat, and he never allowed his tongue to run loose.

Once he went to speak against a Reform candidate in a North Ontario constituency. When he mounted the platform, after having taken too much strong drink and being shaken over a rough track on the train, he became sick and vomited on the platform while his opponent was speaking. Such a sight before a large audience disgusted even many of his friends, and the prospect for the Conservative cause that day was not bright. The opposing candidate, whom we will call Jones, ceased speaking, and John A. rose to reply. What could he say, or how could he act to redeem himself and gain respect or attention? 'Mr Chairman and gentlemen,' he began, 'I don't know how it is, but every time I hear Mr Jones speak it turns my stomach!' The conception was so grotesque and so unexpected, that the audience went off in fits of laughter, and disgust was instantly turned into general good humour and sympathy.

E.B. Biggar, Anecdotal Life of Sir John Macdonald (1891), pp. 192-3

At one time complaints were pretty numerous among prominent Conservative members of the drinking habits of Thomas D'Arcy McGee. A member came to John A. and said, 'You must speak to him. This sort of thing is a disgrace.' After putting them off for some time, John A. went to McGee and said, 'Look here, McGee, this Government can't afford two drunkards, and you've got to stop.'

Akin to this was his remark when the names of the two candidates for Hamilton, at a former election, were submitted to him. One was D.B. Chisholm, a prominent advocate of temperance, and the other was Peter Grant, the brewer. On asking the occupations of the men, Mr Grant was given by mistake as a distiller. 'Where could you get a better combination than that,' said John A. — 'good water and good whisky.'

Though the fact may not be creditable to human nature, Sir John's very weakness was a secret of his popularity with a certain class of men, and he did not hesitate to take advantage of the weakness when the occasion served his purpose. Once he caused great applause in his audience when he said, 'I know enough of the feeling of this meeting to know that you would rather have John A. drunk than George Brown sober.'

In the later years of his life, Sir John was sincerely desirous of promoting the cause of temperance, as far as the sentiment of the people would support it. A preacher in one of his sermons related this:
    'A friend of mine said to him, "Sir John, when are you going to give us prohibition?" The prompt reply was, "Whenever you want it." "But we want it now," said my friend. "Then say so," replied the Premier. "But how shall we say it?" "By sending prohibitionists to Parliament," was the prompt and effective answer.' The preacher thought the Premier's answer was the solution of a difficult problem in a nutshell. 'When the churches do their duty,' said he, 'then the days of the legalized liquor traffic will be few indeed.' The Premier's reply was a good one, and characteristic. While not a prohibitionist in principle himself, he was perfectly willing that the people should have a chance to say whether they wanted it or not. If they voted yes, he, as head of the Government, was prepared to do what he could to pass the law.

Ibid., pp. 193-5

Cab driver Patrick Buckley was ever loyal.

Once Buckley after taking Sir John home, on an occasion when he was somewhat unsettled, drove up amongst a group of members in front of the Buildings, when he was stopped and one of the group said they wished to ask him a question, and as it was very important they hoped and believed he would tell them the truth. Buckley promised he would. 'Then,' said the questioner, 'was Sir John tight when you drove him down just now?' 'What do ye mane?' said Buckley, looking for some road of escape. 'Was he in liquor, — was he drunk?' 'Shure,' replied Buckley, 'I have driven him all these years, and I niver seen him *in betther health* in me life thin today.'

Ibid., p. 243

Macdonald's powers of recovery were remarkable.

After having retired into private life, old Sir Allan McNab, the deposed head of the Conservative party, became somewhat reduced in circumstances and wished to raise money. The Government required land on which to build an asylum for the deaf and dumb, and by purchasing Sir Allan's estate on which 'Dundurn Castle' was built, they would procure a desirable site, and at the same time, by paying a liberal price, help the old man out of his difficulties. It so happened, however, that the transaction was consummated on the very eve of the Government's resignation, and under the circumstances had a suspicious appearance. The Cabinet had passed the order-in-council authorizing the purchase on the very day of their retirement, and the warrant had actually not been issued when the Ministry resigned. On the strength of the order-in-council the deputy inspector general issued the warrant without proper authority, and the title for the land was not obtained. The officer lost his head in consequence when the circumstances became known. A Commission of inquiry was demanded and granted, but when the Commission sat and required John A., he was not to be found. He had disappeared in one of his periodical seasons of dissipation, the prospect of obtaining information was anything but good. His face was sallower than ever they had noticed it, his eyes were bleared, and glanced about in that furtive way peculiar to men in his condition, while the papers quivered in his unnerved hand. The members of the Commission looked at each other and then at him in pity and disappointment, as his testimony was called for. He then began, and without a note to refer to or a moment's hesitation for a fact, he detailed the history of the whole transaction covering a period of twelve to twenty years, giving the most minute particulars with exact dates, all in chronological order and in the most lucid style of narrative. When he had finished, the members of the Commission again looked at each other and at him, but this time it was with wonder and admiration. The spectacle seemed like some performance in magic.

Ibid., pp. 206-7

ON THE FRENCH CANADIANS

Macdonald was very dependent on the support of his French Canadian lieutenants and partners in Confederation. For many years he was so close to George-Étienne Cartier that they were nicknamed the 'Siamese twins' of Confederation, and after Cartier's death Macdonald relied on the support of Hector Langevin, Cartier's successor as leader of the Quebec Tories and a firm supporter of Confederation. Macdonald's view of the French Canadians is well stated in the following extract.

[Macdonald] liked the French Canadians, and his long political success was based heavily on their support. Not even Laurier could dent that—not until after 1885 and really not until after Macdonald's death in 1891. Macdonald's realism comes through very well in a letter he wrote to the editor of the *Montreal Gazette* in 1856:

> The truth is that you British Lower Canadians never can forget that you were once supreme—that Jean Baptiste was your hewer of wood and drawer of water. You struggle, like the Protestant Irish in Ireland, like the Norman invaders in England, not for equality, but *ascendancy*—the difference between you and those interesting and amiable people being that you have not the honesty to admit it. You can't and won't admit the principle that the majority must govern. The Gallicans may fairly be reckoned as two thirds against one third of all the other races who are lumped together as Anglo-Saxons—Heaven save the mark! . . . The only remedies are immigration and copulation and these will work wonders. The laws are equally administered to the British as the French, at least if we may judge by the names of your judges it ought to be so. Lumping your judges of the Queen's Bench, Supreme and Circuit courts, you have full one half British. More than one half of the Revenue Officers, indeed of all offices of emolument, are held by men not of French origin. It would surprise you to go over the names of officials in a Lower Canada almanac and reckon the *ascendancy* you yet hold of official positions. Take care the French don't find it out and make a counter-cry. True, you suffer occasionally from a Gavazzi riot or so, but in the first place you Anglo-Saxons are not bad hands at a riot yourselves, and, in the second place, the

rioters are not Franco-Canadians, nor Canadians of any kind. No man in his senses can suppose that this country can for a century to come be governed by a totally unfrenchified government. If a lower Canada British desires to conquer he must 'stoop to conquer'. He must make friends with the French, without sacrificing the status of his race or language, he must respect their nationality. Treat them as a nation and they will act as a free people generally do—generously. Call them a faction and they become factious.... I doubt very much if the French will lose their numerical majority in L.C. in a hurry ... and I am inclined to think they will hold their own for many a day yet.

Macdonald never really deviated from this. His notes for a speech against Dalton McCarthy show the same policy at work thirty-three years later. Dalton McCarthy had been trying to get the French language abolished in the North West Territories. Now, said Macdonald, what is the point of doing that? There's not much expense in the arrangement as it stands. In any case you can only irritate, since you can't eradicate French that way, or for that matter, any other way. You might as well say 'pills are good for earthquakes'. Leave the French alone; remember a rule of human nature that if you antagonize people you will only make them more refractory.

> P.B. Waite, 'Sir John A. Macdonald: The Man', *Dalhousie Review* 47, no. 2 (Summer 1967), pp. 154-5

Nevertheless French Canadians were not necessarily great fans of Macdonald.

Macdonald ... always prided himself on his ability to work with French Canadians, at least during the Confederation years. Sometimes his mouth ran away with his reason, but this is a common enough failing in politicians. Adolphe Chapleau recalled an occasion where Macdonald told the Cabinet, 'I have always stood by the French', to which Chapleau retorted, 'Don't you think, Sir John, it would be more correct to reverse the proposition, and say: "the French have always supported me"?'

> Alastair Sweeny, *George-Étienne Cartier: A Biography* (1976), p. 143

Internecine strife was a part of Quebec political life. The infighting between Macdonald's faithful French lieutenant and successor to Cartier, Hector Langevin, and the ambitious Tory premier of Quebec, Joseph-Adolphe Chapleau, became fierce after 1882 when Chapleau left provincial politics, won a by-election for the riding of Terrebonne, and took his seat in the federal House. Macdonald attempted to placate both and pleased neither.

Macdonald also needed Chapleau to strengthen his Montreal wing. Langevin had the disadvantage of being from Quebec City, whereas Chapleau was born in Ste Thérèse, just north of Montreal, and had always sat for Terrebonne, the county there. Chapleau was a Montrealer. Madame Quebec seemed not unhappy to be rid of him; a cartoon in *Grip* suggested Chapleau as Madame Quebec's wild boy.

> MME. QUEBEC—It's so kind of you to take him, Sir John! He's nearly brought me to ruin!
> SIR JOHN — Have no fear Madame; under *my* tuition he shall learn prudence, economy, industry and thrift!

So Chapleau was made Secretary of State, a post not devoid of reputation, but in effect he was superintendent of the red tape, parchment, and sealing wax. It was pretty thin pickings. Chapleau was hoping, indeed expecting, that sooner or later he would be put in charge of one of the big spending departments, like Langevin's Public Works. He was never to get one. Chapleau twisted, turned, manoeuvred, tried to undercut Langevin, struck up acquaintances with Quebec Liberals every once in a while, but as long as Macdonald was alive Chapleau remained Secretary of State. He did *not* like it!

The day the dissolution of 1887 was announced, January 15th, Macdonald sent a hurried note to Langevin. 'Chapleau's going to resign, so I must see you tonight. Come in the cab I send this by.' No one can entirely sort out the relations between Chapleau and Langevin, but they were bad. Chapleau revelled in intrigue, positively enjoyed factional infighting; Langevin had little taste for it. If Langevin stopped for lunch in Montreal or to see friends, Chapleau was apt to complain that Langevin was invading his territory. Chapleau complained in October 1886 that Langevin's paper in Montreal, *Le Monde*, got all the patronage, and Chapleau's group at *La Minerve* did all the work. Chapleau wanted the J.J. Ross government of Quebec to fight the Riel issue head on; Langevin advised trying to evade it. Langevin won.

P.B. Waite, *Macdonald: His Life and World* (1975), pp. 192-3

ON NATIVE PEOPLE

John A. was Minister of the Interior and also acted as Superintendent General of Indian Affairs. While on occasion he exhibited an awareness of and appreciation for the culture and rights of the native peoples, it is clear that his political agenda dictated political union of the country, settlement of the west, and the completion of the Canadian Pacific Railway at all costs, even if it meant failing to listen to the case of Indians and Métis, devastating their traditional lands, and ignoring their cultural traditions.

In 1886, on his ride by CPR to Port Moody, John A. was fêted at Regina with a great pow-wow.

The whole journey partook of the nature of a triumphal progress. At almost every town and village addresses were presented to Sir John and the greatest enthusiasm prevailed. At Regina . . . we remained over some days, staying at Government House, holding receptions which in all cases were well attended. At Gleichen the Indians assembled in force, and a great pow-wow was held in our honour, attended by the Lieutenant-Governor in state, Sir John, and other dignitaries. The Indians were marshalled under Crowfoot, head chief of the Blackfeet, Three Bulls, and a third chief whose name I forget. They were gorgeous in war paint and feathers, with exception of Crowfoot. He was in mourning for Poundmaker, who had recently died, and for that reason appeared in undress, which consisted of little more than a dirty blanket round his loins. The Indians began by smoking a filthy-looking pipe, which they passed from one to another, each warrior merely taking a whiff or two. Crowfoot, being invited to state his grievances, began by alluding to the prairie fires caused by sparks from the railway engines, against the continuance of which he strongly protested. He then passed on to the great question of food, which is the staple grievance with Indians on all such occasions.

The interpreter on this occasion rejoiced in the name of Billy Gladstone, and the circumstance suggested a similar scene held at the same place on the occasion of a visit by Lord Lorne, then Governor-General, five years earlier, when there were no railways upon which prairie fires could be blamed. Billy Gladstone was also to have been the court interpreter on this occasion, but something occurred to prevent his attendance, and his place was taken by another whose knowledge of English was limited. Upon the Indian chief being invited to present his complaints, he began by a long harangue, illustrating his remarks by various pantomimic gestures. When at length he stopped for want of breath, Lord Lorne looked towards the interpreter who, feeling the responsibilities of the occasion and realizing the inadequacy of his linguistic attainments, hesitated, shuffled his feet, and finally replied, 'He says he damn glad to see you.' The Indian chief, no doubt wondering at the conciseness of the English tongue, then resumed his speech, and after more pantomimic appeals to the sun, sky, prairie, the Great Mother over the water, and so on, again subsided for want of breath. Again the Governor-General turned to the interpreter, who manifested renewed embarrassment, shuffled his feet as before, and finally replied, 'He say he damn hungry.' In consequence of his more copious diction, which fitted with his great name, Billy Gladstone took more time to translate Crowfoot's speech than did his former *locum tenens*. In substance, both Indians said the same thing—that their people were originally happy and free with plenty of food at all times, that the white man had come in, taken their land, killed off their buffalo, thus depriving them of their means to live and so forth. Crowfoot went on to protest his loyalty, which he had already proved in the rising of 1885, and, Sir John having appropriately replied and having provided a banquet for the occasion together with the presents of pipes, tea, and tobacco, this picturesque gathering terminated. We rejoined our train, and were soon speeding towards the great mountains already fringing the western sky.

Maurice Pope, ed., *Public Servant: The Memoirs of Sir Joseph Pope* (1960), pp. 54-5

Despite the observations of both his secretary and his wife regarding the hardships the native peoples were experiencing and the devastation of the great plains hunting area, Macdonald continued to assume that the ways of the 'white man' would lead them back to prosperity. At the Gleichen pow-wow . . .

Crowfoot brought up the subject of the burned tracts of land and asked John A. what the Government was going to do about this damage done by the 'fire-waggons'. Agnes described the intensity of the scene for her readers: 'When "Our Brother-in-Law" [John A.] answered, he spoke very calmly and was closely scrutinized by Crowfoot as if he would read his very soul.' John A. tried, she said, to explain to the Indians that the railroad was doing much good and that the damage, except in the dry season, was relatively small. Urging the Indians to try to help themselves, he said that they must 'dig and plant and sow like white men, to get good crops. . . . White men worked hard for their food and clothing and expected the Indians to do the same. . . . The Government had already given seed and grain and farming implements; the reserve was fine, rich land; they must work and till it.' . . .

Chief Crowfoot's wife was presented to Agnes.

I made her a little gift. . . She bade me welcome . . . [and] scanning with
something of disdain, my plain travelling dress and dusty appearance,
she enquired if I were not a great 'chief lady'. I assured her I was but a
humble individual brought to the prairies only to look after the
travelling comforts of my lord and master.

Louise Reynolds, *Agnes: The Biography of Lady Macdonald*
(1979), pp. 111-12

Once in a debate on the Indian, Mr Blake jokingly suggested that
when Sir John wished to vacate the office of Indian Affairs, his
friend, Sir Richard Cartwright, would be glad to step into his place;
to which Sir John replied: 'If he knew how much worry these
Indians sometimes cause me I would not congratulate him on the
change.' But Sir John's patience was never exhausted. 'It has been
the fault of our administration,' said he one day, 'that they have
been overindulgent. But what can we do? We cannot as Christians,
and as men with hearts in our bosoms—allow the vagabond Indian
to die before us. Some of these Indians—and it is a peculiarity of
their nature—will hang around the stations and will actually allow
themselves to die, in the hope that just before the breath leaves their
body they will receive some assistance from the public stores.' On
another occasion he said: 'The whole theory of supplying the Indians is that we must prevent them from starving. In consequence of
the extinction of the buffalo, and their not having yet betaken
themselves to raising crops, they were suffering greatly. . . . The
officers exercise every discretion in giving them food to prevent
them from starving, but at the same time every effort was made to
save the public stores, and induce the Indians to become self-
supporting.

'The general rule is that you cannot make the Indian a white man.
An Indian once said to me, "We are the wild animals; you cannot
make an ox out of a deer." You cannot make an agriculturist of the
Indian. All we can hope to do is to wean them, by slow degrees, from
their nomadic habits, which have almost become an instinct, and by
slow degrees absorb them or settle them on the land. Meantime they
must be fairly protected.'

E.B. Biggar, *Anecdotal Life of Sir John Macdonald* (1891),
pp. 176-7

*John A. was entirely aware of the native peoples' lack of preparation
for a democratic vote.*

Mr Watson (on the demoralizing effects of the new Indian franchise
bill as it operated in Manitoba)—'The spectacle presented at the

polling place was disgraceful. Indians walked up to the polls, and on being asked their names did not know. They did not know what name was put on the voters' list. They were afterwards told their names by the person interested in the election of a certain candidate, and told how to vote.'

Sir John—'What was your majority?'

Ibid., p. 156

ON THE BRITISH

Well remembered for his speech 'A British subject I was born, a British subject I will die', John A. always emphasized the need for a strong connection with Great Britain. He attempted to maintain firm ties with the Governors-General and worked hard to gain and maintain British support during the pre- and immediate post-Confederation periods. He also cultivated a friendship with the British Prime Minister Benjamin Disraeli, Lord Beaconsfield. The startling physical resemblance between the two men led to some amusing confusion on Macdonald's visits to England.

Macdonald dined with Disraeli shortly after the latter's pro-Canada speech at Aylesbury in September 1879.

They also, Sir John told me, related their several experiences in early political life; and Lord Beaconsfield added to the charm of the occasion by giving some interesting sketchy descriptions of remarkable characters of years gone by—Count D'Orsay among the number, whom he used to meet in the old days at Lady Blessington's.

'D'Orsay', said Lord Beaconsfield, in reply to a question of Sir John, 'was a strikingly handsome man—as handsome as Saul.'

'An ordinary Englishman', observed Sir John to me, 'would have likened him to Apollo, but Disraeli had rather a way of putting forward his Jewish lineage. I recollect that, among other questions, he asked me how long I had been in public life. "Thirty-five years," I replied. "Ah," said he, "I beat you; I have been forty years, as long as David reigned." '

Joseph Pope, *Memoirs of The Right Honourable Sir John Alexander Macdonald*, vol 2 (1894), p. 206

Macdonald and Disraeli corresponded.

Stadacona Hall, Ottawa, October 7, 1879.

Dear Lord Beaconsfield

Canada has been in a state of pleasurable excitement ever since she received, by cable, the announcement that you had made a speech at Aylesbury in which she was favourably spoken of. Last mail brought us the full report, and your speech has been published *in extenso* by our newspapers, and eagerly read through the length and breadth of the land. The gratification of our people is extreme. They say, truly, that this is the first occasion on which a Prime Minister of England has given prominence to Canada, her capabilities, and her future—the first time that it has been proclaimed by such high authority that England has an especial interest in Canada, can look to her largest dependency for food supply, and become independent of foreign nations. The speech will be worth much to Canada, and will send thousands of strong arms and cheerful hearts to us, instead of adding to the strength of other, and possibly hostile countries.

This is 'Imperialism' in its best aspect, and one might well suppose that every Englishman would rejoice at the prospect held out by it and you. Yet I see that the Opposition press in England are attacking the speech and impugning its accuracy. The attacks must fail, as the statements made by Your Lordship are substantially correct, and will be fully sustained. In one instance you actually understate the advantages held out to the intending settler in Canada. It is not required of him to reduce his 160 acres of 'homestead' or free-grant land 'to perfect cultivation' within three years. He is only required to reside on it for the three years, to put up a habitable residence, and to break up and cultivate such portion of the grant as shall satisfy the Government agent that the occupant really means to be a settler.

There are one or two points of minor importance which may, perhaps, bear correction. In speaking of wages Your Lordship says, 'The rudest labourer will get 12s. a day, and a skilled labourer 16s. or 18s.' Now, as a general rule, agricultural labourers are hired by the month, and not by the day, and they are paid $12 to $16, or even $18 per month, with board and lodging added. Except for a few days in harvest, hiring by the day is not known, then the wages run from $1 to $2 *per diem*, according to the state of the labour market, and the skill of the labourer, board and lodging always added. Again, you mentioned that there is an extensive emigration from the Western States of the United States into 'the illimitable wilderness of Canada'. Now, there always has been, and still is, an annual emigration from the older Atlantic States to those of the Far West, but not, I think, as yet in any great degree to the North-Western Territories of the Dominion. There is already a considerable exodus from the

United States of Canadians who had left their own country and are
now returning sadder and wiser men. Some Americans have also
come to us, and, from the decided superiority of our country for
agricultural purposes, I anticipate, in the not distant future, a large
influx of Yankees—more, perhaps, than, from a political point of
view, is desirable. As yet, however, they have not come in great
numbers. From Western Canada, that is from the Province of Ontario, there has been a very large emigration of farmers to the
Canadian Far West. They are selling their cleared and improved
farms at from $30 to $40 per acre, and afford a great opportunity to
English tenant farmers who may shrink from encountering the
hardships of the wilderness, of purchasing, at very low rates, beautiful farms in good order.

I am satisfied that Messrs. Pell and Read of the Royal Commission, who are now on this continent, will more than sustain your
statements as to the agricultural capabilities of Canada. You have
also near you Lord Elphinstone, who visited our North-West this
year, and has become a large land-holder there. He is, I believe,
about to settle two of his sons there. Your kindness at Hughenden
has emboldened me to do so, and has at the same time increased, if
possible my earnest wishes, as a life-long Conservative, for the
permanence and success of your administration.

> Believe me to be,
> dear Lord Beaconsfield,
> Very faithfully yours,
> John A. Macdonald.

Ibid., pp. 207-9

The physical resemblance between the two men was remarkable.

. . . Sir Charles Dilke has observed:

The first time that I saw Sir John Macdonald was shortly after Lord
Beaconsfield's death, and as the clock struck midnight. I was starting
from Euston station, and there appeared at the step of the railway
carriage, in Privy Councillor's uniform (the right to wear which is
confined to so small a number of persons that one expects to know by
sight those who wear it), a figure precisely similar to that of the late
Conservative leader, and it required, indeed, a severe exercise of
presence of mind to remember that there had been a City banquet
from which the apparition must be coming, and rapidly to arrive by a
process of exhaustion at the knowledge that this twin brother of that
Lord Beaconsfield, who shortly before I had seen in the sick bed,
which he was not to leave, must be the Prime Minister of Canada.

Ibid., pp. 279-80

When Lord Beaconsfield died in 1881, certain English Conservative politicians approached Sir John with a suggestion that he should come over to England and enter the field there, with a view to succeeding the great English statesman, pointing out the higher honours he would obtain, and expressing the conviction that by his natural gifts he would win the position of leader of the Conservative party and of the nation. Sir John declined, and when they asked why, he is said to have replied to this effect: 'That here he was engaged in the development of a nation; there he would be struggling to hold together the fabric of an old one. Here he was building up a new empire—the forces were here forming for the life of a nation—and there was more glory in having a guiding hand in that than striving to preserve from ossification the frame of an old nation.'

E.B. Biggar, Anecdotal Life of Sir John Macdonald (1891), pp. 185-6

The 'colony' on occasion tried to influence the politics of the mother country.

In 1882 ... a series of resolutions were proposed by a private member, acting as spokesman of the Irish Home Rulers on both sides of the House. Sir John Macdonald was in nowise responsible for their introduction. Through his influence they were modified, and, as passed, the address was such as no Unionist could take exception to. The nature and extent of these modifications can best be judged by a comparison of the original resolutions and their final form, which I give, omitting the formal paragraphs.

RESOLUTIONS, 1882.

As originally proposed.

We would most respectfully pray, may it please Your Majesty, that some such form of local self-government may be extended to Ireland, as is now enjoyed by the provinces comprising this Dominion of Canada, and under which Your Majesty's Canadian subjects have prospered exceedingly, so that Ireland may become a source of strength to Your Majesty's Empire, and that Your Majesty's Irish subjects at home and abroad may feel the same pride in the greatness of Your Majesty's Empire, the same veneration for the justice of Your Majesty's rule, and the same devotion to, and affection for, our common flag, which are now felt by all classes of Your Majesty's loyal subjects in this Dominion.

We would further most respectfully pray that Your Majesty would be graciously pleased to take into Your Majesty's favourable consideration the cases of those persons who are now suffering imprisonment in Ireland, charged with political offences, with a view to extending to them Your Most Gracious Majesty's Royal clemency, so that, with their release, the inestimable blessings of civil liberty may be once more restored to all parts of Your Majesty's Empire.

As acquiesced in by Sir John Macdonald.

We desire respectfully to suggest to Your Majesty that Canada and its inhabitants have prospered exceedingly under a federal system, allowing to each province of the Dominion considerable powers of self-government, and would venture to express a hope that, if consistent with the integrity and well-being of the Empire, and if the rights and status of the minority are fully protected and secured, some means may be found of meeting the expressed desire of so many of Your Irish subjects in that regard, so that Ireland may become a source of strength to Your Majesty's Empire, and that Your Majesty's Irish subjects at home and abroad may feel the same pride in the greatness of Your Majesty's Empire, the same veneration for the justice of Your Majesty's rule, and the same devotion to, and affection for, our common flag as are now felt by all classes of Your Majesty's loyal subjects in this Dominion.

We would further express a hope that the time has come when Your Majesty's clemency may, without injury to the interests of the United Kingdom, be extended to those persons who are now imprisoned in Ireland charged with political offences only, and the inestimable blessing of personal liberty restored to them.

The only result produced by this address was a polite invitation to the House of Commons from Mr Gladstone to mind its own business.

Joseph Pope, *Memoirs of The Right Honourable Sir John Alexander Macdonald*, vol. 2 (1894), pp. 228-9

Lord Dufferin was Governor-General of Canada from 1872 to 1878, a period when Macdonald was chiefly Leader of the Opposition and practising law in Toronto. At an event in Montreal, John A. continued to practise his political skills.

During one of the years of Lord Dufferin's administration, that . . . Governor General delivered an address in Greek before the University of McGill College, Sir John Macdonald and Sir Hector Langevin being present with him. One of the reporters wrote in his report: 'His Lordship spoke in the purest ancient Greek without mispronouncing a word or making the slightest grammatical solecism.'

'Good Heavens,' said Sir Hector to Sir John, as they read the report. 'How did the reporter know that?'

'I told him,' replied Sir John.

'But you don't know Greek.'
'True,' answered Sir John, 'but I know a little about politics.'
E.B. Biggar, *Anecdotal Life of Sir John Macdonald* (1891),
p. 223

*John A.'s opinions on the mother country were expressed with
conviction at a banquet held at Queen's University in Kingston.*

'I am satisfied that the vast majority of the people of Canada are in
favour of the continuance and perpetuation of the connection between the Dominion and the mother country. There is nothing to
gain and everything to lose by separation. I believe that if any party
or person were to announce or declare such a thing, whether by
annexation with the neighbouring country, the great republic to the
south of us, or by declaration for independence, I believe that the
people of Canada would say "No". We are content, we are prosperous, we have prospered under the flag of England; and I say that
it would be unwise, that we should be lunatics, to change the certain
present happiness for the uncertain changes of the future. I always
remember, when this occurs to me, the Italian epitaph: "I was well, I
would be better, and here I am." We are well we know, all are well,
and I am satisfied that the majority of the people of Canada are of
the same opinion which I now venture to express here. For the
language which I heard this morning, the language which I have
heard this afternoon, and the language which I have heard to-night
show that, at all events, all who are connected with the University
of Queen's are men in favour of the continuance of the connection
between the Dominion and Great Britain. I say that it would bring
ruin and misfortune, any separation from the United Kingdom. I
believe that is the feeling of the present Parliament of Canada, and I
am certain that any party, or the supposed party, making an appeal
to the people of Canada, or any person attempting to form a party on
the principle of separation from England, no matter whether they
should propose to walk alone, or join another country, I believe that
the people of Canada would rise almost to a man and say, "No, we
will do as our fathers have done. We are content, and our children
are content, to live under the flag of Great Britain." '
Joseph Pope, *Memoirs of The Right Honourable Sir John
Alexander Macdonald*, vol. 2 (1894), pp. 220-1

*There was discussion about the correct title of the Canadian emis-
sary to Great Britain.*

The new Canadian representative in London would prove himself
by deeds, not words; and there was no point in quarrelling about the

importance of his office before it was established. Having won the main point in the argument by getting his new officer accepted by the British government, Macdonald was quite ready to make concessions. He was even prepared to concede something in respect of the new representative's title—something, but not very much. 'Resident Minister' was the title which the Canadian government had first proposed. Because of its obvious implications of diplomatic status, 'Resident Minister' was plainly unacceptable to the British government. But, on the other hand, 'Dominion representative' or 'Canadian representative'—the pale alternatives suggested by the Colonial Office—were completely unsatisfactory to the Canadians. Instead they proposed a new designation, 'High Commissioner of Canada in London'. The British government considered this suggestion for some time in silence; and then, on the last day of January, 1880, the Colonial Office replied that, unless Canada considered the matter of very great importance, the title 'Special Commissioner' might be preferred as more appropriate.

Macdonald would have nothing to do with this last tentative proposal. Galt, he informed Lord Lorne bluntly, was not going to England for any special purpose, 'but to represent Canada's interests generally'. 'Resident Minister' was the best designation on all counts, and since it would have to be conceded some day in any case, why should it not be conceded now? 'It seems to me,' he wrote tartly to Lord Lorne, 'that it is a matter of no importance to the imperial government what title we may give our agent. We might call him "nuncio" or "legate a latere gubernatoris" if we pleased. It is, of course, for the imperial government to settle the status of our agent in England, under whatever title he may present himself. Since the title of "Resident Minister" is objected to, I think we must adhere to that of High Commissioner.' They did adhere to it. . . . On February 7, one week before the opening of the Canadian Parliament, the Colonial Office telegraphed that 'the title of High Commissioner will be recognized under the Great Seal of Canada'.

Donald Creighton, *John A. Macdonald: The Old Chieftain* (1955), pp. 278-80

Socially at ease on either side of the Atlantic, Macdonald was occasionally surprised by his dinner companions.

Sir John was an omnivorous reader: history, biography, travel, philosophy, in fact everything except perhaps natural science. If there was one class of literature he preferred, I think, it was political memoirs, one of his favourite books being Stanhope's 'Life of Pitt'. He also read constitutional works a good deal, and thought much of

Bagehot, respecting whom he used to tell a story. On one of his visits to England he dined at the house of a gentleman whom he knew but slightly. Most of the company were entire strangers to him. The conversation turned on constitutional history, and Sir John happened to remark that he thought Bagehot the best authority on the British constitution. 'I am glad to hear you say that,' said his left-hand neighbour, 'for I am Mr Bagehot.'

Joseph Pope, *Memoirs of The Right Honourable Sir John Alexander Macdonald*, vol. 2 (1894), pp. 270-1

THE TREATY OF WASHINGTON

John A. enjoyed the company of Americans and often visited the United States, especially during his first marriage. But he had no wish to engage in reciprocal trade agreements, and was well aware of the annexation interests of American business, particularly railway men. As early as 1849 he had been pressed to sign the Annexation Manifesto (a petition conceived in Montreal by businessmen angry at Britain for its abolition of preferential duties on Canadian lumber, wheat, and flour, and its decision to consent to the Rebellion Losses Bill) and had advocated instead the formation of the British American League. Later, the major players behind the scenes in the first phase of the CPR negotiations that led to the Pacific Scandal were Americans—a factor not relished by Macdonald.

One of his major diplomatic involvements with the Americans concerned the negotiations between Britain, the United States, and Canada that resulted in the Treaty of Washington (signed 6 May 1871 in Washington, ratified by the three countries involved, and in effect from 1 July 1873 until July 1885, when the United States terminated it). It was important that Canada be a signatory of the Treaty, but the negotiations caused no end of stress to John A., who, ever loyal to the British connection, feared that his British colleagues would sell Canada out in pursuit of their own diplomatic agenda.

Despite his affirmation of the need for strong ties with the mother country, it became clear to Macdonald that, in matters of trade, it would be difficult to keep Britain from giving away the store. He therefore had to contend with the Americans on one hand and the

British on the other. He wrote to Charles Tupper on 1 April:

'I must say that I am greatly disappointed at the course taken by the British Commissioners. They seem to have only one thing on their minds—that is, to go home to England with a treaty in their pockets, settling everything, no matter at what cost to Canada. . . . The effect which must be produced on the public mind in Canada by a declaration from both parties in the Imperial Parliament against our course will greatly prejudice the idea of British connection, as British protection will have proved itself a farce. I do not like to look at the consequences, but we are so clearly in the right that we must throw the responsibility on England.'

> Joseph Pope, Memoirs of the Right Honourable Sir John
> Alexander Macdonald, vol. 2 (1894), pp. 105-6

'I stand alone,' he wrote the Governor-General on April 7th, 'the Americans are constantly depreciating the value of our property, and making absurdly low offers, which my [British] colleagues, in their anxiety for a settlement, are constantly pressing me to yield to.' And as Prime Minister, he would have to take the result, whatever it was, to the Canadian parliament; and be responsible for it.

> P.B. Waite, Macdonald: His Life and World (1975), p. 95

John A. arrived early at a social event connected with the Treaty negotiations. As he waited, alone, for the impending boat trip on the Potomac, he was engaged in conversation by the wife of an American senator.

'I guess you are from Canada.'
'Yes, ma'am.'
'You've got a very smart man over there, the Honourable John A. Macdonald.'
'Yes, ma'am, he is.'
'But they say he's a regu'ar rascal.'
'Yes, ma'am, he is a perfect rascal.'
'But why do they keep such a man in power?'
'Well, you see, they cannot get along without him.'
'But how is that? They say he's a real skalawag, and—'
Just then her husband, the Senator, stepped up and said:
'My dear, let me introduce the Honourable John A. Macdonald.'
The lady's feelings can be imagined. But Sir John put her at ease, saying, 'Now, don't apologize. All you've said is perfectly true, and is well known at home.'

> E.B. Biggar, Anecdotal Life of Sir John Macdonald (1891), p. 196

He signed the Treaty with considerable reservations.

When it was all over, he wrote [11 May 1871] to Sir John Rose a long account of the negotiations. After detailing the circumstances . . . he went on to say:

'I at first thought of declining to sign the treaty. That would have been the easiest and most popular course for me to pursue *quoad* Canada and my position there, and *entre-nous* my colleagues at Ottawa pressed me so to do. But my declining to sign might have involved such terrible consequences that I finally made up my mind to make the sacrifice of much of my popularity and position in Canada, rather than run the risk of a total failure of the treaty.

'It was known here that I was not in favour of accepting the American offer, and, had I refused to sign, it would have been accepted as conclusive evidence that Canada would reject the proposition. The treaty would therefore have gone to the Senate with the Fishery question left, in fact, an open one, and this would have insured its rejection by that body. If the treaty were lost in the Senate, matters would be worse than ever. The hopeful expectation of the people of the United States would be changed to a feeling of great irritation; and, in fact, the conviction would force itself upon everybody's mind, that there was no chance of a peaceable solution of the difficulties between the two countries, and that the only solution would be war, whenever the United States thought they might profitably undertake it. Lord de Grey, on behalf of myself and my other colleagues on the Commission, wrote me a strong letter to the effect that the absence of my name would greatly endanger the acceptance of the treaty. I therefore could no longer hesitate taking the course that I did, and I am quite prepared for the storm of attack which will doubtless greet my return to Canada. I think that I should have been unworthy of the position, and untrue to myself if, from any selfish timidity, I had refused to face the storm. Our Parliament will not meet until February next, and between now and then I must endeavour to lead the Canadian mind in the right direction. You are well out of the scrape.'

Joseph Pope, *Memoirs of The Right Honourable Sir John Alexander Macdonald*, vol. 2 (1894), pp. 138-9

He was attacked by the opposition press in Canada for the position he took in the negotiations.

Sir John Macdonald was not mistaken as to the nature of the reception awaiting him at home. Incited by the *Globe*, i.e. by his old friend George Brown, who greeted him with a storm of obloquy, the whole Opposition press broke out in violent denunciation of the treaty, and of the 'traitor' who had sacrificed Canada to his own ambition. As he has often said, he was Judas Iscariot and Benedict Arnold rolled into one. Sir John met these reproaches with silence. For a whole year he said not a word on the subject, but waited patiently for the effect of time. 'How eagerly was I watched during these twelve months! If the Government should come out against the treaty, then the First Minister was to be charged with opposing the interests of the Empire. Whichever course we might take, they were lying in wait with some mode of attack. But "silence is golden", Mr Speaker, and I kept silence. I believe the sober second thought of this country accords with the sober second thought of the Government, and we come down here and ask the people of Canada, through their representatives, to accept this treaty, to accept it with all its imperfections, to accept it for the sake of peace, and for the sake of the great Empire of which we form a part' [speech in Parliament, 3 May 1872].

Ibid., pp. 139-40

THE FENIANS

American-inspired supporters of Irish independence from Britain, the Fenians were active here and there in Canada throughout John A.'s career, even as late as 1889. When Ireland proved an unlikely immediate venue for an uprising, a group of Fenians tried to invade Canada at the New Brunswick border in April 1866. The raid failed, but it did ensure the Maritimes' interest in joining Confederation. In June 1866 the Fenians raided Quebec at Missiquoi Bay and also enjoyed a brief victory at Ridgeway in Ontario before withdrawing. Thomas D'Arcy McGee, the popular convert to conservatism and one of the best orators of the House, was assassinated in 1868, allegedly by a Fenian. There were two more raids on the Quebec frontier in 1870 and an abortive attempt to muster against Manitoba in the fall of 1871.

The winter of 1884 saw a revival of Fenian activities, quickened by the advent of Lord Lansdowne who . . . had incurred in a marked degree the ill-will of these gentry. Special emissaries were sent on here from Chicago to dog the Governor-General's footsteps with murderous intent. I have seen an intercepted report from one of these ruffians to his chief, in which he described how he lay concealed all day in the woods surrounding Rideau Hall waiting for the Governor-General to come out, but His Excellency did not appear. The fellow adds, 'I could have shot the boy'—meaning Lord Lansdowne's eldest son, Lord Kerry, who was skating on an open rink nearby—'but my heart failed me.'

Some people, particularly those upon whom the responsibility of action did not rest, affected rather to minimize the gravity of the Fenian reports current at that time. Among these I rather think should be included Edward Blake, then leading the Opposition, but from the day on which Sir John called Mr Blake into his private rooms in the Commons, and there showed him two large sticks of dynamite sufficient to have done considerable damage to the Parliament Buildings, which had been found with wires attached immediately outside the window of the chamber in which they were standing, and also gave him, as a Privy Councillor, communication of the report to which I have referred above, I think he became disposed to regard the matter more seriously. At any rate, those responsible for the Premier's safety saw to it that he was suitably guarded and never suffered to drive home alone, especially late at night.

> Maurice Pope, ed., *Public Servant: The Memoirs of Sir Joseph Pope* (1960), pp. 47-8

LOUIS RIEL AND THE RED RIVER REBELLION, 1870

Educated for the priesthood as well as in law, Louis Riel was the leader of the Métis people in the region that was to become Manitoba. It was his unfortunate fate to be a principal in the Red River Rebellion and the victim of one of Canada's greatest episodes of unreason.

In preparation for the transfer of the Hudson's Bay Company lands to Canada, set for 1 December 1869, the federal government had appointed William McDougall Lieutenant Governor and sent surveyors to the Red River settlement. Concerned for their land and language rights, the Métis organized a National Committee, with Riel as secretary, that stopped the surveyors and prevented McDougall from entering Red River—so far, peacefully. They then invited local delegates to discuss a 'list of rights'. Meanwhile, the federal government decided to delay the transfer of the lands.

McDougall, however, ignorant of this change in plans, went ahead without authorization and proclaimed Canadian sovereignty in the territory on 1 December.

As indicated in the first of the following selections, this rash action exacerbated a difficult situation. On 7 December the Métis imprisoned an armed group of Canadians who had gathered at Fort Garry to protect supplies intended for the surveyors. Riel declared a provisional government, and late in December a commission of three men sent by the federal government—Abbé J.B. Thibault, Col. Charles de Salaberry, and Donald A. Smith of the Hudson's Bay Company—arrived in Red River. Riel called another convention, at which delegates were named to take the list of rights to Ottawa.

By late January some of the men the Métis had imprisoned had escaped (the others were released), among them a surveyor named Thomas Scott. Regrouping to continue their resistance, several of them were arrested again, and two were condemned to death. One was spared, but Scott was executed on 4 March.

The Red River delegates sent to Ottawa succeeded in having the main features of the list of rights incorporated in the Manitoba Act (12 May 1870, with a transfer date of 15 July). When General Garnet Wolseley arrived to assist the new Lieutenant Governor, Adams G. Archibald, in the summer of 1870, Riel fled to the United States. Thus ended the first phase of a great Canadian debacle in which Riel was cast by militant English-speaking Protestant Canadians as the 'murderer' of Thomas Scott.

John A. described the situation at the end of December. (William MacTavish was Governor of Rupert's Land; John Stoughton Dennis, the chief of the survey party that had trespassed on Métis lands.)

Ottawa, December 31, 1869.

My Dear Rose,

I have yours of the 13th. McDougall has made a most inglorious fiasco at Red River. When he left here he fully understood that he was to go as a private individual to report on the state of affairs at Red River, but to assume no authority until officially notified from here that Rupert's Land was united to Canada. He wrote to that effect to Governor McTavish immediately on his arrival at Pembina, stating that he would take no action until officially notified.

Notwithstanding this, from mere impatience at his uncomfortable position at Pembina, and before he could possibly have received instructions in answer to his report of being stopped on the way, he chose to assume that, on the 1st of December, the surrender was made by the Company and the Order in Council passed by the Queen, and that the Order in Council was to appoint the day of its issue as the day of the Union. He issued a proclamation under the Great Seal of the new province, formally adding it to the Dominion. He then entered into a series of inglorious intrigues, particulars of which I do not yet know, with the Swamp Indians near Red River, and with the Sioux Indians at Portage la Prairie, and sent the irrepressible Stoughton Dennis, in his capacity of 'Conservator of Peace', as he dubbed him, to surprise the Stone Fort. Dennis took possession of the fort, and held it for a little while, and then, as I understand it, after having first summoned all the loyal residents to join him, published a proclamation declaring the inexpediency of their organizing themselves on the rumour that Riel was going to send a deputation to treat with McDougall. What has become of Dennis I do not know, but it is said that he has abandoned the Stone Fort, and is lurking somewhere. All these movements aroused Riel, who collected his forces, and has a large band at Fort Garry, estimated variously at from 300 to 700 men.

By the way, I forgot to mention that Col. Dennis, while at Fort Garry, consulted the Recorder, Black, as to the advisability of declaring martial law. Did you ever hear such frenzy?

Riel, in order to starve McDougall out, took possession of the Hudson's Bay post, two miles from Pembina, and McDougall thereupon retreated to St Paul, where I understand he will be to-day.

All this has been done in the direct teeth of instructions, and he has ingeniously contrived to humiliate himself and Canada, to arouse the hopes and pretensions of the insurgents, and to leave them in undisputed possession until next spring. He has, in fact, done all in his power to prevent the success of our emissaries, who were to arrive at Pembina on Xmas Day, and who would, I think, if things had been kept quiet, have been able to reconcile matters without any difficulty. As it is now, it is more than doubtful that they will be allowed access to the Territory or intercourse with the insurgents.

If my fears should be realized, the only thing left is the preparation of an expedition in the spring, via Thunder Bay. All this I tell you, of course, in confidence.

McDougall has weakened our case enormously with the Imperial Government, but we must put the best face possible on matters. We have undoubted information that the insurgents have been in communication with the Fenian body in New York, and letters have been interchanged. . . .

By the middle of January we may expect to hear from Donald Smith, the Hudson's Bay man, and from Mr Thibault; but, as I fear they will be unsuccessful, we must at once address ourselves to preparations for the spring. In this view, we must know what Her Majesty's Government will do, and most likely we shall next week address a despatch to Lord Granville on the subject. . . .

Believe me, yours sincerely,
John A. Macdonald

Joseph Pope, *Memoirs of The Right Honourable Sir John Alexander Macdonald*, vol. 2 (1894), pp. 59-61

Donald Smith of the Hudson's Bay Company proved more efficacious as a mediator.

Fort Garry, 28th December, 1869.

My Dear Sir John,

Last evening about five o'clock, I drove up to the gate of Fort Garry, and finding several armed men there, was requested not to enter until they should communicate with their Chief. In a short time Mr Riel appeared, and asked me into his 'Council'. He and they were very affable, polite, full of regrets, &c., but ultimately requested me to take an oath that I should do nothing to undermine the 'Government now legally established'. This I, of course, peremptorily declined, but gave my word of honour that I would not go without the gates of the Fort till the morrow, and that meanwhile I would do nothing with the view of restoring the Government of the Hudson's Bay Company. I was then permitted to go to Governor MacTavish's house, and have since had no restraint put on me, further than having to remain within the walls—and without permission, none, whether connected with the Hudson's Bay Company, or not, are permitted to go out.

Nothing can be more serious than the present state of affairs here, the power being entirely in the hands of Mr Riel and his party. Rev. Mr Thibault is said to be under arrest at the R. Catholic mission opposite, and there is not the slightest chance that Mr deSalaberry will be permitted to communicate with the insurgents.

The drift of the whole thing is evidently annexation. . . . The action taken by Col. Dennis is reprobated on all hands, and the proclamation on the 1st of December, seeing that no transfer had actually taken place, was unquestionably a great mistake. But with regard to all this, Mr MacDougall, whom I met on his way out to St Paul, would no doubt have kept you fully informed. Governor MacTavish's health is much improved, but he is still very weak and unable to leave his room. . . .

I write very hurriedly, everything being in such confusion here, but trust by next mail to have something more definite to report.

> I have the honour to be,
> faithfully yours,
> Don. A. Smith.
> Sir Joseph Pope, *Correspondence of Sir John Macdonald* (1921),
> pp. 114-15

George-Étienne Cartier, co-architect of Confederation, was sent to London to negotiate a solution to the problem.

> Westminster Palace Hotel
> Saturday, 6th March, 1869.

Mr Dear Macdonald,

... On Thursday last Lord Granville sent to us a note in which he said he would try again to settle the matter on the basis of some modified proposals, if we are willing to encourage him in so doing. . . . My dear Macdonald, I am acting as cautiously and moderately as possible. I am happy to report to you that generally McDougall and myself are in perfect accord. You must have seen by the tenor of my letters that we were in better hands with the last ministry to settle the H.B. question. . . .

> Your devoted colleague,
> Geo. Et. Cartier.
> Ibid., pp. 91-2

Macdonald could be a stickler for form, as in this letter to the Lieutenant-Governor of Manitoba.

> Ottawa, 18th November, 1870.

My Dear Archibald,

I have seen your despatch about the appointment of a Council for Rupert's Land and the North West, and also the one enclosing the ordinance for the prevention of small-pox.

We are completely at sea here as to the authority under which you think you have a right to make the appointments and to pass the laws. We do not know of the existence of any Executive or Legislative Council with you, except the Council of Assiniboia. It is well, we think, that to avoid any doubt, a Council should be appointed under our Act of 1868 to aid you in the administration of the affairs of the unorganized territories.

By the way, I see that you style yourself 'Lt. Governor of Rupert's Land and the North West Territories'. Now your appointment under the Act of last session, and your Commission, constitute you 'Lieutenant-Governor of the North West Territories.' The distinction is a small one, but is to be observed. Rupert's Land and the North *Western* Territory are united to Canada by the name of *North West Territories*. I would suggest your opening separate books under your two Commissions, and keeping your correspondence altogether as distinct as if your Commission were to two different persons. You seem to be getting on very well and I have no doubt will have much satisfaction in your future Government.

We are looking anxiously for your report as to Indian titles both within Manitoba and without; and as to the best means of extinguishing the Indian titles in the valley of the Saskatchewan. Would you kindly give us your views on that point, officially and unofficially? We should take immediate steps to extinguish the Indian titles somewhere in the Fertile Belt in the valley of the Saskatchewan, and open it for settlement. There will otherwise be an influx of squatters who will seize upon the most eligible positions and greatly disturb the symmetry of future surveys. I have a strong idea that in order to relieve you from your numerous and harassing duties, a special Commissioner to deal with Indian Treaties should be appointed to act in concert with and subordinate to yourself as Governor. He would not be authorized to do anything of himself, but his whole time and attention would be directed to the one subject of dealing with Indian matters under your general superintendence.

Pray let me hear from you on this point at once. I am glad to say that my health is keeping up very well.

> Believe me,
> Yours sincerely,
> John A. Macdonald.

Ibid., pp. 140-1

When Riel won a by-election in 1873, few could have expected that he would actually go to Ottawa and sign the members' roll. Expelled from the House on a motion by Ontario Orangeman Mackenzie Bowell, he fled to the United States and, though re-elected in the general election of 1874, did not try to take his seat a second time.

The Clerk of the House, Alfred Patrick, had not known who Riel was until he was leaving his office. It had all happened quite casually. That afternoon Dr Jean-Baptiste Fiset, the newly re-elected representative of Rimouski, had come into his office and asked him if he would swear in a new member. Patrick replied that he would be pleased to do so. Dr Fiset then asked whether the roll might not be taken into another room. This, Patrick said, could not be done; the practice of signing the roll in his office would have to be followed.

Dr Fiset glanced about anxiously. He went to the door and looked out. It occurred to Patrick for a moment that he was acting somewhat strangely. Growing a little impatient, he asked Dr Fiset whether he really wished to be sworn in or not. Dr Fiset said that he did and that he had a friend with him.

He then brought in a stranger, who 'had a heavy whisker, not exactly black'. Patrick administered the oath to both of them. They both said solemnly: 'I do swear that I will be faithful and bear true allegiance to Her Majesty Queen Victoria.'

Having taken the oath, the two men signed the members' roll. 'I did not pay particular attention, as I was in a hurry,' Patrick later stated, 'and did not look at the roll until they were leaving the room. To my astonishment I saw the name "Louis Riel". I looked up suddenly, and saw them going out of the door. Riel was making a low bow to me, and I did not get a sight of his face . . . Mr Fiset whispered to me, "Do not mention this, and do not say anything about it." After it was done, I went to the Premier at the Privy Council, and related to him the fact, at which he appeared to be astonished.'

Edgar Andrew Collard, Canadian Yesterdays (1955), pp. 42-3

SEPARATE SCHOOLS

Canada has historically experienced considerable conflict over the issues of language and religion, notably in the area of separate schools.

Macdonald, ever the pragmatist, recognized the claims of both sides. In 1855 he introduced and carried forward a Bill on Behalf of Separate Schools for the Province of Canada; in 1863 he supported the Scott Act establishing a system of separate schools; and he guaranteed the rights of separate schools in the BNA Act of 1867.

In addition, the Act assigned responsibility for education to the provinces, and protected the legitimacy of the denominational schools that existed in the provinces when they joined Confederation. What it left unstated, however, was that those denominational schools established by custom and not by law were not guaranteed the same right to exist.

After the Act five different administrative systems developed. In Quebec, a predominantly Roman Catholic province, a system of Protestant and Catholic schools evolved, while Ontario provided separate schools for Roman Catholics. In the Manitoba Act of 1870 Macdonald intended to secure these rights for the Roman Catholics of Manitoba. Nova Scotia, Prince Edward Island, and New Brunswick developed informal arrangements for the funding of denominational schools.

A convert from Anglicanism to Methodism, Egerton Ryerson was Superintendent of Education for Canada West from 1844 to 1876. He believed in a strong system of common schools in which education would be universal, compulsory, and religious (Protestant), and for years he had struggled with the Anglicans, led by Bishop John Strachan, and the Roman Catholics. His agreement was essential if John A. was to work towards compromise on educational issues in the pre-Confederation period.

Quebec 8 June 1855

My dear Sir

Our Separate School Bill which is as you know quite harmless, passed with the approbation of our friend Bishop Charbonnel [Roman Catholic Bishop of Toronto, 1850-60], who before leaving here formally thanked the Administration for doing justice to his Church.

He has got a new light since his return to Toronto, and now says the Bill won't do. I need not point out to your suggestive mind that in any article written by you on the subject it is politic to press two points on the public attention:

1st That the Bill will not injuriously affect the Common School system. This for the people at large.

2nd. That the Bill is a *substantial boon* to the Roman Catholics. This to keep the Papists in good humour.

You see that if the Bishop makes the R. Catholics believe that the Bill is of no use to them there will be a renewal of an unwholesome agitation which I thought we allayed.

I send you the Bills.

Yours very faithfully
John A. Macdonald

P.S. Recd your telegraph.

J.K. Johnson, ed., *The Letters of Sir John A. Macdonald 1836-1857*
(1968), pp. 276-7 (Contributed by Dr Colin Pearce)

He wrote to the Rev. James Quin of the Roman Catholic Church in St Stephen, New Brunswick:

Ottawa, 29th May, 1873.

Reverend and Dear Sir,

I fear that the pressure of sessional business prevented me from answering your note.

You will have observed how the School Question ended. It is the bounden duty of the Government of the Dominion, in the first place, to support the Constitution. The Constitution would not be worth the paper it is written on, unless the rights of the Provincial Legislatures were supported. It is not a matter for the consideration of the Governor General whether the Legislature of any Province acts wisely or unwisely. The simple question is: had it jurisdiction? Was it competent to pass the law? Now the Governor General had been instructed by Her Majesty's Government, from whom he must take his orders, that the School Law was within the jurisdiction of the New Brunswick Legislature.

It follows as a matter of course that if the jurisdiction existed at Fredericton, it did not exist here, and that neither the Parliament nor the Government of the Dominion had any constitutional right to interfere.

In the discussion that took place last session, I expressed as strongly as I could my opinion as to the want of wisdom displayed by the Legislature of New Brunswick in the school legislation. I spoke in the hearing of the leading members of the New Brunswick Government.

It appears to me, however, that the Catholics, if they pursue a wise course at the next election, will be masters of the position. They should not agitate the School Question too much, or they will raise a Protestant sentiment against it; they should simply use their influence in favour of those Candidates who will promise to do them justice. In the balance of parties in your Province, it seems to me that the Catholics are strong enough to carry their point. Such a policy, to be successful, must, however, be carried out quietly.

Believe me,
Reverend and dear Sir,
Yours very faithfully,
John A. Macdonald

Sir Joseph Pope, *Correspondence of Sir John Macdonald* (1921), pp. 213-14

Separate schools were a provincial issue. On that Macdonald remained firm, as he made clear to a member of the Manitoba legislature.

'You ask me for advice as to the course you should take upon the vexed question of separate schools in your province. There is, it seems to me, but one course open to you. By the Manitoba Act, the provisions of the BNA Act (sect. 93) respecting laws passed for the protection of minorities in educational matters are made applicable to Manitoba, and cannot be changed; for, by the Imperial Act confirming the establishment of the new provinces, 34 & 35 Vict., c. 28, sect. 6, it is provided that it shall not be competent for the Parliament of Canada to alter the provisions of the Manitoba Act in so far as it relates to the province of Manitoba. Obviously, therefore, the separate school system in Manitoba is beyond the reach of the Legislature or of the Dominion Parliament.'

> Joseph Pope, *Memoirs of The Right Honourable Sir John Alexander Macdonald*, vol. 2 (1894), pp. 248-9

'OLD TOMORROW'

Macdonald allegedly earned this nickname from an Indian chief. In his early years as Prime Minister his delaying of decisions until 'tomorrow' was often useful in allowing problems to cool down.

It is perhaps significant that during Macdonald's lifetime many believed that his nickname 'Old Tomorrow' was given him by a western Indian chief—either Poundmaker or Crowfoot. In Blackfoot the name is Ap-e-nag-wis. Indian chiefs had good reason to resent Macdonald's habit of putting problems off until tomorrow— over and over again! Macdonald knew about his nickname. When it was rumoured that he was to be elevated to a British peerage, he was asked what title he would take. With a perfectly straight face he replied: 'Lord Tomorrow.'

> Donald Swainson, *John A. Macdonald: The Man and the Politician* (1971), p. 130

During the Confederation debates Macdonald was known for his policy of delay. This exchange took place on 7 March 1865.

Hon. Luther Hamilton Holton [Châteauguay]—I say it has always been a theory of my own, and facts are rapidly demonstrating the truth of that theory, that this Government was formed in consequence of the emergencies of certain gentlemen who were in office, and desired to retain office, and of certain other gentlemen who were out of office and who desired to come in. I believe that the whole constitutional difficulties, or alleged constitutional difficulties, of this country arose from the personal or rather the political emergencies in which certain hon. gentlemen found themselves, from causes to which I shall not now advert. (Hear, hear.) Well, sir, feeling that this scheme has failed—feeling that the pretext upon which they have held office for six or nine months is about to fail them, they devise other means, as a sort of lure to the country, whereby office may be kept for a further period. I admit the dexterity with which the thing is done—a dexterity for which the Hon. Attorney General [Canada] West has long been famous in this country. His theory is: 'Take care of to-day—when to-morrow comes we will see what can be done'—and by adhering to this maxim he has managed to lengthen out the term of his political existence. That, I believe, will be acknowledged to be the theory upon which the hon. gentleman acts.

Hon. Atty. Gen. Macdonald—And a very sensible theory it is. (Laughter.)

P.B. Waite, ed., *The Confederation Debates in the Province of Canada/1865* (1963), p. 135

It was the subject of considerable jest in the House.

Mr Mitchell (the Hon. Peter, insisting on the discussion of one of his motions)—'If the minister (Sir John) will say to me, "Come to my office and talk the matter over quietly", then I have nothing more to say. The right hon. gentleman was kind enough the other day to send me candies across the House. I was very much obliged to him, and accepted them as an indication that the olive branch was extended to me; and although we have not been as cordial for the last year or two as we ought to have been as public men . . . if he is willing to talk the matter over privately, I will withdraw my objections to the motion. But if he does not, I can assure him that every time the Government move to go into committee of supply, I shall move an amendment for the purpose of discussing my grievances.'

Sir John—'Well, like Davy Crockett's coon, I must come down. I will be glad to sit down with the hon. gentleman and go over these matters with him, and I shall always have a sufficient assortment of candies for his use.'

Mr Mitchell—'Will the hon. gentleman kindly name the day?'

Sir John—'I won't say "To-morrow"!'

E.B. Biggar, *Anecdotal Life of Sir John Macdonald* (1891), p. 158

Certainly the strategy was useful in situations requiring tact.

Macdonald's whole administration from about 1882 onward reflects increasingly his willingness to believe that all troubles are temporary and that, in a little while, like sparks, they will pass. 'Time and I are a match for any two men,' he used to say. A good example of this technique is the story about a man whose name is unknown but whom we can call Dobson. It dates from 1879:

> ... one fine morning Dobson appeared at the office of Sir John in Ottawa. 'Why, I know your face,' began Sir John. 'Stop now, don't tell me, you are Dobson, and I stopped all night at your house in the campaign of 1878, and I told you on leaving, if ever you wanted anything, to come right to me. Take a seat. I'm glad to see you. How's your wife? Good. And what can I do for you?' Feeling at home and flattered at his reception, Dobson opened out in a confidential drawl: 'Well, yes, Sir John, that's the p'int. You see I kind o' failed in business here a month or two ago, and my friends thought as there was no Assign-ee ap'inted for our country, I sought to git the place: so I tuck a notion I'd come down and see you about it.' 'What!' replied Sir John, perking himself up and looking at the top of his interviewer's head, 'a man with a head like yours, and with ability such as you have, to take the paltry position of assignee! Why your talents would be simply thrown away in a place like that. No, no! You just wait a while, and we'll give you something better than that.' Carried away with this high estimate of his abilities by the Premier of Canada, Dobson agreed that it would be better to wait until a more suitable vacancy occurred, and departed a proud and self-satisfied man, content to wait for the high honour of the future. Meantime the office was given to a presumably better man, and the day never came when a sufficiently dignified position was open for Dobson.
>
> P.B. Waite, 'Sir John A. Macdonald: The Man', *Dalhousie Review* 47, no. 2 (Summer 1967), p. 152

It also worked on the Jesuits' Estates Act.

'Old Tomorrow', in short, did not get his nickname for nothing. The truth is that it is a serious and difficult matter to decide when, or how, or—still more important—if, a particular problem is to be redressed. There is no use mounting a charger and hitting issues head on; usually you do not need to. You can often work your way around issues and outflank them. Macdonald on the Jesuit Estates is a good example. The Jesuits' Estates Act was an Act of the Quebec legislature, perfectly within its competence and broadly agreed to in advance by both Protestants and Catholics within the province of Quebec. But the language of the preamble to the Act was admittedly provocative, and in any case it took very little to provoke Ontario Protestants, at least those of that day, into demanding disallowance of the Act. A mighty tempest arose, with the 'drum ecclesiastic', as Macdonald put it, beating across Ontario. The Government at Ottawa held its peace. Mercier, the Premier of Quebec, in Ottawa on other business, had an opportunity in the intervals of a formal occasion to whisper to Macdonald, 'Are you really going to disallow our Estates Bill?' Macdonald whispered back, 'Do you take me for a damn fool?' And the Jesuits' Estates Act never was disallowed.

Ibid., p. 153

ILLNESS, 1870

On 6 May 1870, at his office in the House of Commons, John A. was suddenly stricken with what turned out to be an attack of gall-stones. He lay where he fell and was thought to be dying. Although the illness was grave enough to sideline him until the autumn of 1870, his ever-present sense of humour surfaced from time to time.

After his first collapse he was laid out for dead, and the doctors said they could do no more. Lady Macdonald, on the first news, flew to the office and bent over his dying form in an agony of sympathy. He lay there with limbs relaxed and helpless, and only an occasional gasp escaped his lips. Life seemed ebbing away. The next day the clerks were all removed from this part of the Eastern Block, so that no harsh footfall should grate upon his exhausted nerves, and the officers of the garrison, who then had their quarters on Parliament Hill, forbade the bugle to sound. At last, as hours lengthened into days, Lady Macdonald, bending over him, could distinguish faint whispers. But she could do little for him but watch and wait. One day, knowing nothing better to do, she took a flask of whiskey and rubbed some of it over his face and chest. 'Oh, do that again,' he whispered, 'it seems to do me good.' Soon after this he began to recover, but towards the end of the month took a relapse. From this he again slowly recovered, and was at length removed in a little to more comfortable quarters in the Speaker's rooms of the House of Commons.

E.B. Biggar, *Anecdotal Life of Sir John Macdonald* (1891), pp. 106-7

When beginning to recover from his critical illness in 1870 . . . Dr Grant allowed him half an oyster at a meal. As his appetite returned he begged for more, but the doctor said it would be dangerous to indulge himself, and added, 'Remember, Sir John, the hopes of Canada are now depending on you.' 'It seems strange,' replied the invalid, 'that the hopes of Canada should depend on half an oyster.'

Ibid., p. 233

As a result of this illness, John A.'s friends, ever mindful of the disarray of his fiscal affairs, banded together and set up a trust fund of $67,500, chiefly for his wife and invalid daughter should they be left penniless by his untimely death.

... Sir John, in repelling some charges brought against him in connection with the Northern Railway [1877], told the story in simple but touching language, as follows: — 'And now as to his own case. The hon. gentleman had said it was a suspicious circumstance that the road had subscribed to his testimonial. It was always unpleasant to have personal matters brought up in this way; but in the vicissitudes of public life one must expect that sort of thing. It would be remembered that in 1870 he was struck down with an illness supposed to be mortal. This being made known, his friends began to consider what would become of his family. He did not like to speak of this, but he supposed he must. His friends finding it exceedingly probable that his family would lose their head and protector, began to consider what could be done. On inquiry they found — whether through his own fault, or his own devotion to public business — that he would leave them but a slender provision. He himself was perfectly unconscious of what was going on around him, and it was then, as he understood it, the movement was commenced. It was taken up vigorously, not in the idea that it was to do any good to him, but to those to be left behind. It was feared that he was far beyond the reach of pecuniary needs, and that the places which knew him then would know him no more. After recovering consciousness he was taken to Prince Edward Island, where he stayed the whole summer. This movement was never hinted to him, and he never heard of it in any way till his return to Ottawa in the fall, when he saw statements in the papers. It was not till Mr McPherson asked his approval of the names submitted as trustees of the fund that he had any specific information of the matter. He had only to mention these names — Col. Gzowski, Hon. G.W. Allan and Col. Burnet — to show that they would not allow anything connected with it as far as they knew to touch their honour or the honour of his family.'

Ibid., pp. 108-9

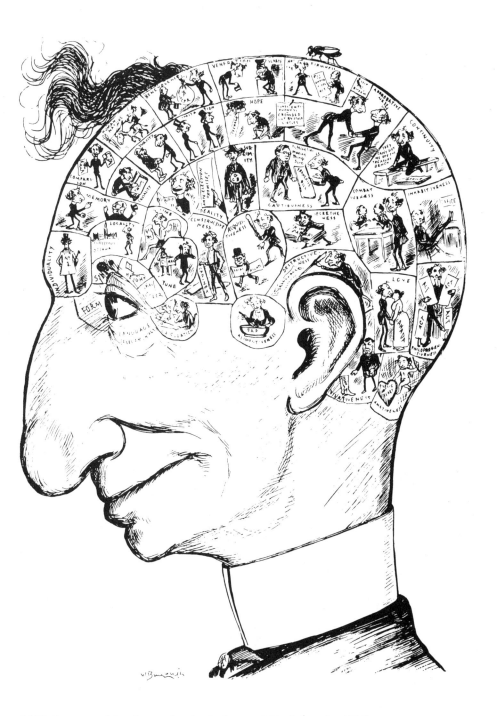

J.W. Bengough's phrenological chart of Sir John A., 1887.

Portrait, 1842.

Isabella Clark Macdonald.

Lady Agnes Macdonald.

Bellevue, Kingston.

Earnscliffe, Ottawa.

In middle age.

Bengough on the Pacific Scandal, August 1873.

BLACKWASH AND WHITEWASH.

*Bengough again, on the Royal Commission investigating the
Pacific Scandal, September 1873.*

Poster used during the election campaign of 1891.

Mrs Eliza Grimason.

In 1883.

The funeral of Sir John A. Macdonald, 10 June 1891.

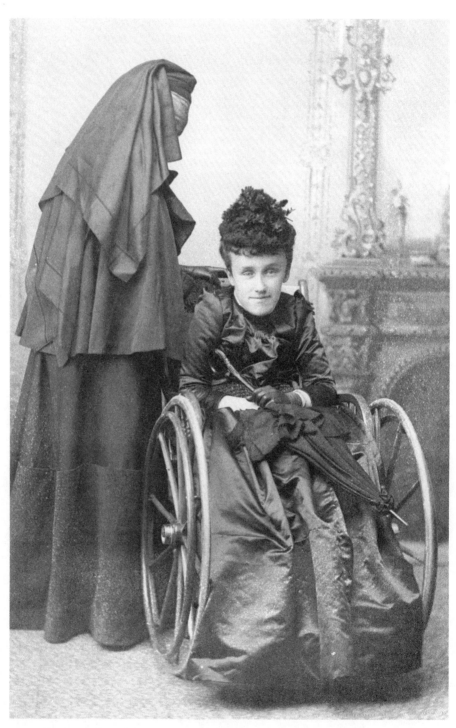

Baroness Macdonald and Mary, 1893

THE PACIFIC SCANDAL

The scandal that erupted in 1873 over relations between the government and a group of railroad promoters led by Sir Hugh Allan defeated the administration and almost crushed John A. The Conservatives had been desperate for money to fight the 1872 general election. What hung in the balance above all was the crucial transcontinental railroad project. As Macdonald wrote to his Minister of Finance, 'I am ... exceedingly desirous of carrying the elections again; not from any personal object, because I am weary of the whole thing; but Confederation is only yet in the gristle, and it will require five more years before it hardens into bone.' The Pacific railroad would be the backbone of the nation.

Together with Cartier and Langevin, Macdonald solicited some $360,000 in campaign funds from Allan and the railway consortium. In return, his judgement likely clouded by exhaustion and drink, Macdonald awarded Allan the contract to build the Canadian Pacific Railroad, with the stipulation that Allan rid himself of his American partners. Unknown to Macdonald, however, Allan had used American money to bribe the government to obtain the charter for the railway, and the American partners were unwilling to be dumped.

Political blackmail resulted. In March 1873 the Montreal office of Allan's solicitor, J.J.C. Abbot, was rifled by a clerk, and highly damaging evidence stolen that revealed pay-offs by Allan to the Tory election fund. This evidence was sold to the Liberal opposition for $5000.

The Liberals broke the scandal in the House in April, and damning evidence was printed in Grit newspapers in July. The government managed to withstand a royal commission inquiry begun in August, but could not survive further revelations in Parliament in October. The 1872 election had returned the government but with a reduced number of seats; its survival depended upon the independent members or, as Macdonald called them, 'loose fish'. Facing certain defeat, he tendered the resignation of his administration on 5 November 1873.

Alexander Mackenzie formed a Liberal government. Allan's company fell apart, the railway dream was shattered, and John A.'s political life was in ruins. Because Mackenzie's government thought the project too costly, particularly during the economic depression of the 1870s, there was to be no revival of the Pacific railroad scheme until 1880.

The railway bill that Cartier had introduced in 1872 was intended to block American interests.

On April 26, Cartier strutted around his office and regaled a number of MPs, civil servants, and junior clerks with the nature of the measure he was about to propose to Parliament: 'Here', he bellowed, 'is a bill that has attraction for a man!' Holding the printed act above his head, he filled them all with his infectious happiness: 'Here are ideas! We are going to tie the oceans together . . . More than that, we are going to bring together the China of Asia and the Lachine of Montreal. A hundred victories carried over the opposition please me less than the mere presentation of such a bill. This bill is my pride and joy.'

At that very moment, Macdonald sauntered in, with his hands in his pockets, and catching the mood of the moment, smiled and said, 'Well, ready? Let us have another field day.' He cocked his head, turned around, and marched down the hall swinging his arms like a toy soldier. Cartier fell in behind him, followed by the members, and together they trooped down the corridors of Parliament to the House of Commons.

The Chamber was full. At the appointed time, a smiling Cartier rose from his seat, pointed at a small set of papers on his desk, and 'begged leave to introduce a small Bill under a modest and humble title. It was a Bill respecting the Canadian Pacific Railway. (Hear, hear) . . . To a great extent this measure is an enabling Act, empowering the Government to make agreements with companies incorporated, or hereafter to be incorporated, for the purpose of building a railway from Lake Nipissing to the Pacific coast.' As Cartier explained it, the government intended to have strict control, by this Act and previous railway acts, over the financing and construction of the line. Control would be exercised largely through Orders in Council by the cabinet, without going before the Commons. The company, and therefore the cabinet, would have strict control over any branch line either to or from the United States. *This was the key to Cartier's whole plan.* Although he did not elaborate, this provision would effectively bar the Northern Pacific or the Vermont Central from tapping any of Canada's North-West trade.

Parliament was asked to approve a land grant of fifty million acres, given in alternate blocks twenty miles deep on each side of the road, and a cash subsidy to the line of $30,000,000. According to Cartier, this sum could be raised easily through bonds and land sales, without any increase in taxation.

George W. McMullen [an American member of Allan's consortium], watching Cartier from the visitor's gallery, realized the game was up. Or was it? He slipped out to the nearest telegraph office and wired Jay Cooke that it was imperative they should have an immediate meeting of their 'Canadian Railway project association'. McMullen knew that if the Canadian cabinet were to have strict control over branch lines (the Pembina-Fort Garry line was of course the important one) then the present Canadian cabinet would have to be replaced with men more receptive to their own proposal. The Vermont Central ring had reached the same conclusions.

On June 1, 1872, after a long though not particularly bitter debate, Cartier's bill received third and final reading. The Opposition appeared to agree in principle with the carrying out of the 'bargain' made with British Columbia, yet did not feel that the length of time nor the cash subsidy were realistic, and objected to the cabinet being given the power to control the destiny of the railway. Yet the bill was so airtight that no amendments were seriously considered. It was a masterpiece of law-making, and when the Speaker signalled unanimous passage of the act at two o'clock in the morning, a delighted Cartier rose from his seat and crowed, 'All aboard for the West!' The House rose as one man and gave him a long and grateful cheer.

Alastair Sweeny, George-Etienne Cartier: A Biography (1976), pp. 276-7

The scandal broke on 2 April 1873.

... Macdonald watched with disdain as that annexationist and small-time railway promoter, the member for Shefford, Lucius Seth Huntington, known in the House for his smiling manner and 'agreeable' speeches, rose to put the case for the prosecution. What better man to do it! A year previously, Macdonald had suggested to a newly elected member, W.H. Gibbs, that 'a party, like a snake, is moved by its tail. The tail of the Grit party is the Annexation section.' If any man represented that tail, it was Lucius Seth Huntington. Macdonald listened, scarcely concealing his disgust, as Huntington, in his nasal drawl, without explanation and with only the faintest of smiles playing across his bland face, moved, since he was 'credibly informed' and believed that he could 'establish by satisfactory evidence' that, since

an understanding was come to between the Government and Sir Hugh Allan and Mr Abbott, MP, —that Sir Hugh Allan and his friends should advance a large sum of money for the purpose of aiding the elections of Ministers and their supporters at the ensuing General

Election—and that he and his friends should receive the contract from
the construction of the Railway; that accordingly Sir Hugh Allan did
advance a large sum of money for the purpose mentioned, and at the
solicitation, and under the pressing instances of Ministers; that part
of the monies, expended by Sir Hugh Allan in connection with the
obtaining of the Act of Incorporation and Charter, were paid by the
said United States Capitalists under the agreement with him, that a
committee of seven should be struck to enquire into the whole affair.

When Huntington resumed his seat, a pall of silence descended
over the House. Macdonald was silent, and his entire caucus sat
poker-faced as the eyes of the opposition flickered over them,
searching for any sign, any break in unanimity. There was little;
they had all heard the rumours. The motion, treated as a confidence
vote, was called, and at division, the House split exactly on party
lines, 107 Conservatives to seventy-six Liberals. Unfortunately for
the Conservatives, their supporters included a large number of
lukewarm independents, who, if they were to defect, could easily
put Alexander Mackenzie into office.

   ... [Macdonald] moved for a Select Committee to meet behind
closed doors, composed of three Conservatives, and the Liberals
Blake and Dorion, whom he might be able to trust with the truth.
The motion was passed, and Macdonald sat back to see what
developed....

What [Cartier] and Macdonald did not fully recognize was Abbott's deep involvement with the Vermont Central ring. They did
not know at this point that the money telegrams had been 'stolen'
and were in Huntington's hands. The only danger, as Macdonald
saw it, lay in Sir Hugh Allan's deliberate lies to the Americans in
some of his letters, especially his brazen statements that he had
'made an agreement' with the government, that he had been 'promised' a majority of the stock.

Ibid., pp. 314-15

A committee was appointed to review the issue.

On Tuesday, the 8th of April, the following resolution was carried
on the motion of Sir John Macdonald:

That a select committee of five members (of which committee the
mover shall not be one) be appointed by this House to inquire into,
and report upon, the several matters contained and stated in a resolution moved on Wednesday, the 2nd day of April instant, by the Hon.
Mr Huntingdon, member for the county of Shefford, relating to the
Canadian Pacific Railway, with power to send for persons, papers and

records, to report from time to time, and to report the evidence from time to time, and, if need be, to sit after the prorogation of Parliament.

Joseph Pope, *Memoirs of The Right Honourable Sir John Alexander Macdonald*, vol. 2 (1894), p. 165

On the 6th of May the recommendation of the committee was concurred in by a vote of one hundred and seven to seventy-six. It then having been ascertained and admitted by all parties that the committee could not sit after prorogation, and that the House could not confer that power upon it, it was arranged that the House, after disposing of the business of the session, should adjourn to a period beyond the 2nd of July, the day appointed for the meeting of the committee, giving sufficient time for the committee to complete their report on the inquiry entrusted to them.

The day of re-assembling was finally fixed as the 13th of August; but it was distinctly stated by Sir John Macdonald that the meeting on that day would be merely a formal one, that no business would be transacted beyond the reception of the report of the committee; that the members need not return, and that none would be required save the Speakers of both Houses in the chair, and the members of committee, who were to make their report, which would be read and published and would go before the country with the evidence.

Ibid., pp. 166-7

The death of Cartier:

It was on the afternoon of May 20th, 1873, that the news of Sir George Etienne Cartier's death in London became generally known in the capital of the Dominion. Only a few days before it had been reported that he was making satisfactory progress and was soon to return to Canada, so that the announcement of his death came as a shock. . . . In the Commons, which had been the scene of Cartier's greatest triumphs, the scene was particularly striking. Nearly every member was in his seat, and the galleries were crowded, when shortly after three o'clock after ordinary business had been disposed of, Sir John A. Macdonald amidst the most profound silence rose in his place and said:

> Mr Speaker, I have a painful duty to fulfil to this House. I have received a telegram this morning from Sir John Rose, which I read to the House.
> 'Sir George (Cartier) had a relapse last Tuesday and he died peacefully at six o'clock this morning. His body will be sent by Quebec steamer on the 29th.

Rose.'
I feel myself quite unable to say more at this moment.

Sinking into his seat, his eyes suffused with tears, and his whole frame shaking with emotion, Cartier's lifelong colleague bowed his head upon his left arm, while his right rested upon the desk of Cartier, which adjoined his own.

John Boyd, *Sir George Etienne Cartier, Bart.* (1914), p. 338

The fatal telegram:

Sandford Fleming had been appointed as engineer-in-chief of the Pacific Railway in April 1871 and had begun surveys that summer, which were now already ramified extensively. But Macdonald had not forgotten that construction *had to start officially* by July 20, 1873. . . .

The opposition had grown increasingly angry over delays. Finally they bought, from Abbott's clerk, really damaging letters and telegrams stolen from Abbott's office. These were published in three opposition papers, on Friday, July 18, 1873: the Toronto *Globe*, the Montreal *Herald* and the Quebec *L'Événement*. They were devastating.

Macdonald to Abbott, St. Anne de Bellevue, from Toronto, August 26, 1872. Immediate. Private. I must have another ten thousand. Will be the last time of asking. Do not fail me. Answer today.

P.B. Waite, *Macdonald: His Life and World* (1975), p. 103

The damning money letter, later paraded by the opposition as evidence of the 'deal' made between Cartier and Allan, is as follows:

Private and Confidential   Montreal, 30th July, 1872

Dear Sir Hugh [Allan], — The friends of the Government will expect to be assisted with funds in the pending elections, and any amount which you or your Company shall advance for that purpose shall be recouped to you.

A memorandum of immediate requirements is below.

Very truly yours,
(Signed),
Geo. E. Cartier

NOW WANTED

Sir John A. Macdonald	$25,000
Hon. Mr. Langevin	$15,000
Sir G.E.C.[Cartier]	$20,000
Sir John A. (add'l)	$10,000

Hon. Mr. Langevin $100,000
Sir G.E.C. (add'l) $30,000

Alastair Sweeny, *George-Etienne Cartier: A Biography* (1976), p. 289

Caught by the opposition in scandal, Macdonald put the blame on his now-deceased colleague Cartier.

On September 4, 1873, the Royal Commission began its hearings in the Parliament Buildings in Ottawa, but without the presence of McMullen, Foster or Huntington, Macdonald was unable to bring out the whole story of the Pacific Scandal. Perhaps he did not really want to . . . How else can we explain what is probably nothing more than a bare-faced lie, in the following letter written by Macdonald to Lord Dufferin:

> It is too evident . . . from the evidence that has come out before the Commissioners, that Sir Hugh Allan took undue advantage of the failing health and waning mental faculties of Sir George [Cartier] . . . Not until after his death, and the evidence was produced, were any of his colleagues aware of his insane course. As I have already said, it showed too clearly that mind had broken down as well as body. Of course I can say this to you only, as I would rather suffer any consequence than cast reflection on his memory before the public, or say anything that would have even the appearance of an attempt to transfer any blame that may attach to these transactions to one who is no longer here to speak for himself. No member of the Government here knew or had any suspicion of the nature of the arrangement made between Sir George and Sir Hugh Allan, or of the papers signed by the former until they were recently published. I certainly did not.

. . . Most Canadians were content to leave it at that, to blame the debacle on a dead man who could tell no tales. Cartier's demise was indeed a convenient one, although I would argue that, had he lived, he would have played the game a little differently, a little more dangerously than Sir John A.

Ibid., p. 324

John A. made his exit on 3 November 1873.

Finally on Monday night, November 3rd, Macdonald made the speech of his life and, in a sense, for his life. Without a major defence he was finished as a public man. Most people believed he was probably finished anyway. He owed it to himself, to his party, to try. He rose to his feet shakily at 9:00 P.M. looking as if a breath would knock him over. Peter Mitchell, his Minister of Marine and Fisheries, kept him going on gin and water. The House was packed.

The galleries were packed. Macdonald said plainly there had been no corrupt bargain. He denied that Sir Hugh Allan had ever been promised the charter in return for campaign funds. That was probably true. Macdonald said that the uses of campaign funds were well known to members on both sides of the House.

Macdonald's defence got better and stronger as he went along. Lady Dufferin was sitting in the gallery—Lord Dufferin could not, constitutionally, be there—listening spellbound to Macdonald. So was twenty-six-year-old Lord Rosebery. After five hours Macdonald concluded:

> I leave it [the decision] with this House with every confidence. I am equal to either fortune. I can see past the decision of this House either for or against me, but whether it be against me or for me, I know, and it is no vain boast to say so, for even my enemies will admit that I am no boaster, that there does not exist in Canada a man who has given more of his time, more of his heart, more of his wealth, or more of his intellect and power, such as it may be, for the good of this Dominion of Canada.

. . . Wednesday morning, November 5, 1873, a council was called for nine o'clock. There was no Sir John then, or at ten o'clock, and finally John Henry Pope, the Minister of Agriculture, was deputed to go and get him at Earnscliffe, the house that Macdonald had rented three years before. Pope found him in bed reading a novel. By the time Macdonald had arrived on the scene, about eleven-thirty, the members of the cabinet had virtually decided to throw in the sponge. According to Peter Mitchell, all that Macdonald said was, 'I suppose I shall have to go to Rideau Hall and hand in your resignations.' That was what Macdonald quietly announced to the House that afternoon when it met at three o'clock. The House was anything but quiet after that.

P.B. Waite, *Macdonald: His Life and World* (1975), pp. 104-6

He was not in the House that night, when Donald Smith defected to the Grits.

The large galleries were crowded to suffocation on that clear autumn night, of November 5, 1873. There was not even standing room in the space usually allotted to the public. There was a strange lack of order or control. The Government was willing enough, if they were to win, that all the citizens of Ottawa and visitors to the capital should witness their triumph. If they were to lose it mattered little to them who saw it. On both sides of the Speaker's Chair the uninvited public pressed a way, as also at the four corner entrances of the Chamber. They ranged against the walls behind the members' seats, some even venturing to sit on the arms of members' chairs. Neither members nor officials noted this invasion into the sacred precincts of the Chamber, or if they noticed, cared to interfere.

Apparently the last word had been spoken, and the clear voice of the Speaker, slightly tremulous, was heard: 'Are the Members ready for the question?' Almost before the echoes of his voice died away, Donald A. Smith rose amid strained and intense stillness.... His hearers, perhaps, knew better than he the fates that were dependent upon his views. If he stood by the Government the crisis might be postponed. To denounce them meant the crushing out of the last hope that Sir John Macdonald might have of weathering the storm. No wonder there was not a vacant chair in the House so soon as the word was passed out that Donald A. was on his feet. He began in a somewhat hesitating and doubtful manner.... As he proceeded every eye in the House was turned towards him, and every ear strained. He expressed his regret that it had been found necessary to establish a case against the Government by the aid of the confidential documents which had undoubtedly been purloined from the possession of Sir Hugh Allan. He thought that the sanctity of private correspondence should never have been violated. He believed that nothing could justify a third party in receiving and retaining private and confidential correspondence, without the written consent of the sender and receiver.

The Tories waited for no more, radiant smiles illumined their faces, they shook hands with one another, and the Opposition was correspondingly silent. The Government benches broke into loud and enthusiastic applause. The Tory Whip excitedly whispered to those behind him to repair to the restaurant of the House. He was quickly followed by a score or more of Members, including three members of the Government, hurling defiant sneers at the front Opposition Benches as they passed. At the restaurant they filled their glasses 'To the health of Donald A.' For a few minutes the faint echoes of an enthusiastic crowd engaged in opening champagne bottles, mingled with strains of 'Rule, Britannia!' and 'God Save the Queen' reached the Chamber.

... While Tories found interest in these proceedings in the restaurant, Donald A. Smith continued his speech. His tone suddenly changed. It ceased to be mildly condemnatory of the means by which the present situation had become acute. There was an indication of harshness, and then he reached a phrase beginning with 'But'. It was evident that he was preparing to convince himself. The matter that followed set the Liberals cheering. Suddenly the noise of the 'loyalists' outside ceased. A messenger had reached the restaurant with the alarming intelligence: 'Donald A. has gone over to the Grits', a favourite term of derision then applied to the Liberals. There was a hurried return to the Chamber, many glasses of champagne being left untasted. The dismay of the returning party, which had left so joyously a few minutes previously, covered them as with a garment.

W.T.R. Preston, *The Life and Times of Lord Strathcona* (1914), pp. 82-5

After announcing the resignation of his Ministry, Sir John Macdonald moved the adjournment of the House. He then went over to his office, directed his secretaries to pack up his papers, drove home, went upstairs to his bedroom, and remarked quietly to Lady Macdonald, 'Well, that's got along with.' 'What do you mean?' said she. 'Why, the Government has resigned,' he replied, arraying himself in his dressing-gown and slippers, and picking up two or three books from a table close by. 'It's a relief to be out of it,' he added, as he stretched himself on the bed, opened a volume and began to read, intimating that he did not wish to be disturbed. That was all he said on the subject at the time, nor did he allude to it again.

Joseph Pope, *Memoirs of The Right Honourable Sir John Alexander Macdonald*, vol. 2 (1894), pp. 195-6

The election of 1874 resulted in a resounding Tory defeat.

IN OPPOSITION, 1873-78

The years in opposition allowed John A. to develop his Toronto law practice with his son Hugh John. The defeat and disgrace of the Tories coincided with a severe economic recession, which hampered the work of the incumbent Liberals under the stolid, upright, sober, at times ferocious Alexander Mackenzie. It was during this period of defeat that Macdonald developed and refined the key ideas of his National Policy, which were popularized in the period prior to the election of 1878.

John A.'s defeat in the election of 1874 is aptly described by the Liberal journalist John Willison.

I was among those who gathered in the telegraph office at Greenwood on the night of the general election of 1874, when the Mackenzie Government carried the country by an overwhelming majority. It was known at an early hour that all the Toronto seats had been taken by the Liberal party and until midnight victory followed victory. There was a faint cheer from the stricken Conservatives when it was announced that Sir John Macdonald had carried Kingston. The incident of the night which I chiefly remember was the picturesque declaration of a gloomy and profane Conservative when this news was received, that he hoped not another candidate of the party would be elected since 'John A.' alone would be a match for all the d----- Grits that could be crowded into the Parliament Buildings. It is curious now to recall the settled conviction among Liberals that Sir John Macdonald never could rise again. For the moment he was discredited, and almost dishonoured. There is reason to think that his removal from the position of Parliamentary leader was considered. But he had the patience, the wisdom, and the resource to repair his broken fortunes. He had not wholly alienated the affection for himself which lay deep in the hearts of Conservatives, while among the stable elements of the country there was always a strong reserve of confidence in his prudence and patriotism. In Canadian history there is no other such illustration of the charm of a man, the resource of a politician and the camaraderie of human nature as the restoration of Sir John Macdonald affords.

Sir John Willison, *Reminiscences Political and Personal* (1919), pp. 27-8

The Conservatives were shattered. They were reduced to 67 in a 206-seat House. Macdonald narrowly escaped defeat in Kingston. . . . Was it not really time to quit? He walked down Sparks Street disconsolately one morning in February or March 1874 into the offices of the Ottawa *Citizen*. The *Citizen* was at that time run by the Holland brothers. They stopped work to talk to him. 'Boys,' said Macdonald, 'I want you to publish an editorial paragraph in today's Citizen announcing my resignation of the leadership of the Conservative party.' The party, Macdonald said, could never again come to power with him as leader. It would always be known, as long as he headed it, as the 'Charter Seller's' party. The elder Holland threw down his pen. Such a resignation would be an admission that Sir John was guilty. 'Sir John,' he emphasized, 'my pen will write no such announcement, nor will it be published in the Citizen.' Macdonald listened. He did not resign, not yet. A few weeks afterwards an uproarious banquet at the Russell House showed Macdonald how thoroughly he was still entrenched in the hearts and confidence of the party.

P.B. Waite, *Macdonald: His Life and World* (1975), p. 110

During the session of 1874 and 1875, the Conservatives made little or no fight in Parliament, it being in accordance with Sir John Macdonald's tactics to conceal as far as possible the numerical weakness of his party, by avoiding divisions in the House. . . . he was content to bide his time, assisting in the legislation, much of which had been framed by himself, and quietly awaiting an opportunity for striking a blow. In due time that opportunity arrived. In September, 1875, the appointment of Mr Thomas Moss, MP, to the Ontario Bench, created a vacancy in the representation of West Toronto. Sir John felt that to carry this metropolitan constituency in the face of both the Ottawa and Ontario Governments would be the signal to the rest of the Dominion that the tide had turned. The task, however, was no easy one; few believed it possible, and it required all his persuasion to induce Mr John Beverley Robinson to take the field in the Conservative interest. To the astonishment of the Ministry, Mr Robinson was successful by a sweeping majority. His victory marks the beginning of the reaction which culminated on the 17th of September, three years later.

> Joseph Pope, *Memoirs of The Right Honourable Sir John Alexander Macdonald*, vol. 2 (1894), pp. 199-200

In opposition John A. remained lively.

Mr Young, a ministerialist, speaking of the depression then existing, and which the Opposition blamed the Government for causing, said the depression was confined principally to three interests, the manufacturing, the lumbering and the mercantile. 'Exactly,' interjected Sir John; 'that is, every possible interest except the agricultural and the ecclesiastical.'

> E.B. Biggar, *Anecdotal Life of Sir John Macdonald* (1891), p. 123

The following extract from a speech of Sir John's on the budget of 1876 gives a good sample of the pleasant raillery of which he was a master: 'I heard the threat, the dire threat, that the member for Montreal would go into opposition . . . I thought I could see a smile, a gentle, placid smile, pass over the countenance of my hon. friend, who knows his power so well. My hon. friend from Montreal is like ancient Pistol—he can speak brave words, but, like the same ancient Pistol, he can eat the leek. My hon. friend the Premier was quite satisfied that although the member for Montreal was very brave just now, and although

> He casts off his friends
> As huntsman his pack,

For he knows with a word
He can whistle them back,

they would give him their confidence as they had done hitherto. If the Government are never displaced until through the arm or the accident of my hon. friend from Montreal, they will remain in office much longer than either the wishes of the Opposition or the good of the country require. My hon. friend from Montreal Centre gave me a warning that, unless I accepted this offer at once, there would be no use in throwing my net for him. Well, Mr Speaker, I have caught some queer fish in my time, but I am afraid my hon. friend is too loose a fish for me to catch.'

Ibid., pp. 123-4

Though the 'old guard' still supported him loyally,

. . . there were dark days also, when even those who afterwards enrolled themselves in the guard, passed by on the other side. If ever there was a man in low water, it was Sir John as I saw him one day in the Winter of 1875, coming out of the House into the bitter air, dressed in a Red River sash and coat, and the old historic mink-skin cap, tottering down the hill to the eastern gateway alone, others passing him with a wide sweep. The lesson of Sir John's life is that he pulled himself out of those days and trials into higher and more solid footing. But Sir John's real 'old guard' were not the men who stood with him at Ottawa, but the greater old guard who stood and fought for him in every township, year after year, and to whom a call by name or a nod of the head was all the recompense they got and yet the recompense they most prized.

Sir John Willison, *Reminiscences Political and Personal* (1919), p. 186

The Mackenzie government was defeated on 17 September 1878.

About half-past seven in the evening of that day Mr [Luther] Holton, in accordance with a custom of many years standing, 'dropped in' to what was familiarly known in Montreal as the 'back office of the *Herald'*. It was rather early, and he sat down on a bench somewhat apart from the younger members of the party, who were making merry in the centre of the room. Presently the news began to come in. Its import was soon divined by the subdued manner of the once noisy group. Without moving from his position, Mr Holton gathered that the news was bad; but he said not a word, nor had the ever-swelling tide of disaster that came rolling in about nine o'clock the effect of breaking his silence. At length he rose quietly, buttoned his coat, drew on his gloves, struck his stick on the floor, and with the single observation, 'Well! John A. beats the devil,' he passed out into the silent night. I have heard Sir John Macdonald tell this story himself.

Joseph Pope, *Memoirs of The Right Honourable Sir John Alexander Macdonald*, vol. 1 (1894), p. 326

The Conservatives won a huge majority. The numbers cited in the following anecdotes vary, but the final count was 140 Tory seats, to only 65 for the Liberals.

In the erstwhile Liberal province of Ontario, Sir John Macdonald captured no less than sixty-three seats out of eighty-eight. In Quebec the majority was equally decisive, and in the new Parliament, the leader of the little band of forty-five—'the old guard', as he used affectionately to call them—found himself supported by one hundred and forty-six members, out of a house of two hundred and six. This unparalleled revulsion of popular feeling surprised no one less than him to whose personal magnetism, apart altogether from questions of trade and tariffs, it was largely due. Yet it was not until the eve of the battle that Sir John could be prevailed upon to give his opinion as to the result. He had a rooted objection to counting upon the future, and especially to speculating upon the chances of an election contest. 'An election is like a horse-race,' he used to say, 'in that you can tell more about it the next day.' On this occasion, although he has told me he felt as sure as one could feel of anything that had not occurred, that the Mackenzie government was doomed, he maintained his habitual reserve far into the summer. Lady Macdonald has related that, during the eventful campaign of 1878, she could not obtain the slightest intimation of what he thought the issue of the fight would be. Towards the end of July it became absolutely necessary, for domestic reasons, that she should know whether they were to continue to occupy their Toronto house or not. Accordingly she brought the subject up, and, explaining the circumstances under which she desired to know, pressed him to give her some hint of what he thought was going to happen. Then for the first time he spoke. 'If we do well, we shall have a majority of sixty; if badly, thirty.' He had eighty-six.

Joseph Pope, *Memoirs of The Right Honourable Sir John Alexander Macdonald*, vol. 2 (1894), p. 202

'The day of the General Election', writes [Edmund] Meredith, just returned to town from a holiday at Rivière du Loup, on September

17, 1878, 'Arthur brought home the startling news that the Conservatives had triumphed.' So amazed was Meredith, along with everyone else—the Conservatives included—that it wasn't until the next day that he really believed what had happened. 'The Conservatives would appear to have a large majority, say 40.' But Macdonald himself, as Meredith couldn't resist adding with a certain relish, 'has been defeated by a large majority at Kingston!' In the end, by the time the last ballots from faraway Manitoba and British Columbia had been counted, and Macdonald himself acclaimed hastily to a seat at Victoria, the Tory majority had mounted to the incredible figure of 78. At half-past one on the afternoon of October 9, Macdonald, seemingly a very different Macdonald from the trembly, ashen-faced figure who'd surrendered his government five years earlier, was once again sworn in as Premier. 'He can certainly drink wine at dinner without being tempted to exceed which hitherto he has never been able to do,' wrote Dufferin to Carnarvon.

Sandra Gwyn, *The Private Capital* (1984), p. 135

THE NATIONAL POLICY

The seeds of Macdonald's National Policy were sown in the election campaign of 1872 and germinated during his years in opposition (1873-78), which happened to coincide with a serious depression. 'Protection' became the rallying cry of the lively political picnics initiated by the Tory organizers in Ontario in 1876, and it emerged as the winning platform in the election of 1878. After the depression of the 1870s, this policy would raise tariffs and reinforce Canadians' confidence in their fledgling country.

The protectionism that was to become the basis of the National Policy was part of Macdonald's appeal to working men in the election of 1872.

Sir John Macdonald stood forth as a friend and saviour of the working man. Without hesitation, and in his usual accomplished manner, he had confirmed and generalized James Beaty's stand; and thus the Liberal-Conservative party appeared suddenly as a new colonial embodiment of Disraeli's Tory Democracy. On June 19 John Hewitt, corresponding secretary of the Toronto Trades Assembly, wrote to Macdonald informing him that the Canadian unions would like the privilege of making a presentation to Lady Macdonald 'and a slight token of our appreciation of your timely efforts in the interests of the operatives of this Dominion'. On the night of July 11 a great crowd of working-class people assembled in the Toronto Music Hall. The jewelled gold casket was presented to Lady Macdonald by J.S. Williams, president both of the Toronto Trades Assembly and the Toronto Typographic Union; and Sir John, who spoke in reply on behalf of his wife, took advantage of the occasion to make a direct and forceful appeal to Canadian labour. He told them how glad he had been to prevent 'the barbarous resurrection of a disgraceful old law'; he invited their suggestions and advice in the further improvement of the Canadian labour statutes; and he ended by emphasizing, in his own characteristic facetious fashion, the association which had come into being between the working class and himself. 'I ought to have a special interest in this subject,' he told them, 'because I am a workingman myself. I know that I work more than nine hours every day, and then I think I am a practical mechanic. If you look at the Confederation Act, in the framing of which I had some hand, you will admit that I am a pretty good joiner; and as for cabinet-making, I have had as much experience as Jacques & Hay themselves.' . . .

All that winter Macdonald had been deeply preoccupied with the party platform. The whole matter of policy had come up with the founding of the *Mail*; and Sir John had given the subject his unremitting attention. He had come back from his tour in the 'West' (Western Ontario) with the firm conviction that tariff protection would be a popular policy to advocate. 'It is really astonishing,' he told George Stephen, the future president of the Canadian Pacific Railway, 'the feeling that has grown up in the West in favour of the encouragement of home manufactures. I am sure to be able to make considerable capital out of this next summer.' Many of the party stalwarts were dubious, but Sir John was full of confidence. 'The paper must go in for a National policy in Tariff matters,' he told T.C. Patteson, the first editor of the *Mail*, 'and while avoiding the word "protection" must advocate a readjustment of the Tariff in such a manner as incidentally to aid our manufacturing and industrial interests.' On July 13, [1872] at Hamilton, in the first great public meeting of the campaign, Macdonald and Hincks announced the new party platform of 'incidental protection to home industry'.

D.G. Creighton,'George Brown, Sir John Macdonald, and the "Working Man",' *Canadian Historical Review* 24 (1943), pp. 374-5

[The] Liberal-Conservative party hit on the happy phrase 'National

Policy' to describe their protectionist views. Macdonald himself introduced the programme as an amendment in the budget debate, March 7, 1878. On March 12 the amendment was defeated, but the Liberal-Conservative party had declared its principles for the future.

> I move: That the Speaker do not leave the Chair, but that this House is of the opinion that the welfare of Canada requires the adoption of a National Policy, which, by a judicious readjustment of the Tariff, will benefit and foster the agricultural, the mining, the manufacturing, and other interests of the Dominion; that such a policy will retain in Canada thousands of our fellow countrymen now obliged to expatriate themselves in search of the employment denied them at home, will restore prosperity to our struggling industries, now so sadly depressed, will prevent Canada from being made a sacrifice market, will encourage and develop an active interprovincial trade, and moving (as it ought to do) in the direction of a reciprocity of tariffs with our neighbours, so far as the varied interests of Canada may demand, will greatly tend to procure for this country, eventually, a reciprocity of trade.
>
> James J. Talman, *Basic Documents in Canadian History* (1959), p. 114

Patteson's Mail *later committed a journalistic blooper that did nothing to win Catholic support for the protectionist cause.*

[Harry] Good, as Patteson's revising proof-reader, was one of those responsible for an historical blunder in connection with Sir John Macdonald's adoption of Protection as the National Policy. John Maclean, the earliest Canadian advocate of this economic measure, was at that time an editorial writer on the *Mail*, and had written many articles on the subject which Patteson had quietly pigeon-holed. One day Sir John who was then in opposition, walked into the office and announced that Protection was henceforth to be his policy. He asked that the *Mail* publish a good strong editorial defining what it meant, for Protection was not the familiar word to readers fifty years ago that it is today. Maclean was sent for and instructed to herald the new policy. He was so elated over the triumph of his ideas that he went out and celebrated a little, a step that, while it did not obscure his mind, did affect his handwriting. The printers had especial difficulty in making out the long, unfamiliar word beginning with 'p'. Finally the late Edward F. Clarke, who was chief proof-reader, thought he had found the correct solution; as an Orangeman he was sure that the word was 'protestantism'. Harry Good passed this interpretation, and the *Mail* came out the next day with a leader announcing that 'Canadian interests demand more protestantism', and that Sir John would give it to them. No wonder Mr Patteson, a few years after, gave up newspaper work because his nerves could not stand the strain.

Hector Charlesworth, *Candid Chronicles* (1925), p. 152

The 1879 tariff debate dragged on interminably, and it was not until third reading that Macdonald perked up and entered the fray.

Alexander Mackenzie, as if he too had become bored to tears by the subject, devoted most of his final speech on the tariff to a discussion of constitutional points and economic theories as advanced by such writers as John Stuart Mill and Goldwin Smith. Macdonald made the obvious retort that Goldwin Smith, who had made a stump speech in aid of the Conservatives on the eve of the election of 1878, was a repentant ex-free-trader, who had been converted from his previous doctrinaire Liberalism by the bitter experience of five years of Liberal rule. The memory of those five appalling years, Macdonald insisted, would keep the Canadian people safe in the 'abiding city' of Conservatism for a good many lustrums to come. It might be, he went on, that in some distant future, and from some height of lofty impartiality, he would look down and see the position of the parties in the Canadian Parliament reversed. But that spectacle, he concluded, would not be in his time.

Mackenzie was on his feet in a moment. A thin, tight-lipped smile appeared and vanished on his face.

'I would merely remark,' he said briefly, 'the honourable gentleman does not mean he would look downwards. He would look upward.'

The House laughed. But Macdonald would not permit this laugh to be the last.

'I always look up to my honourable friend,' he answered urbanely, and the incident closed. That night the Tariff Bill passed its third reading.

Donald Creighton, *John A. Macdonald: The Old Chieftain* (1955), p. 263

One of the themes of the National Policy was the settlement of the west. The need to provide wives for the settlers was clear, but assisting the immigration of women from elsewhere created new problems.

While Protection was everywhere the rallying cry, other questions arose, among them the absurd charge of French domination. The

Government's railway, North-West, and immigration policies were also under fire. A feature of the last-named came in for some adverse criticism. This was a system of assisting female immigration to this country with the object of providing wives for the prairie settlers, among whom there was a great shortage of women. This scheme, however excellent it might be in theory, did not work well in practice. A number of loose characters took advantage of its provisions to get out to Canada, and Sir John Macdonald, who as Minister of the Interior was specially responsible for the execution of this policy, decided to discontinue it. Amongst its warmest advocates was a certain MP, for many years a strong and consistent Protectionist, who after the National Policy had been placed on the statute book, feeling his occupation gone, took up this immigration scheme as an outlet for his surplus energy, and pressed it strongly upon the Government. One evening as the gentleman in question was waiting in my office for Council to break up, in order to learn the decision of the Government as to the continuation or abandonment of this policy of assisted immigration, Sir John walked into the room and seeing him, said, 'I'm sorry, Angus, but my colleagues and I have talked over the subject, and we have come to the conclusion not to go on with the assisted immigration, at any rate for this year.' Then, seeing the look of disappointment on his old friend's face, he put his hand kindly on his shoulder and added: 'You know, Angus, we must *protect* the Canadian w----s.'

> Maurice Pope, ed., *Public Servant: The Memoirs of Sir Joseph Pope* (1960), p. 38

THE CPR

When Macdonald returned to power in 1878, the completion of the CPR was an urgent priority. The transcontinental rail line was one of the three prongs of the National Policy of economic development, the others being western settlement and tariff protection. The Canadian Pacific Railway Company, incorporated in February 1881, received the government's contract with generous public support including $25 million in cash and 25 million acres of land. The Company was organized by Donald A. Smith (later Lord Strathcona) together with J.J. Hill and George Stephen; W.C. Van Horne was the general manager of construction. In the spring of 1885 the incomplete line was used to transport troops to suppress the North-West Rebellion, enabling Sir John's government to justify further financial support to the beleaguered company, and the 'last spike' *was driven at Craigellachie in Eagle Pass, BC, on 7 November 1885. The first through passenger train left Montreal 28 June 1886, arriving in Port Moody, BC, on 4 July.*

The great majority of this [1878] parliament of individualists belonged to Macdonald. Could he keep them all in line? The job of maintaining party discipline would not be easy; and, Macdonald knew, the debate would be exhausting. [George] Stephen, who was already convinced that what was good for the CPR was good for the country, naively supposed that the business would be disposed of by Christmas, 'otherwise a season may be lost'. Macdonald knew better. 'Surely,' Stephen wrote, 'the Opposition will not be foolish enough to take a line to damage us in the country, too.' But the Liberals' whole strategy was to save the country from Stephen.

The debate, which began in early December and ran until the end of January, was the longest ever held until that time and one of the longest in all the history of the Canadian parliament. During that period, more than one million words were uttered in the House of Commons on the subject of the Canadian Pacific Railway contract —more words by far than there are in both the Old and the New Testaments. Though the proceedings were not immune from the kind of bitter, personal invective that marked the polemics of the period, there was a very real sense of the importance of the occasion. Tupper, when he put the resolution to the House, called it 'the most important question that has ever engaged the attention of this Parliament' and speaker after speaker on both sides echoed these words when it came his time to stand up and be counted. They realized, all of them, that once the contract was committed, the small, cramped Canada they knew could never again be the same. Some felt the nation would be beggared and ruined, others that it would blossom forth as a new entity. All understood that a turning point had been reached.

Goldwin Smith, who was opposed to any project which attempted to split the continent in two, understood one aspect of the coming debate. 'Seldom has any country been summoned to deliberate upon an enterprise so vast in comparison with its resources, or so vitally connected with its fundamental policy,' he wrote in the *Bystander*. 'What is truly momentous, and makes this a turning point in our destiny, is the choice which our people are now called upon to make between the continental and the anti-continental system, between the policy of antagonism to our neighbours on the south and that of partnership.'

Goldwin Smith was talking in extremes when he used words like 'antagonism' but he managed to catch the sense of the issue. To

Macdonald, 'partnership' meant something perilously close to en-
gulfment; to the Liberals, it was not a danger but an economic asset.
The echoes of that argument have yet to be stilled.

Pierre Berton, *The National Dream* (1970), pp. 441-2

Stephen sat in the pleasant library of his house in St James's Place.
He felt triumphantly elated. Even in that autumn of disaster, there
was still hope; and today was a day of hope confirmed. He and his
cousin, Donald Smith, by pledging their own personal credit once
more, had just secured a loan of fifty thousand pounds for the
railway. And now, with Macdonald committed in principle to a
further instalment of government aid, Stephen could almost bring
himself to believe that a way would be found through the blind
jungle of difficulties which faced him. Once again the partnership
of company and government, the partnership of Donald Smith,
John A. Macdonald, and himself, had triumphed. They were all
Scotsmen, all Highlanders, all, ultimately, sons of the same river
valley. Macdonald's ancestors, on his mother's side, had come from
Strathspey; and Stephen and Smith had been born in little towns
close to the river in the land dominated by the Clan Grant. Stephen's
fierce hatreds, his black discouragements, his radiant exaltations,
were all legitimate parts of the rich inheritance he had received
from Speyside; and unlike Macdonald, who had no personal memory of the country of his forbears, he was steeped in recollections of
the land by which he had been shaped. He remembered the river
itself, winding onward, peat-black between the high banks, and
brown, like old ale, over the shallows. He remembered the great
rock which had given the Clan Grant its rallying-place and its battle
slogan. The rock of defiance. Craigellachie.
  Stand fast, Craigellachie!
  He would beat them! He and Macdonald and Donald Smith
would beat them yet! Blake, the hated *Globe*, the Grand Trunk
Railway scribblers, the 'bear' speculators in New York—the whole
malignant host of the Canadian Pacific's enemies—he would beat
them all. He took a telegraph form, addressed it to Donald Smith in
Montreal, and wrote a message of three words only:
  'Stand fast, Craigellachie!'

Donald Creighton, *John A. Macdonald: The Old Chieftain*
(1955), pp. 397-8

One of Sir John's speeches, which at the time caused many to wear a
broad smile, was that which he made when he returned from Europe, after having been unsuccessful in getting a British or Continental Syndicate to take up the Canadian Pacific, but having, never-

theless, succeeded in placing the completion of the road in the hands of Mr George Stephen (now Lord Mountstephen) and his Canadian associates. Sir John was expected by the Quebec train, *en route* for Ottawa. He was received at the then Hochelaga depot by a number of members of Parliament and citizens prominent in commerce, among whom were Mr Thomas White, afterwards Minister of the Interior, Mr M.H. Gault, member for Montreal West—both of whom have since passed over to the majority. The late Premier was never more airily jocose than in referring to the success he had had in getting his syndicate. His speech was important, and strangely enough the only short-hand reporter present was Mr James Harper, then correspondent of the Toronto *Globe*, who, wedged in the mass of jocular Conservatives, was able to take the speech verbatim, and preserve it in the columns of the *Globe*. Then it was that Sir John spoke that sentence of which so much irreverent fun was made in Ontario newspapers, that the time would come when Canada's teeming millions would remember that it was the Conservative party which had given the country its great railway. 'I shall not be present,' said Sir John. 'I am an old man,' he continued, 'but I shall perchance look down from the realms above upon a multitude of younger men—a prosperous, populous, and thriving generation —a nation of Canadians, who will see the completion of the road.' Mr Harper says that these words produced a sort of lull in the jollity of the crowd as the Premier's manner was quite reverent when he used them, and there was less jollity afterwards during the short interval within which Sir John remained and chatted with his friends before the train started. Sir John, however, not only lived to see the road finished, but to ride over it from end to end.

E.B. Biggar, *Anecdotal Life of Sir John Macdonald* (1891), p. 218

LATER YEARS IN GOVERNMENT

Though there was an obvious fondness for the increasingly ailing, crotchety, and ineffectual old gentleman, Sir John's later years were undistinguished. Ethics were often neglected.

The Government thought nothing of holding up important legislation, such as the Franchise Bill of 1885, until late in a session, when members had to choose between passing the bill hastily, or prolonging their sojourn in Ottawa at great inconvenience to themselves. For several years after Confederation, important departmental reports were tabled late. A cabinet member in 1873, debating an Opposition argument that 'the payment of money to contractors in excess of the contract sum is a gross violation of public duty', admitted candidly that the Government had taken 'a liberal view' of contracts; his defence was that while the Government would have been safe if it had kept to the letter of the contracts, the work would not have been completed. Macdonald, while Leader of the Opposition, drew the sum of $6,600 from a public fund, not only without ministerial sanction, but without ministerial knowledge that the fund existed. Until the establishment of the Auditor General's office, governments commonly transferred surpluses from one branch of the administration to another that needed money, though a clear violation of the law was involved. In 1878 the Finance Minister, Sir Richard Cartwright, agreed cheerfully with an Opposition criticism that lapsed votes for money were actually being spent after having been revived by Order in Council.

> Norman Ward, 'The Formative Years of the House of Commons,
> 1862-91', *Canadian Journal of Economics and Political Science*
> 18 (1952), p. 450

Aside from the completion of the CPR and the passing of the Jesuits' Estates Act, there were few positive accomplishments. Macdonald's tendency to put action off until 'tomorrow' did much to escalate the Riel Rebellion of 1885, and his decision to execute Riel led to the alienation of many French Catholics. It was a time too of challenge to Macdonald's concept of centralized federalism, as the provincial premiers successfully fought in the courts against Dominion primacy over provincial powers.

Patience was his watchword.

Patience. The world was not made in a day, or in two days. And the world is not changed overnight. Macdonald could never have been a true Reformer: he felt that changes do not really change things as they really are. One may reform this, or reform that, but human nature will always find holes in a system: work around it, through it, under it, somehow. No human device could block the basic iniquities of human nature. Not that human nature was good or bad. You had to take men as they were. Don't expect anything from them; don't count on love, or loyalty, or honesty. Be grateful when you encounter love, loyalty, or honesty, but don't be surprised or mortified if you don't find them. This was not cynicism, although some alleged it to be; it was a strong-grained realism. 'There is no gratitude to be expected from the public', Macdonald wrote

Stephen in 1888, 'I have found that out years ago.' And there was no reason to be bitter about it. It was the way the world was. 'A good carpenter,' he told T.C. Patteson in 1874, 'can work with indifferent tools.' So, he went on, stop attacking Cumberland (the Managing Director of the Northern Railway); at least don't attack him more than you can help. 'We may want to use him hereafter.'

That sounds unscrupulous. Perhaps it was. But it is part of the something else about Macdonald: he was always willing to forgive and forget. Unlike some of his celebrated Highland forebears, he did not nurse grudges. Life was too short. Oh, no doubt it was hard to work with Brown in June, 1864, in the Great Coalition, after all the bitternesses that had passed between them in the 1850s: but work Macdonald did. 'A public man', he told Chapleau in 1885, 'can have no resentments.' Chapleau would have been a better man if he had listened; but then, no doubt, he would not have been Chapleau. One of Macdonald's favourite sayings, when something unfortunate but irreparable had happened, was 'It's done. There's no use crying over spilt milk.' Forget, and go on.

P.B. Waite, 'Sir John A. Macdonald: The Man', *Dalhousie Review* 47, no. 2 (1967), pp. 144-5

Joseph Rymal, a Reformer from Hamilton Wentworth and the wit of the house, held Macdonald in great respect for a long time.

Probably one of the best tributes ever paid to Sir John upon his power of influencing and managing men was given by Mr Rymal in a speech in 1882, in which he took the Government to task for maladministration and encroachment upon provincial rights.

After saying that, unless the rights of the Provinces were better respected, Confederation would fall to pieces like a rope of sand, he proceeded to say: . . . 'It may be doubted if Canada could exist any length of time without the services of her greatest statesman, the leader of the present Government. He is a man of extraordinary ability, I admit; as a manager of men I have never seen his equal. I have often wondered how it was that he was able to so completely mould the character and shape the actions of the men who supported him. Whether it is magnetism or necromancy, whether it is the inherent strength that he possesses, or whether it is the weakness of the gentlemen he leads, I am bound to say that, as yet, that question is unsolved in my own mind. Among his supporters are a great many able men, and I will not go so far as to say there are not even a great many good men; but good or bad, able or unable, weak or strong, he wraps them around his finger, as you would a thread.

E.B. Biggar, *Anecdotal Life of Sir John Macdonald* (1891), pp. 130-1

*But Rymal changed his opinion of John A. after the Redistribution
Bill of 1882, which was intended to 'hive the Grits', or break off large
chunks of traditionally Grit areas in order to weaken their forces
and work to the advantage of the Tories.*

The 'gerrymander bill' . . . affected his [Rymal's] own constituency,
by throwing over one of his strongest townships into the adjoining
riding. This was the process known as 'hiving the Grits', and fore-
shadowing as it did his defeat, Mr Rymal denounced it in the
strongest language. 'To tell me,' said he, 'that this change was not
made with a political purpose! Why, I have read the Arabian Nights'
Entertainments, the Travels of Sinbad the Sailor, and of Gulliver,
but any of those narratives would commend themselves to my faith
and judgment more than that statement of my hon. friend (Sir
John). . . . I think the feelings of an outraged people will revolt at
such scheming as this. I have not the patience to express my feelings
on this subject. I feel a little like the man addicted to a great deal of
profanity, who was driving a wagon-load of pumpkins up a hill.
Some of the boys, thinking they would hear some tall swearing,
lifted the tailboard of the wagon. He drove his oxen till he got to the
top of the hill, when he looked back and saw the pumpkins rolling
down the hill, and the boys waiting to hear what he would say. But
he said nothing. One of the boys asked, "Why don't you swear?"
"Why," said he, "I could not do justice to the occasion." So I feel.
The amenities of the House would be outraged were I to give
expression to my feelings, but if any honorable gentleman wishes to
talk the matter over with me outside, I will give him some strong
opinions.' . . .

Mr Rymal, however, still went on pouring out his wrath and
sarcasm, and concluded with these words: 'I am as sure as that I am a
living man, that there was no other reason for removing the keystone of that old organization of Wentworth, than the fact that for
forty-five years at least it had much to do with returning a Reform
representative. I quite understand the answers which inspired the
Hon. First Minister when he said to me privately on the floor of the
House a night or two ago, with a pretty hard expression at the
commencement of his sentence: "We meant to make you howl."
Well, he has made us howl, and some of us will do more howling yet
before the next election . . . The First Minister desires to go down to
his grave honored and respected, and gladly would I see any man
who has devoted so many years of his life to the public service
depart in that way. But there are some acts of the right honorable
gentleman's career to which I must refer. His leadership of the Tory

party was obtained, as I was told by the man he supplanted [the reference is to Sir Allan McNab], by intrigue and deception. Having obtained power in that way, by a cunning and deceptive heart, he signalized his public career by acts that are not unworthy of notice. . . . I will suppose that the Honorable First Minister was about to organize his followers into a band of musicians, and he were to ask me what instruments they should play. I would say to him, "Let everyone play the lyre, because the band master would not have much trouble in making experts of them." '

Ibid., pp. 132-3

Nor was Rymal the only Liberal outraged by the bill.

The Redistribution Bill was introduced late in the 1882 session—a habit of Macdonald's, increasing now as he grew older, especially with controversial legislation. It was presented for first reading on April 28. When it came up for second reading on May 6, Blake quickly noted it was substantially different from the first bill. The Speaker ruled, rightly, that the process had to begin all over again. Even before first reading there had been a great spate of representations from Ontario Conservative members and those who hoped to be Conservative members; between first and second readings there had been another flood from those who wanted this township taken off or added. The meeting at which these were sorted and settled was stormy and violent, and one member averred he had not heard so much profanity since the caucus on Letellier's political execution.

That the Gerrymander of 1882 was bitterly resented by the Liberals is an understatement. G.W. Ross, Liberal MP Middlesex West, whose constituency was one of the many operated upon, suggested that the Redistribution Bill be replaced by one more frankly worded, 'An act to bull-doze the Liberal Party of Canada and for other purposes.'

Peter B. Waite, *Canada 1874-1896* (1971), pp. 114-15

While the Opposition developed its bright stars, notably Laurier, the government withered away, and even the question of a likely successor was not resolved. (John A. favoured the distinguished former jurist John Thompson, but his wishes were not to be immediately obeyed.) In the past his tendency to delay had been useful, but now it exacerbated problems that required expedient resolution. The polarizing effects of the North West crisis of 1885, the hanging of Riel, and the Jesuits' Estates question might have been avoided had John A. not let things slide.

Flashes of his old sagacity emerged on the franchise issue, but too late.

In 1885 the Cabinet was a mess; Macdonald admitted that himself. He got his old friend Alexander Campbell to stay on, but in agreeing to do so, Campbell wrote: '. . . let me say how much I hope we may get on without this eternal yielding to everyone, who has, or thinks he has, control of a few votes . . . The constant giving way to truculent demands and our delays and the irritation and mischief which they produce are in everybody's mouth. . . .' Of course this was easy counsel from a Senator. Still, it was a real and palpable problem, and Campbell said a lot more in a letter written about the same time to T.C. Patteson:

> Things have been going badly in the Ministry for a year or more. Macdonald has lost his grasp and does nothing he can help. Putting off, his old sin, has increased upon him until it has become an irritation to have relations with him . . . he retains his old power of dealing with his followers and his keen insight into motives of action—but for the work of government and of legislation he is gone I think . . . he wasted months before bringing it [the Franchise bill] in at all; simply, I believe, from feeling that he only had a very hazy view of the subject, and a desire for more time, with his usual reliance on the hurry of the House at last . . . tell me what you think and tear up this letter.

Patteson agreed. 'He was always timid and yielding,' he said, 'and if he has ever taken a bold stand I think it was because he had a bold man at his elbow at the time.'

P.B. Waite, 'Sir John A. Macdonald: The Man', *Dalhousie Review* 47, no. 2 (Summer 1967), p. 151

September 8, 1885.

Dear Lord Carnarvon,

. . . The Chief subject of contest was a Franchise Bill for the Dominion; and as it is, in my opinion, the completion of the Federal Constitution which you had so great a hand in constructing, I am sure you will take an interest in knowing that that constitution has at last been perfected. *Ex necessitate*, the Act of 1867—your Act— provided that the provincial franchises, until altered by the Federal Parliament, should be used for Dominion representation. As they did not greatly differ, those franchises were allowed to continue until now. But the provinces had begun to tinker at their electoral franchises, and in some cases legislated with the direct object of

affecting the returns of the Federal Parliament, so that the independence of that Parliament was threatened, to such a degree that it
had to be dealt with.

Our radicals, or Grits, as they are called, violently opposed the
change, as they had got possession of several of the provincial
Legislatures, and could alter the franchises in those provinces at
will. For two months and a half they used every means of obstruction, but patience and firmness defeated obstruction in the end. On
one occasion the House sat from three o'clock p.m. on Thursday
until Saturday night at twelve without adjournment.

With the Canadian Pacific Railway finished and my Franchise Bill
become law, I feel that I have done my work, and can sing my *Nunc
dimittis*. Lady Macdonald joins me in kind regards to Lady Carnarvon and yourself.

Believe me,

> Your Excellency's very faithful
> servant,
> John A. Macdonald.

The main principles underlying Sir John Macdonald's Franchise Act
are (1) uniformity of the suffrage, and (2) the recognition of a
property qualification as determining the right to vote. He desired
uniformity because he believed that, in a young country like Canada, composed of divers elements, whatever assimilates the political conditions of the various provinces ought to be sought after and
promoted.

> Joseph Pope, *Memoirs of The Right Honourable Sir John
> Alexander Macdonald*, vol. 2 (1894), pp. 246-7

*Macdonald's colleagues became increasingly dissatisfied with his
policy of delay.*

Undoubtedly, part of the trouble lay in the fact that Macdonald, like
most men, became less willing and less able to change as he grew
older. And while timid in the face of real votes and real pressures, he
had come, by the mid-1880s to dominate and sometimes to tyran-
nize the Cabinet. John S. Thompson, the newly-arrived Justice
Minister from Nova Scotia, was not one to accept the old man's
views without question. 'I showed fight,' he wrote to his wife in
1867, 'and refused to agree to an opinion of his on a legal question.
Of course the poor old fellow is worried to death but I do not care for
him and I am so determined to let him see it that I could insult him
at every turn while he keeps it (his gruffness and bad temper) up.

This is unheard of heresy here because the practice is to worship
him from afar even when he is ugly.'

P.B. Waite, 'Sir John A. Macdonald: The Man', *Dalhousie
Review* 47, no. 2 (Summer 1967), p. 151

IMMIGRATION

*In a vast, new, and almost empty country, immigrants were ob-
viously needed. But some were more welcome than others. The
Chinese, for instance, were subjected to increasing discrimination
after the economic depression of the 1870s, when they were blamed
for undercutting wages. By the mid-1880s British Columbia had
imposed numerous restrictions on the Chinese and was pressing
the federal government to limit their immigration. Although he did
not support such a move, Macdonald's motives were frankly
utilitarian.*

. . . the federal government had resisted any restriction for fear that
a labour shortage might jeopardize the completion of the CPR. Prime
Minister Macdonald was echoing such concerns when he frankly
told the House of Commons in 1883:

> It will be all very well to exclude Chinese labour, when we can replace
> it with white labour, but until that is done, it is better to have Chinese
> labour than no labour at all.
>
> Peter S. Li, *The Chinese in Canada* (1988), p. 29

*His attitude towards Jewish immigrants was no more human-
itarian. Although there had been Jewish families in what was to
become Canada as far back as the 1750s, the first mass migration of
Jewish refugees from Europe to North America began in the 1880s.
The persecution of Jews in Russia was long-standing. When they
began arriving in droves as refugees in France and England, distinguished citizens in all walks of life began raising funds to assist
them. On 2 February 1882 the Lord Mayor of London held a public
meeting at which prominent British Jews such as the Rothschilds
and Herman Landau, the London representative of the CPR, headed
the drive for relief funds. Present at this meeting was Sir Alexander
Tilloch Galt, in his capacity as Canada's first High Commissioner
to Great Britain. He had already suggested in his correspondence to
John A. that some of these homeless Jews might be settled in the
west to help with railroad construction and to settle thinly popu-*

lated regions. Macdonald thought this a good idea and agreed to
make land available to them. In Montreal, relief committees were
formed by a number of Jewish and Christian groups, and as a result
of their efforts the first Russian Jewish immigrants arrived at Win-
nipeg on 26 May 1882.

A week before the Mansion House meeting, on January 25, 1882,
High Commissioner Galt had written privately to Prime Minister
Macdonald, informing him of his intention to join the relief com-
mittee and broaching a possible Canadian interest:

> The Jewish persecution in Russia has induced me to write Rothschild
> suggesting that I would like to discuss with him the feasibility of
> removing the agricultural Jews to Canada. I have only sent my note
> to-day. It seems not a bad opportunity of interesting the Hebrews in
> our North West.

A second private letter, the day after the Mansion House protest,
elaborates the suggestion with considerable persuasiveness:

> 3 February, 1882.
> My dear Macdonald,
> As I mentioned in my last note I have had more or less conference
> with the leading Jews in regard to Emigration from Russia to Canada
> and at their request I have consented to act on the Mansion House
> Committee to which I was nominated at the very influential meeting
> held on Wednesday.
> From what I learn these Russian Jews are a superior class of people,
> partly farmers, but generally trade people. Most of them were well off
> and though many have been ruined, still my opinion is that a large
> proportion will still be found with sufficient means to establish
> themselves in Canada or the United States if Russia will let them go.
> I found the American Jews were actively promoting emigration to
> the United States and I thought what was good for them could not be
> bad for us.
> When the Committee meets I will know what their ideas are and
> may perhaps be able to suggest some mode by which we may get a
> share. The Jews are really now so influential in Europe, that there can
> be no harm in cultivating them.

Galt was exaggerating the extent to which the proposed immigrants might be expected to arrive with financial means. A small
number may have been relatively 'well off' before the destruction of
their Russian or Polish homes, and many were skilled in various
trades, but in material goods very few had more than their meagre

personal possessions, and the funds raised in Britain were urgently needed to help the Russian Jews make the long voyage across the Atlantic.

Macdonald ... moved quickly, advising the Marquis of Lorne, Governor General of Canada, on February 20, 1882, that Galt 'has been attending to the Jews,' and adding, 'I hope something will come of this. He will be instructed to act for the Immigration Department, and we are quite ready to assign the Jews lands.'

Despite this declaration, however, the Jews who arrived in Winnipeg in May and June found that no land had yet been provided for them, and repeated representations were made to the Dominion government to fulfil its agreement without further delay. Galt himself wrote again to Macdonald, this time from Montreal, on July 7, 1882:

> My dear Macdonald,
> I wish you would read the enclosed and determine how far the view of the Jewish Committee can be met.
> I think it of great importance, especially in view of my return to London, and future influence with leading Jews there & in Paris, that you should find the means of giving a district for settlement to these people. It cannot fail to have a good effect.
> Could you give them the spare Mennonite Townships or if this cannot be done, might not some of the Colonization Companies be called on peremptorily to take this land or *leave* it. It seems absurd to have the whole district covered with bogus applications (in many cases) to the exclusion of bona fide settlers.

The Colonization Companies Galt mentions were privately organized concerns for whom the government had reserved close to three million acres of land, on condition that they bring to Canada the hundreds of thousands of immigrants the new country needed. The scheme was unsuccessful, attracting scarcely twelve hundred settlers. Between 1884 and 1891 the terms of the contracts were re-examined and many of the companies dissolved for their failure to fulfil the agreement.

A rather cynical and derogatory footnote appears in a further private letter from Macdonald to Galt, on February 28, 1882:

> The Old Clo' move is a good one—A sprinkling of Jews in the North West would do good. They would at once go in for peddling & politics and be of much use in the new country as cheap jacks and chapmen.

Macdonald's offhand witticism about the 'Old Clo' move' echoes the familiar stereotype of the Jewish peddler. . . .

Harry Gutkin, *Journey Into Our Heritage* (1980), pp. 28-31

THE RIEL REBELLION, 1885

The Métis in the Saskatchewan Valley, concerned that their rights were not being respected, invited the exiled Louis Riel, now an American citizen, to return and lead their cause. Ill and impulsive, still unrecovered from a severe mental breakdown in the 1870s, Riel occupied Batoche, armed his supporters, formed a provisional government, and sought the surrender of Fort Carlton. Defeated within two months, he was tried as a traitor and hanged over the strong protest of French Canadians, who sought clemency for him on the grounds of insanity. Macdonald, coasting through his final years in government, clearly underestimated the backlash that Riel's execution would cause, and the subsequent schism between French and English has had lasting effects. It sent droves of formerly Conservative French Canadians into the ranks of the Liberal party, and in the long run was to help Laurier's cause a great deal.

His mishandling of the Riel affair was one of Macdonald's greatest tactical mistakes.

The Métis were exasperated.

Petitions were sent to Ottawa, but no useful answers were received.

In their bitterness and frustration the Métis sent a delegation to the self-exiled Louis Riel, asking him to return to Canada to lead his people. Riel agreed. With his family he travelled north from the United States in July 1884 to resume his role as Métis chieftain. Within a short time he headed a broadly based protest movement. White farmers were discontented because of the lack of both responsible government in the Northwest Territories and representation in Ottawa. They felt that the CPR should run westward through the northern park belt, not through the southern part of the district. Like Manitobans, they wanted cheap freight rates, subsidies, and rapid economic development. The Plains Indians—set aside on reservations that were much hated by a people who were once free and remained proud—were without buffalo. Many were desperate for want of food and starvation was not unknown. Indians, white settlers, Métis—all were discontented. Initially all looked with favour upon the leadership of Riel.

Donald Swainson, *John A. Macdonald: The Man and the Politician* (1971), p. 129

Macdonald and the Governor-General clearly differed in their

impressions of the seriousness of the rebellion. Nevertheless, John
A. took counsel from the Queen's representative.

Government House,
Ottawa, August 31st, 1885.

Dear Sir John,

Thanks for your letter of the 28th which I have read with attention.

We are, I think, entirely at one upon the general principle, but I am not sure that I should apply it as you do in Riel's case. I still think that there are features in that case which give it an aspect distinct from that of ordinary criminal cases.

You regard the recent outbreak in the N.W. as a merely 'domestic trouble' which should not be 'elevated to the rank of a rebellion'.

The outbreak was, no doubt, confined to our own territory and may therefore properly be described as a domestic trouble, but I am afraid we have all of us been doing what we could to elevate it to the rank of a rebellion, and with so much success that we cannot now reduce it to the rank of a common riot.

If the movement had been at once stamped out by the N.W.M. policy, the case would have been different, but we were within an ace of an Indian war; the progress of the outbreak and its suppression has been described in glowing language by the press all over the world: we brought up troops from all parts of the Dominion: those troops have been thanked by Parliament: they are to receive an Imperial medal. Will not all this be regarded as placing the insurrection in a category quite different from that of the Rebecca riots with which you compare it? No one would have proposed to confer a medal upon the troops or a decoration upon the Commanding Officer engaged in the suppression of these.

I should not like to go a step further than could be helped in facilitating an appeal to England, and there would no doubt be an objection to the postponement of the execution by directions set from Ottawa at this stage. On the other hand, assuming that the Court of Queen's Bench refused to order a new trial, and that thereupon Riel at once appeals to the Privy Council, could we hang him before that tribunal had disposed of his application?

It seems to me that if there is any feeling at all on the subject in the Dominion (and I observe what you say as to the extent of this) that feeling would be greatly embittered and prolonged by such a course.

I should much prefer that whatever is done should take place as much as possible in the ordinary modes of procedure and as little as possible by direct intervention on the part of the Government. Under the section of the N.W. Territories Act to which you refer me

(S. 76. s.s. 8) the Stipendiary is required to postpone the execution from time to time until his report has been received and *the pleasure of the Governor thereon communicated to the Lieutenant-Governor.*

If in the interval between the termination of the proceedings at Winnipeg and the date fixed for the execution, we become aware that Riel has appeared by counsel before the Judicial Committee, my 'communication' to the Lieutenant-Governor might be deferred. Whereupon the Stipendiary, without special instructions, would, I apprehend, postpone the execution.

What do you say to this?

> I am,
> Dear Sir John
> Yours sincerely,
> Lansdowne.

> Rivière du Loup.
> September 3, 1885.

Dear Lord Lansdowne,

I fear that you *have me* with respect to the character given to the outbreak. We have certainly made it assume large proportions in the public eye. This has been done however for our purposes, and, I think, wisely done. Still it was a rising within a limited area, and was confined to a small number of persons. It never endangered the safety of the State, nor did it involve international complications. True it involved the danger of an Indian war, and in that would be similar to the arson of a small house, in the vicinity of a powder magazine.

What I ventured to suggest in my letter was that the persons convicted at Regina, should be dealt with as guilty of municipal and not political offences.

I quite agree with Your Excellency that if notice is given of an intention to appeal to the Judicial Committee, it would not do to hurry the execution as it were—in order to prevent such appeal.

The mode suggested by Your Excellency of deferring the signification of your pleasure, without any positive action on the part of the Government, seems the best solution of the matter.

I shall be obliged by Your Excellency not mentioning your views to anyone. These things do get out in an extraordinary way, and if it were suspected that there was a prearranged intention of postponing the execution of the sentence, there would, I fear, be a popular burst of indignation in Ontario and the Northwest, that may as well be avoided.

Believe me

> dear Lord Lansdowne,
> faithfully yours,
> John A. Macdonald.
> Sir Joseph Pope, *Correspondence of Sir John Macdonald* (1921),
> pp. 356-8

Macdonald's decision to execute Riel, carried out on 16 November 1885, was not a popular one, but it reflected his idea of justice.

Like Alexander Campbell, who was Minister of Justice until September 24, 1885, the Prime Minister had a narrow view of the law. Riel was a traitor. After his first offence he was pardoned. Now he must pay the full penalty and die. French Canada might accept Riel's death after the fact. J.A. Chapleau, who almost resigned from the cabinet to lead a Quebec agitation against Ottawa, changed his mind after looking over the brink, explaining to Macdonald: 'I prefer the risk of personal loss to the national danger imminent, with the perspective of a struggle in the field of race and religious prejudices. We will have to fight, perhaps to fall. Well I prefer, after all, to fight and to fall in the old ship and for the old flag.' Quebec, reasoned Macdonald, was loyal. It would swallow the execution and stand by the Conservative party, as it always had. . . .

Within Quebec a wave of indignation greeted Riel's hanging. The provincial Conservative Party was in power. Guided by Chapleau it refused to declare war on Ottawa. That left an opening for the Liberals, led by the ultra-nationalist Honoré Mercier. The provincial Conservative government was ridiculed for not assaulting the federal régime. As a consequence many ultra-Conservatives deserted their party and supported Mercier. Early in 1887 he formed a new provincial government, with the help of some ultra-Conservatives or Castors. The Conservative Party was publicly split and, like Humpty-Dumpty, was never properly put back together.

> Donald Swainson, *John A. Macdonald: The Man and the Politician* (1971), pp. 136-8

TO BRITISH COLUMBIA VIA CPR

In 1886 the Macdonalds travelled to the west coast on the CPR. The enthusiasm of both was contagious, and John A. used every opportunity to stop and casually campaign.

In fact, it was Agnes's second trip, as she had spent the previous Christmas-New Year's period travelling with friends to within 500

miles of the coast. She commented on the trip in a letter to her
sister-in-law Louisa Macdonald:

As for me I have been to the summit of the Canadian Rocky Mountains by CPR. . . . It was by far the most interesting and delightful trip I ever made in my life. I asked Judge & Mrs Brooks to go as my guests & took a butler & maid & we had besides a car porter who is also cook. . . . We started off quietly, very few had any idea I was going away at all. . . .

We were absent 16 days and nights, spent 2 days & 2 nights at Winnipeg, two more at Canmore (in the mountains) & half a day & night at Port Arthur & travelled all the rest. Every day was a pleasure & a new interest. . . .

The CPR were ever so good to me. Mr Van Horne said I might go where I liked. . . . Altogether it was too delightful.

What astonished me was the comfort & ease of the railway, its strict punctuality, its quiet & prompt management & its little motion. We read, played games, wrote letters, all generally with great ease & this on a line far away in an almost uninhabited country & in depth of a Canadian winter. . . .

Ottawa seems so dull & tame & stupid & old after that wonderful new western world with its breadth & length & clear air & wonderfully exhilirating atmosphere that always seems to lure me on! . . .

Louise Reynolds, Agnes: The Biography of Lady Macdonald
(1979), p. 105

On the second trip she decided to view the mountains from the
vantage point of the train's cowcatcher.

The idea of the Prime Minister's wife riding the cowcatcher caused the crew no little consternation. What was she going to sit on, for example? This question she answered for them by choosing an empty candle-box, which she then placed on the buffer beam. The next thing to do was to have Agnes obtain John A.'s permission. When she approached him:

> The Chief, seated on a low chair on the rear platform of the car, with a rug over his knees and a magazine in his hand, looked very comfortable and content. Hearing my request . . . he pronounced the idea 'rather ridiculous', then remembered it was dangerous as well, and finally asked if I was sure I could hold on. Before the words were well out of his lips, and taking permission for granted by the question, I was again standing by the cowcatcher . . . and asking to be helped on.

At least some members of the Prime Minister's staff were as nonplussed as the crew by Agnes' unorthodox choice. Pope, for one, did not approve and wrote of Lady Macdonald's 'characteristic imprudence'. (As there was never any other mention of Agnes being imprudent, it seems more likely that he meant 'impulsive', for she was that.) . . .

On the last morning of the cowcatcher trip, Pope had reason to be upset. The danger that cattle might be on the track was ever-present, but on this particular day it was a number of young pigs that appeared just in front of the train. All except one managed to get out of harm's way, but that one was hit by the train and Pope declared that it passed between his body and the post he was holding. Had either of the passengers on the cowcatcher been hit by the animal, the impact could have been fatal. Pope rightly decided that this mode of transportation was not for him: 'I have not ridden on a cowcatcher since.' Agnes was aware of the possible danger of her exposed position but much less worried about it. On that morning, she wrote, she was admiring the scenery when 'There was a squeak, a flash of something near, and away we went. . . . The Secretary averred that the body had struck him in passing; but as I shut my eyes tightly as soon as the pigs appeared, I cannot bear testimony to the fact.'

The ride on the cowcatcher gave Agnes too much pleasure to leave room for fears. 'Enthroned on a candle-box with a soft felt hat well over the eyes, and a linen carriage-cover tucked around me from waist to foot . . .', she turned to the Superintendent who shared her 'peril' and decided that some word of comfort was necessary for him: 'This is *lovely quite lovely*; I shall travel on this cowcatcher from summit to sea.' The poor Superintendent only surveys me with solemn and resigned surprise. "I-suppose-you-will", he says slowly.'

When the summit was passed and the rivers began to flow westward down towards the Pacific, the steam was shut off and the brakes put on. The sixty-ton engine glided into the pass of the Kicking Horse River, making a descent of 2,800 feet in only twelve miles.

> With a firm right hand grasping the iron stanchion, and my feet planted on the buffer-beam, there was not a yard of that descent in which I faltered for a moment. . . . There is glory and brightness and beauty everywhere, and I laugh aloud on the cowcatcher, just because it is all so delightful. . . . Halted at Pallister, The Chief and his friends walked up to . . . make a morning call. I felt a little 'superior' and was rather condescending. Somewhat flushed with excitement but still anxious to be polite, I asked 'would the Chief step up and take a drive'? To the horror of the bystanders, he carelessly consented. . . . There was general consternation among our little group of friends . . .

—The Chief rushing through the flats of the Columbia on a cow-catcher! . . . It is a comfort to the other occupant of the buffer to find someone else wilful.

. . . When they emerged from one . . . tunnel, they saw a party of young English sportsmen, standing and looking in understandable amazement at the sight

> of a lady, bareheaded and with an umbrella, seated in front of an engine, at the mouth of the tunnel in the Gold Range of British Columbia! I am sorely afraid I laughed outright at the blank amazement . . . and longed to tell them what fun it was; but not being 'introduced, you know', contented myself with acknowledging their presence with a solemn little bow—which was quite irresistible under the circumstances!
>
> Ibid., pp. 113-15

The appearance of the great man was a surprise to at least one of his loyal supporters.

Sir John had quite a reception at Winnipeg, where a large number of people assembled to receive him. Among the crowd gathered round the car was an enthusiastic young Tory who was cheering with all his might. Upon Sir John's appearance the enthusiasm became tremendous. When the lull came, the young Tory, who evidently had never seen Sir John before in his life, remarked in a low voice to a friend standing by, 'Seedy-looking old beggar, isn't he?' and then resumed his cheering with redoubled vigour, as though determined that his private impressions should not be allowed to interfere with his party loyalty.

> Maurice Pope, ed., *Public Servant: The Memoirs of Sir Joseph Pope* (1960), p. 53

At Regina he expressed his opinion of the landscape.

On his visit to the Pacific Coast in 1886, Sir John stopped off a short while at Regina. As every one knows, that ambitious capital of three great territories lies in the midst of a dead level plain, extending in every direction farther than the eye can reach. While the Premier was standing at the railway station, he was approached by one of Regina's gushing sons, who asked him 'what he thought of the prospect?' swinging his arms around, so as to indicate the vast plain by which they were surrounded. With many a twinkle in his eye, and the quiet smile for which he was noted playing about his mouth, he said in slow and measured tones, 'If you had a lit-tle more wood, and a lit-tle more water, and here and there a hill, I think the prospect would be improved.' There was an awkward pause in the conversation till a new topic was propounded.

E.B. Biggar, *Anecdotal Life of Sir John Macdonald* (1891), p. 231

MACDONALD'S MEMORY

John A.'s memory was legendary. He could recall faces, names, family attachments, events, passages in literary works in a flash, often in the most unlikely moments. This ability, combined with a remarkable political sensitivity to people and issues, ensured him many votes.

How Macdonald actually managed his Cabinet meetings must now be nearly a closed book, but there are hints here and there. One suspects that he listened much, perhaps not giving the impression that he was, and that he stepped in either to sum up, or to make plain what was the sense of the meeting, or occasionally, as in the case of Charles Tupper, or his son Charles Hibbert Tupper, to make quite clear where final responsibilities and power lay. Macdonald's general role is well put by a bluff old Nova Scotian, A.W. McLelan, who wrote him: 'Often when [the Executive] Council was perplexed . . . you had made things smooth and plain. I thought of the expression of an old farmer about my father, "There are wheels in that man that have never been moved yet".' This was certainly a feeling that John A. Macdonald gave to many people: the immense richness and variety of his inner resources. . . . There is a wonderful little note in the Patteson Papers about this. T.C. Patteson, former editor of the Toronto *Mail* and at the time Postmaster of Toronto, had got into a literary squabble with some friends, and promptly scribbled a note to the Prime Minister of Canada: 'What is the next line to, "Ye gentlemen of England who sit at home at ease"? Please endorse answer.' And on the back of this note is written, in Macdonald's clear flowing hand, 'Ah, little do you think upon the dangers of the seas.' This in January, 1890. There the letter lies, in the Patteson Papers in the Archives of Ontario, a curious reflection of Macdonald's eclectic knowledge of literature and history. He would lay himself up for days with sherry and Dickens, in the days when he was living a quasi-bachelor life. And he remembered what he read, as he remembered names and faces. He always seemed to have a story from Sheridan, or Trollope, or Dickens at hand, to say nothing of innumerable stories from less respectable sources.

P.B. Waite, 'Sir John A. Macdonald: The Man', *Dalhousie Review* 47, no. 2 (Sept. 1967), pp. 146-7

While living at Kingston, [Macdonald] went out into the country to a farm house near Adolphustown on business, and while waiting for the horses to be brought to the door, sat reading a book. When told the vehicle was ready, he dropped the book and came away. Nine years afterwards he visited the same house, and going to the bookcase took down the same book and turning to a certain page, said: 'There's the very word I read last when I was here nine years ago.'

Mr Bell, of the *Belleville Intelligencer*, met Sir John in 1872, and did not see him again till 1885, when he was one of a deputation to interview the Premier on a political question. Having only exchanged a few words and been in his presence a few minutes on the first occasion, Mr Bell was proceeding to introduce himself, when Sir John anticipated him and said: 'Oh! I know you. You are Mr Bell, the *Intelligencer* man.'

When on his visit to Vancouver in 1886, a man came up to Sir John out of the crowd and began to introduce himself by saying: 'Sir John, I suppose you don't remember me.' 'Oh, yes,' replied the Premier, without hesitation. 'I met you at a picnic in 1856, and you may remember it was a rainy day.' 'Yes,' said the man, 'that was the very occasion'.

Once he and a friend were walking together, when a working man stopped before them. Sir John, after shaking hands, said, 'Well, D---, it is sixteen years since I met you. By the way, how is your boy?' The man agreed as to the time, and said his boy was better. After they parted and went on, the friend said to Sir John, 'Of course that was a chance hit.' 'No,' said he, 'I remember when I met him before he was in great distress about his little boy, who was suffering from a lame back.'

At a political meeting at Napanee in 1882, when he ran for Lennox, Sir John noticed a gentleman on the platform, and after looking at him for a moment asked, 'Isn't your name Ruttan?' 'Yes,' replied Dr Ruttan, for it was he who was addressed, 'but I never met you, Sir John. How did you know me?' 'By your likeness to your brothers,'

replied he. 'But it must be a long time since you have seen them,'
observed the doctor. 'Yes,' answered Sir John, 'it is now forty years.'
> E.B. Biggar, *Anecdotal Life of Sir John Macdonald* (1891),
> pp. 207-9

CAMPAIGN STORIES

*Political campaigns in the nineteenth century were unregulated
and often chaotic. Until the ballot was introduced in 1874, electors
simply 'spoke to' the candidate of their choice; that is, they voted
orally. This 'choice' was often made on the basis of which candidate
had offered the voter the most pleasing bribe. If a candidate had
paid a voter the astronomical sum of $5 to vote for him, it was fairly
sure to be done; after all, the vote could be heard. Money was just
one way of bribing electors, however; booze, promises of jobs, and,
on occasion, violence were other inducements. After the introduction of the ballot people quickly developed the facility of verbally
supporting one candidate while voting for another.*

*There are many campaign stories about Macdonald. The picture
that emerges is one of astounding wiliness and a chameleon-like
ability to adapt to circumstances. Always humorous, often poig-
nant, delving into his extraordinary memory on many occasions,
John A. was ever working, ever planning a way to garner more
votes. And, in spite of his weaknesses, he was a grand success.*

*In the 1878 general election, Sir John A. was knocked unconscious
at a violent mass meeting in Montreal's Dominion Square.*

The federal election was only a few days away when posters were
put up announcing the meeting. These posters read:

A MASS MEETING
will be held on
SATURDAY EVENING
IN
DOMINION SQUARE
To give an opportunity to
Rt. Hon. Sir John A. Macdonald
To address the
MANUFACTURERS, MERCHANTS
AND WORKING MEN
OF MONTREAL,
ON THE LEADING ISSUES OF THE DAY . . . .

Chair to be taken at 7.30 p.m.
In the event of unfavorable weather
The meeting will be held in the
SKATING RINK

Despite the thoughtful provision at the poster's close, there was no
rain on that Saturday night. The sky was unclouded and a full moon
silvered the grass and the trees of Dominion Square. There was
additional illumination, for lamps hung from the platform on the
northern side, while locomotive reflectors at the corners of the
square sent clear broad beams over the assembly. And it was a vast
assembly, with thousands of admirers, detractors and undecided
persons mingled together to see and hear the eminent man, who had
been for five years in opposition in Ottawa, but who now claimed to
be on the way back to power.

Montrealers took their politics with full appetites in those days.
The meeting opened, as announced, at seven-thirty, and it did not
close until eleven o'clock. Sir John A. himself was to speak for an
hour and a half, and other speakers were to supplement him.

Perhaps, however, the length of the meeting was drawn out by the
interruptions which were made. Alfred Perry was there, and wherever Alfred Perry was to be found, things were not likely to be
tranquil. In 1878 he was a considerably older man than in 1849,
when he had been a leader of the mob that burned down the old
Parliament Building in St Ann's Market. But age had not greatly
bowed down his youthfulness, and in the Dominion Square meeting he was nearly at his aggressive prime.

Perry had become as vehement a Liberal as he had once been a
Tory. To the meeting he came accompanied by his disturbers of the
peace. More than this, with quaint inventiveness, he had devised a
sort of horn, which made a loud, piercing sound, much like the
scream of a soul at the limits of anguish.

The meeting had hardly begun when the horns were sounded and
Perry and his men showered the brilliant group on the platform
with eggs and other missiles, harder, if less expansive. Then came
the onslaught, as the platform was actually stormed. In the fight
which ensued, someone struck Sir John on the head, and for a few
moments the eminent Conservative leader lay on the platform
unconscious, while his friends and his foes battled above him.

But Sir John was a resilient campaigner. When order had been
restored and he had regained his consciousness, the meeting proceeded with an effective speech in Sir John's best manner. The
election was being fought out on the vigorous lines of Conservative
protection versus Liberal free trade. Since a serious depression then
darkened the industry for the country, Sir John A.'s 'National

Policy' for the protection of Canadian industries was being presented as the hope of the people.

His final point was made with serious energy. He pictured the human cost of undefended industry. 'And I have seen,' he said, 'the poor men returning from Hay's manufactory in Toronto, with their heads hanging down in despair, a miserable half-dollar in their pockets . . . when, at the next door, there were the culls and refuse of the United States market selling for what they could fetch.'

Despite all the racket and interference of Perry and his followers, it had been a stirring speech. When the meeting had closed with three cheers for the Queen and three for Sir John, the crowd began streaming over the square on their way home.

With his remarkable urbanity, Sir John made his way through the crowd to the same Alfred Perry who had tried his best to ruin the rally. He examined Perry's strange horn, and said that he would like to take out a patent for it, so that it could be used only by Conservatives. As he turned to go away, he made his parting thrust. 'You know, Fred,' he said, 'I think that your bark is worse than your bite.'

Edgar Andrew Collard, *Canadian Yesterdays* (1955), pp. 76-8

On the 28th August [1878], Sir John went East to Cornwall to a meeting, and by a coincidence Mr [Oliver] Mowat went on the same train down to Glengarry to help Mr [Alexander] Mackenzie at one of his picnics. It appeared that Sir Richard Cartwright had been expected at Mr Mackenzie's picnic at Alexandria, in that county, but failed to appear. His non-appearance was attributed by the Conservatives to the anger of the Highlanders at some real or supposed insult he had given them. Sir John went from Cornwall to the little village of St Andrews, seven miles distant, where in the churchyard of the little Roman Catholic church reposed the remains of his old antagonist, John Sandfield Macdonald. In his speech here, his audience being composed chiefly of Scotchmen, Sir John turned the Cartwright incident to account in the following way: 'The last and worst thing they had said of him was, that he was a Scotchman, a descendant of a Highlander and a thief. Why, Mr Cartwright, who made this charge was a Highlander himself, and his ancestors might have stolen cattle—and the instinct might remain with him. He seemed to forget that, and it seemed to have slipped his memory, that his leader, Mr Mackenzie, was also a Highlander, and had shown himself quite as great an adept at stealing as he (Sir John) had. Mr Cartwright was told by his leader to be at Alexandria, but he had not gone, as he heard some Scotchmen had gone there to meet him. Well, he had shown a little more sense than the man who attacked the laird of Camlogie. The laird of Camlogie, while crossing a bridge, was insulted by a man. For this insult he threw the man into the water and nearly drowned him. Some friends of the laird asked him if he did not know the danger of throwing the man into the water. "A weel," said the laird, "I did na think ony mon wad insult the laird o' Camlogie on a bredge if he could na swem." (Laughter.) Mr Cartwright evidently could not swim, so he got out of the way of the Highlanders of Alexandria.'

> E.B. Biggar, *Anecdotal Life of Sir John Macdonald* (1891), p. 173

Just after the [1878] elections he went down to Quebec to bid an official good-bye to one of the ablest and most popular Governor-Generals Canada ever had—Lord Dufferin. While here he was pressed to attend a meeting and give an address, which he consented to do. He expressed his regret that he could not address them well in the French language—the language of his great friend, his 'alter ego', who had been called his Siamese twin—Sir George E. Cartier. He (Sir John) considered himself an English-speaking Frenchman, as Sir George E. Cartier considered himself a French-speaking Englishman. After the elections just over it was impossible to find a Rouge in Quebec or a Grit in Ontario, even if a reward were offered for them, so complete was the victory. The Grits were like the Dodo —extinct. A story was told in Toronto of two Grits or Rouges—for they are as much alike as a crocodile and an alligator—who met the day after the election. One of them said to the other, 'Didn't you Grits get a good licking?' and his companion replied, 'Yes, didn't they!' You might know the Grits now by their wearing longer faces than anybody else. It was said that the Hon. George Brown, editor of the *Globe*, of whom they had all heard, had gone three times a week to the same barber for twenty years, always paying him ten cents to be shaved. On the morning after the election, however, the barber demanded fifteen cents instead of ten, because he had never seen his face so long before.

> Ibid., p. 174

'Sir John has got his war paint on and wants us all to take the field in Ontario,' Thompson wrote to his wife in Halifax two weeks after Macdonald's return from the West. A September 1886 by-election in Haldimand, a constituency in Ontario that had been Liberal since long before Confederation, had been held by the Liberals, notwithstanding great Conservative efforts to take it. It was the time to strengthen the government with Ontario voters. In any Dominion election, ground would probably be lost in Quebec. On October 30th, the cabinet decided to have the elections before another session of Parliament was called, and expected to go to the polls in

January and probably secure an overall majority of about twenty-five. By November 1886, Ontario announced a provincial election and the Conservative campaign went vigorously forward into Ontario.

Macdonald and three or four cabinet ministers spent almost two solid weeks campaigning in the last half of November. The pace was ferocious. Macdonald was astonished. He went through meeting after meeting with ease. 'Sir John surprises me,' Thompson wrote to his wife, 'he goes through all these hardships quite gaily . . . ' The Dominion ministers, Macdonald, Thomas White, and Thompson, together with W.H. Meredith, the leader of the Conservative opposition in Ontario, installed themselves in a special Grand Trunk car, lived there and slept there, like gypsies. Thursday, November 18, 1886, they travelled from Palmerston to Goderich in a perfect blizzard all day. At every station there was a crowd, sometimes with a brass band, who always cried out for 'John A.'. Thompson would watch Macdonald go out, 'shake hands everywhere with everyone, and kiss all the girls and . . . come back to the car covered with snow.' When they arrived at Goderich at 10:30 P.M. there was a torchlight procession which the Dominion ministers were too exhausted to attend, so they gave Meredith to the natives as a peace offering.

The next day the blizzard subsided into wind; they drove twelve miles in open carriages northeast to Dungannon, arrived perished from cold, to have the crowd there take out the horses and themselves haul the carriages through the crowded streets of the village. Then back to Goderich for another five-hour meeting until 1:00 A.M. On Saturday they were in Hamilton, to the biggest meeting so far, a very rough crowd. Thomas White could not manage them at all. They stamped their feet until they got Macdonald but even he had a difficult time. 'You have to say very wicked things,' said Thompson frankly. 'You cannot hold such crowds as we have had unless you give them your best and your worst.' They often felt like travelling minstrels, from railway car to meetings and back again, often in dirty clothes; and in spite of their own exhaustion, both of mind and body, were 'supposed to be quite up to the boiling point of excitement which prevails among the audiences.' At Stratford the press was so thick that Thompson's guide was stopped dead, and when he was on the point of being suffocated by the pressure, by shouting and cursing he got himself lifted up bodily by the crowd, was hoisted over their heads and handed forward to the platform amid deafening cheers and laughter.

When the general election of February 22, 1887 was over Macdonald was still firmly in the saddle. Quebec's 65 seats broke even,

33 Conservatives, a retreat from the 51 of 1882. But Nova Scotia returned to the fold—rather dishing the repeal movement—and Ontario held firm; altogether Macdonald could look forward to a comfortable 35-seat majority.

P.B. Waite, *Macdonald: His Life and World* (1975), pp. 182-4

At a banquet which followed the public meeting [in Brantford, 1886] in the evening, Sir John in his speech said he was in the position of the great French writer, Voltaire, who after many years' absence from Paris returned there a hero, worshipped by the people. He had been driven from the Paris he loved so well by the despotic power of Louis XV. On his return he visited the theatre, and was crowned with a chaplet of roses. He was an old man, and he said feebly 'My friends! you smother me with roses,' and he died the next day. It appeared the people of Brantford were determined to smother him with roses, but he did not intend to die, nevertheless. (Laughter.) He was not quite so old as Voltaire, and he was a good deal tougher.

E.B. Biggar, *Anecdotal Life of Sir John Macdonald* (1891), p. 170

When the late David Thompson was sitting for Haldimand, in the days when the record of the riding was an unbroken series of Liberal victories, he was laid aside for nearly a whole session through illness. He got down to Parliament at last, and told the story of his reception as follows: 'The first man I met on coming back was Blake. He passed me with a simple nod. The next man I met was Cartwright, and his greeting was about as cold as that of Blake. Hardly had I passed these men when I met Sir John. He didn't pass me by, but grasped me by the hand, gave me a slap on the shoulder, and said, "Davy, old man, I'm glad to see you back. I hope you'll soon be yourself again and live many a day to vote against me—as you always have done!" Now,' continued Mr Thompson with genuine pathos, 'I never gave the old man a vote in my life, but hang me if it doesn't go against my grain to follow the men who haven't a word of kind greeting for me, and oppose a man with a heart like Sir John's.'

Ibid., p. 190-1

Mr Peak, an officer of one of the Canals, was appointed by the Mackenzie Government, and when Sir John came back to power again, an enemy of the officer thought he would take advantage of the opportunity to get him out. The most serious charge that could be brought against the officer was that he had bought a coffin for a poor deceased workman and paid for it with Government money. Sir John received the accusation, but, as usual, did not say what would be done. Meeting the officer some time after, Sir John alluded to the charge in no censorious way and added: 'I hope you made the coffin big enough.' Laughing off the rest of the charges he asked the officer after his daughter, of whose beauty he had heard. The officer was so struck with Sir John's broad-mindedness, and so pleased with the compliment to his daughter, who was his special pride, that he became a devoted political follower of the Conservative Premier.

Ibid., p. 191

In a more cunning way he met the intrigues of another of his own partisans, who just before an election demanded, as the price of his important services in his county, that Sir John should turn out from his position a certain postmaster—a worthy man against whom nothing of a serious nature could be brought. The intriguant coolly told Sir John he proposed to trump up charges against the postmaster, and wished it understood that when the postmaster was ejected he was to have the place. 'All right,' said Sir John. 'When you get him out you shall have the place,—but wait till after the election.' Presumptuously interpreting this as an assurance that the old postmaster would be discharged on any sort of complaint, the would-be supplanter went to work with a will in the election, the Conservative being returned. After the election he preferred some trumpery charge against the postmaster, which of course the Postmaster General refused to entertain. Finally he came to the Capital, and going to Sir John claimed the old postmaster's place, reminding Sir John of what he had said. 'Well, did you get old — out?' asked Sir John. 'No,' replied he. 'Well,' said Sir John, 'as soon as you get him out, you shall have the place.' 'But the Postmaster General won't listen to me,' he complained. 'Oh! well, then I'm afraid I can't do anything. I can't interfere,' explained Sir John with a delightful assumption of innocence and helplessness.

Ibid, pp. 191-2

The Premier [John A.], talking once with a friend on the peculiar customs of different people, related that on a visit to the West [1886] a reception was given him at which a Bishop from Belgium was present. As the party were being escorted by a body of men in Highland costume, the foreign Bishop, seeing the bare legs and kilts, asked why these men were without trowsers. He replied that it was just a local custom, and that whereas the people in some

places took off their hats as a mark of honour to distinguished
guests, the people here took off their trowsers.

Ibid., p. 204

On a trip from Fredericton to St John down the River St John three
summers ago, a genial gentleman of the latter city was deputed to
show the Premier the points of interest on that beautiful and romantic river. The steamer was to stop at Gagetown, and when they were
nearing that place our guide asked him if he intended to make a
speech, as it was expected that a large crowd would gather at each
stopping place. 'I can't tell till I see the crowd,' he answered. As the
steamer came into the wharf, a large crowd was seen, and the
landing place was gay with flags and decorations. When the steamer
was made fast, he said, 'I am going to speak,' and coming to the
vessel's side delivered one of his short and happy speeches, which,
of course, was well received. At the next place, as they were steam-
ing up to the wharf, our guide asked the same question, and he
returned the same answer—'I can't tell till I see the crowd.' When
the boat was made fast he said, 'I'm going ashore,' and immediately
went out on the wharf, where he spoke privately to all within reach,
patting a child on the head here, giving a flower to another there,
and kissing a third, while not forgetting attentions to the grown
ladies. When the steamer proceeded on her way our guide asked
him, 'Will you tell me, Sir John, why you spoke at Gagetown and
not here?' 'Why,'' said he, 'they were mostly men at Gagetown, and
they were nearly all ladies and children here.'

Ibid., pp. 210-11

At another small stopping place on the trip a knot of people were
gathered, and among them was a good old negro who did service as a
local preacher on Sundays, and on the week days made himself
useful by working about the wharf and warping the steamer in
when she arrived. He was now dressed up in his best clothes, with a
silk hat brighter, if possible, than his beaming face, and when the
boat was made fast, he stood in an attitude of intense expectancy,
thinking Sir John might notice him. The Premier did not observe
him, however, till he was nudged by Lady Macdonald, when he
arose and made the old man a very emphatic bow, in which there
was a slight suggestion of effect. The action sent a thrill of exalta-
tion through every fibre of the old negro's frame, and he bowed back
till he nearly bowed himself off the pier. Sir John had no information about the negro, but his friends said the bow was a stroke of
policy in its way, for the old negro was both well known and well
liked.

Ibid., p. 211-12

PATRONAGE

It is extremely difficult to put the political morality of Macdonald's era into historical perspective. There can be no doubt that corruption, bribery, and party patronage were rampant; nor that John A. was a rogue by any standard. He never denied that. In fact, he assumed that the power of dispensing the plums of patronage was essential to building a party and a nation. What he did deny was that he ever lined his own pockets, and the evidence supports his claim.

By contemporary standards, the level of political corruption under Macdonald's auspices was truly shocking. On the other hand, in nineteenth-century Canada the patronage system was generally regarded as normal. In politics, as in other areas of human activity, most people naturally prefer the company of friends to that of enemies. The problem for politicians and commentators alike has always been to determine the point at which patronage and preferment harm the public interest—itself a slippery concept. The boundary between ugly corruption and normal patronage is always indistinct, a fuzzy line that moves with the shifting standards of the time and the eye of the beholder.

Perhaps all that can be said with assurance is that insistent demands for patronage consumed much of Macdonald's time and often irked him, but that he regarded it as necessary, and played the game with consummate skill.

Here is Pierre Berton's assessment of political morality in Macdonald's day.

Elections in post-Confederation Canada were fought with money and, often enough, it was the candidate who spent the most who cornered the votes. Dollars spoke louder than ideas and out-and-out bribery was not uncommon. At the end of the decade a contemporary historian wrote that 'bribery at elections was scarcely regarded as an offense; both parties resorted to it freely and almost openly.' During the seventies so many elections were controverted because of bribery that a kind of gentleman's agreement existed between the parties to keep them to a manageable number. As late as 1874, there were official charges of bribery before the courts in no less than twenty-nine constituencies in Ontario and Manitoba. Charles Clarke, who was clerk of the Legislature of Ontario, recalled that 'for many years before Confederation, and after its creation, elec-

toral corruption, gross intimidation, bludgeon arguments and bru-
tal force had been employed at various elections to the detriment
and loss of electoral strength by one or other of the opposing
candidates.' Of the early seventies, Clarke wrote that 'nearly every
active politician who had experience in Canadian Parliamentary
elections was aware of the existence of bribery and intimidation. So
common was this experience that, although never seeing money
actually exchanged for a vote, its use was as well known to me as was
the existence, say, of the Queen of England, or the fact that she
occupied the throne.'

In those days, before competing electronic pleasures, politics was
the major pastime in city and village. The entire country was almost
totally partisan which meant that, in the absence of any really
burning issue, it was difficult to change a man's mind unless, in the
euphemism of the period, you 'treated' him—to a drink, a bottle, a
dinner or a five-dollar bill. (In one election wagonloads of voters
were paid off in the unnegotiable five-dollar bills of a defunct bank.)
Treating was against the law, as was the practice of driving or
dragging reluctant voters to the polls, but these expensive customs,
as Macdonald himself admitted, were common to both parties. And
each charged the other with committing identical crimes. Goldwin
Smith, at a political picnic, drew a farmer aside to ask him what was
the difference in principle between his party and the opposition.
'He was a long time in answering but at last he replied: " We say the
other fellows are corrupt." '

Pierre Berton, The National Dream (1970), pp. 91-3

Macdonald came to political maturity when politicians considered
patronage normal and necessary. Political men of the nineteenth
century described it as 'the patronage', and thought it as natural an
outgrowth of politics as laws, regulations, and dissolution of
Parliament. . . .

Politicians, including Macdonald, drew the line at bribery of
elected officials. Even Macdonald's most remorseless critics, who
accused him of perverting every other acceptable standard of political behaviour, conceded that he had never indulged in corrupt
practices for personal gain. He so stiffly dismissed an offer of a
thousand dollars a year for four years in a letter from a supplicant in
Sarnia, who desired the position of county registrar for his son, that
the chastened supplicant wrote back five days later (the post office
worked fast in those days), 'I assure you it was in an unguarded
moment that I wrote my letter . . . [and] I beg humbly of you to
forgive the error I have fallen into. Depend on it, it will never
happen again. . . .

Alexander Mackenzie and Oliver Mowat might insist that politics should be tinged with the precepts of a higher calling; Macdonald considered them foolish for so believing. He was a political
man to the tips of his fingers.

Jeffrey Simpson, Spoils of Power (1988), pp. 66-7

John A. could keep a petitioner dangling.

[Colonel Playfair] agitated for a colonization road from Perth north-
west to Buckshot Creek, above Trout Lakes. After many disap-
pointments he was informed that the work would be commenced,
and, his heart being in the enterprise, he applied to John A. for the
superintendency of the road. He was put off from time to time till at
last he came to the Capital in a state of indignation, and determined
to give John A. a piece of his mind. But John A., like the proverbial
flea, was not to be found when he wanted to put his finger on him.
At length, he heard a council meeting was being held, and thither
the colonel repaired. A man of his fine presence and military bearing was not to be put off by the man on guard at the door, and John
A. was called out—and came. 'God bless my soul, Col. Playfair, is
that you!' exclaimed the minister, grasping him with both hands.
'How are you? I'm so glad to see you. By-the-bye, colonel,' he went
on, after the greetings were over, 'we have just been discussing in
council a military matter that we cannot decide. Now you, with
your great military experience and your memories of Salamanca and
Talavera will be able to solve the question.' The colonel drew
himself up and looked grave. 'The question is,' said John A., 'how
many pounds of powder put under a bull's tail would blow his horns
off?' and John A., who had been edging towards his office, disappeared through the door and could be seen no more. 'And is this the
result of all I have come for?' ruminated the disgusted and disheart-
ened colonel as he drove his old mare home with the mail (for he
held amongst other offices that of mail carrier from Perth to Playfair); and with muttered imprecations he sat down on arriving home
to open the mail bag. The first letter he took out was an official one
addressed to himself, and it contained the appointment he had
despaired of.

E.B. Biggar, Anecdotal Life of Sir John Macdonald (1891),
pp. 199-200

It will be remembered that after the Conservative party in Parliament had committed itself to Protection the leaders addressed
many political demonstrations throughout the country. Referring
to these demonstrations Mr Joseph Rymal said that he was re-

minded of one who went to and fro on the earth many years ago, tempted the people with false promises, took the Saviour into a high mountain, showed Him the Kingdoms of the earth and declared that He should possess these and the glory of them if He would fall down and worship him. Failing to make the application Sir John, who always maintained good relations with Rymal, interrupted with the remarks, 'You did not finish the story about the man who went up into the high mountain.' Rymal retorted, 'That was not a man, that was the devil; the other tempter did not go to the top of the mountain; he went round the country holding picnics and tempting the people.'

Sir John Willison, *Reminiscences Political and Personal* (1919), p. 183

The bestowal of royal honours in Canada was, as a student of his correspondence cannot fail to have observed, a subject to which Sir John Macdonald at all times attached a good deal of importance. In his view 'the monarchical idea should be fostered in the colonies, accompanied by some gradation of classes', and no better way of effecting this desirable result, in his judgement, existed than by a judicious distribution to fit persons, of Imperial distinctions. In pursuance of this policy, he suggested to the Governor-General in the early part of 1888, the name of President Daniel Wilson of Toronto University for a mark of royal favour, in the form of a Knight Bachelorship. President Wilson saw fit to decline this honour when it arrived, not ... for any want of sympathy with the principle of associating Canadians in the bestowal of Imperial distinctions, but because the proposed honour was not a KCMG! On the announcement of his declinature of the honour becoming known, the radical press acclaimed him as a 'sturdy democrat' who cared not for trumpery 'tin pot titles', but was content to remain a plain citizen of Canada. This hugely amused Sir John Macdonald, who, however, never divulged the truth. Eventually, the 'sturdy democrat', finding that he could not persuade the authorities to give him a riband and star, accepted the minor dignity, and was known as Sir Daniel Wilson till the day of his death.

Sir Joseph Pope, *Correspondence of Sir John Macdonald* (1921), pp. 410-11

The fulminations of Macdonald's opponents, in and out of politics, against his use of patronage rolled off his back and apparently left the electorate profoundly unimpressed. Richard Cartwright, an acerbic Liberal and a penetrating critic, described what his party confronted. 'In Ontario,' he said, 'there was scarcely a riding in

which Sir John could not count on a score of men occupying more or
less influential positions, [all] of whom either owed their appointments to him, or had been under obligations to him of one sort or
another, or of whom he knew something they would not care to
have made public.' For all Macdonald's sins, and Cartwright considered them to be many, 'he had one considerable merit in that he
rarely canted about the purity of his motives or made much pre-
tence of being better than he was.' Upon Macdonald's death, Sir
Daniel Wilson, then president of the University of Toronto, described him as a 'clever, most unprincipled party leader [who] had
developed a system of political corruption that has demoralized the
country. Its evils will long survive him . . . Nevertheless he had
undoubtedly a fascinating power of conciliation, which, superad-
ded to his unscrupulous use of patronage, and systematic bribery in
every form, has enabled him to play off province against province
and hold his own against every enemy but the invincible last
antagonist.'

Goldwin Smith, the quite brilliant if headstrong political com-
mentator, roared from his Toronto lair:

> The task of his [Macdonald's] political life has been to hold together a
> set of elements, national, religious, sectional and personal, as motley
> as the component patches of any 'crazy quilt', and actuated, each of
> them, by paramount regard for his own interest. This task he has so
> far accomplished by his consummate address, by his assiduous study
> of the weaker points of character, and where corruption was dispen-
> sable, by corruption. It is more than doubtful whether anybody could
> have done it better than he has done . . . By giving the public the full
> benefit of his tact, knowledge and strategy, he has probably done the
> work for us as cheaply as it was possible to do it. Let it be written on
> his tomb, that he held out for the country against the blackmailers
> until the second bell had rung.
>
> Jeffrey Simpson, *Spoils of Power* (1988), pp. 96-7

Patronage also carried with it responsibilities. One of [Mackenzie]
Bowell's old Belleville acquaintances was Lewis Wallbridge. He
wanted a job on the bench. Finally he got one; in 1882 Wallbridge
was made Chief Justice of Manitoba, a part of the world, it is
probably safe to say, he had never laid eyes on. The trouble was that
Lewis Wallbridge had very bad teeth, some missing, and some
others looking as if they should be. Macdonald was concerned with
the dignity of the Manitoba bench. . . .

> The great question of teeth or no teeth, I find, is some what difficult to
> solve.

Whilst I agree with you that it would add much to the appearance, and perhaps dignity, of the Bench, if the Chief Justice had a mouth of good teeth, still when you consider the extreme egotism of the Chief Justice of Manitoba, and the difficulty of approaching him upon a subject of such *gnashing* importance, you will see the difficulty. . . .

However I set three or four at him, — our friend Dan Murphy among the number—who said that he would induce Wallbridge to consent provided I would 'pledge a quarter's salary in *advance'* —which of course I did—still I have very great doubt of his succeeding. . . .

P.B. Waite, *Macdonald: His Life and World* (1975), pp. 188-9

Some amusement was caused in the House one day upon a motion by Mr McMullen asking for a return showing the sums paid to Mr J.E. Collins for services rendered to the Government, and asking what the nature of the services were. Mr Collins, who had written a political life of Sir John, was employed in some capacity in Sir Hector Langevin's office, but it transpired that the length of service was but sixteen days, for which Mr Collins only received twenty-eight dollars. The motion, however, gave Sir Richard Cartwright an opportunity for a few jibes on the subject, in the course of which he made this quotation from a passage in the writings of Mr Collins: 'Sir Hector's replies are always full and almost invariably satisfactory, but he never says more than is necessary and pertinent; never opens doors through which eagle-eyed opponents may enter, and give worry to the Minister and his Government. Two ministers there are who are always opening their mouths too wide—Mr Caron (Sir Adolphe) and Mr Pope. Mr Blake, Mills, Casey or some Oppositionist will first worry them off their guard, get them to make statements they didn't intend to make, and so put the Government "in for it". On these occasions you can notice Sir John fidgeting in his chair, annoyed at the blundering and indiscretion.'

After Sir Richard had chaffed Sir Hector some time, he said he understood that Mr Collins was the Collins who had already immortalized himself by producing a life of the right hon. gentleman opposite.

'No,' replied Sir John, 'he has immortalized me.'

'That work', went on Sir Richard, 'was couched in equally chaste and elegant language, and no doubt it will be very satisfactory to the hon. gentleman's friends, because I observe from it that in all the acts of the hon. gentleman's career which evil-minded persons have misinterpreted, he has been actuated by the purest and most patriotic motives, and has even sometimes allowed his reputation to be tarnished for the general welfare of the country. It is a happy association of ideas, and what a lamented friend of mine called the "eternal fitness of things", that a gentleman who in his life has done justice to so many John Collinses, should at last find a John Collins to do justice to him.'

    Sir John laughed at this as heartily as anyone in the House.

E.B. Biggar, *Anecdotal Life of Sir John Macdonald* (1891),
pp. 153-4

THE LAST CAMPAIGN

Macdonald's last campaign resembled that of an old Roman general, with homage being paid in greater and greater measure as he toured selectively, as much as his health would permit.

Speaking at a dinner at the Tory Albany Club in January 1891, he hinted that the last campaign was nearing.

In a short speech . . . he said: 'As you are all Conservatives, there is no need to try and convert you—that effort will have to be reserved for the unregenerate Grits. Their fright, when they hear rumours of a dissolution, is most amusing, for although they have been valiantly proclaiming that they wanted the opportunity to appeal to the people, they immediately begin to abuse the Governor General, and call upon him to refuse a dissolution. They have as many aliases for their policy as a thief has excuses for his wrong-doing. It has been commercial union, unrestricted reciprocity, and latterly tariff reform; but there is another name by which it must be known, and that is annexation—which is treason. But we are prepared for them. We have a Minister of Justice at Ottawa and an Attorney General at Toronto who will certainly put the law in force.' (Laughter.) He then declared that the Government were going to stand by the [National] policy they introduced in 1878.

E.B. Biggar, *Anecdotal Life of Sir John Macdonald* (1891),
p. 273

On 9 February 1891 an election manifesto made his position clear, ringing with cries of patriotism, protection, and loyalty to the Crown.

'For a century and a half this country has grown and flourished under the protecting aegis of the British crown. The gallant race who first bore to our shores the blessings of civilization, passed by an easy transition from French to English rule, and now form one of the most powerful law-abiding portions of the community. These pioneers were speedily recruited by the advent of a loyal band of British subjects, who gave up everything that men most prize, and were content to begin life anew in the wilderness, rather than forego allegiance to their sovereign. To the descendants of these men, and to the multitude of Englishmen, Irishmen and Scotchmen who emigrated to Canada that they might build up new homes without ceasing to be British subjects—to you, Canadians, I appeal, and I ask you what have you to gain by surrendering that which your fathers held most dear? Under the broad folds of the Union Jack, we enjoy the most ample liberty to govern ourselves as we please, and at the same time we participate in the advantages which flow from association with the mightiest empire that the world has ever seen. Not only are we free to manage our own domestic concerns, but practically we possess the privilege of making our own treaties with foreign countries, and in our relations with the outside world we enjoy the prestige inspired by a consciousness of the fact that behind us towers the majesty of English.

'The question which you will shortly be called upon to determine resolves itself into this: Shall we endanger our possession of the great heritage bequeathed to us by our fathers, and submit ourselves to direct taxation, for the privilege of having our tariff fixed at Washington, with a prospect of ultimately becoming part of the American Union?

'I commend these issues to your determination and to the judgement of the whole people of Canada, with an unclouded confidence that you will proclaim to the world your resolve to show yourselves not unworthy of the proud distinction you enjoy of being numbered among the most dutiful and loyal subjects of our beloved Queen.

'As for myself, my course is clear. A British subject I was born; a British subject I will die. With my utmost effort, with my latest breath, will I oppose the veiled treason which attempts by sordid means and mercenary proffers to lure our people from their allegiance. During my long public service of nearly half a century, I have been true to my country and its best interests, and I appeal with equal confidence to the men who have trusted me in the past, and to the young hope of the country, with whom rests its destinies in the future, to give me their united and strenuous aid, in this my last effort for the unity of the Empire, and the preservation of our commercial and political freedom.'

Ibid., pp. 273-5

John A.'s last great campaign speech in Toronto was delivered in the Academy of Music building on 17 February 1891. An unprecedented success, the rally was described the next day in the Empire.

'As was expected, the gathering was of such stupendous proportions that all attempts to accommodate the numbers were practically useless. As the throng from office and workshop were returning home at six o'clock they encountered on the principal
thoroughfares a stream of people already flocking townwards. The
street cars, even at this early hour, were jammed. Admittance to the
Academy commenced a few minutes after six o'clock, when the
supporters of Conservatism, who had been fortunate enough to
obtain tickets, were admitted by the stage door. That narrow entrance was not even then found equal to the press, and recourse was
had to a rear door off Dorset street that led to the basement. At 6:30
the theatre was partially filled, while outside was an immense
throng awaiting admittance. A mass of men and women surged and
crowded against the main doors, bearing down every obstacle in
their way. Police were powerless to make any orderly arrangement
for admittance. Shortly after seven o'clock the main doors were
opened, the waiting crowd entered with a rush and a shout, and in a
few seconds the whole building was completely filled. It was then
discovered how small a fraction of the multitude were accommo-
dated within the building. What could be done was done. Every
available inch of room was occupied. With the additional chairs
2,000 were seated in the theatre, 300 were crowded on the stage,
and fully 1,000 more were jammed in passages and spaces behind
the seats. There were nearly 4,000 inside, but outside there was a
mass that numbered between 15,000 and 20,000. At 7:20 every
entrance to the building had to be closed, still the crowd outside
surged and jostled in good nature. In the press the large gas lamp in
front of the theatre was carried away, and the rupture in the gas
main interfered with the gas inside the theatre, rendering necessary
the use of electricity.

'At 7:35 two carriages drove up in front of the theatre, the first
containing Sir John Macdonald, Mr W.R. Brock, chairman of the
meeting, Col. Fred. C. Denison, and two members of the reception
committee of the Young Mens' Liberal Conservative Club. Between
the pavement and the stage entrance a solid mass of humanity was
wedged, rendering admittance almost impossible. Appeals were
made to the crowd to clear an opening for the chieftain, but so dense
was the force for yards on either side that an opening was nearly a
physical impossibility. At length, after waiting nearly ten minutes,
during which many demands for a speech were made from Sir John,
the chieftain and Mr Brock managed to make their way to the door
and to enter the theatre. A few minutes later and the Premier stood
on the platform, surrounded by a sea of cheering, shouting faces,
that could find no way adequately to express their enthusiasm.

Whirlwind after whirlwind of applause and cheers shook the building. Hats, handkerchiefs, flags were waved in indescribable enthusiasm. When the audience were tired of cheering they sang 'For He's
a Jolly Good Fellow'. It was fully ten minutes before the multitude
had given vent to their magnificent welcome to the Premier.
Nothing could better prove the secure position the noble chieftain
occupies to-day. Premier of the Dominion, he is premier also of the
hearts of his fellow-countrymen. When the ovation had at length
temporarily ceased, Mr W.R. Brock, who fulfilled his duties as
chairman in a conspicuously able manner, rose to open the meeting,
only to be interrupted by the entrance of Sir Charles Tupper, which
was the signal for another magnificent ovation of enthusiasm and
applause.

'The emblems placed around the theatre added a bright and in-
structive aspect to the scene. As a background to the stage, crowded
with its influential auditors, were the mottoes: "Hail to Our Chieftain", and "No United States Senators Need Apply"; while appropriately hung between these scrolls were three shields with the
words, "The Old Flag", "The Old Leader", "The Old Policy". The
stage pillars and boxes were adorned with the mottoes: "God Save
the Queen", "Disloyalty is at a Discount", "Welcome to the Cabinet", "Progressive Legislation", "We Welcome Our Leaders", "Encourage Home Talent", "Canadian Labour for the Canadians". The
railing of the balcony was covered with these bannerets: "Ottawa,
Not Washington, Our Capital", "Canada for the Canadians", "Ontario, Quebec, Nova Scotia, New Brunswick, Prince Edward Island,
Manitoba, British Columbia, N.W. Territories—A Noble
Heritage", "A Fair Measure of Reciprocity", "No Tariff Discrimination Against Great Britain".

'The stupendous crowd of 20,000 men and women who thronged
King street, between York and Simcoe, completely baffled every
effort of control. They were there. . . .

Mr Coatsworth first addressed the meeting and was followed by
Sir Charles Tupper, who made one of the most brilliant speeches of
his life, and was rewarded by the hearty applause of a very appre-
ciative audience, which lasted for some minutes after he had resumed his seat. The chairman, Mr W.R. Brock, after restoring order,
then addressed the assemblage of citizens in these words: 'Ladies
and gentleman,—I want to say one word to this vast audience. We
all admire the Premier of Canada. (Loud cheers). We all respect the
Right Honourable Sir John Macdonald, and the Liberal Conservatives love John A. (Vociferous cheers).

At this juncture the old man stood up, and as, in the fulness of his
years, he leaned slightly forward there was a sudden outburst from

the audience that fairly shook the building from its vaulted roof to its foundations. The entire gathering rose and yelled. Handkerchiefs, hats, umbrellas, walkingsticks, programmes, and in fact everything within reach, were waved by the audience. The enthusiastic uproar was deafening. The grand old hero stood there motionless as his heart throbbed within his honoured breast. . . . It was a proud minute for Sir John. . . . When the cheering had subsided, someone shouted:

'For he's a jolly good fellow.'

It's a question whether any Canadian was ever before honoured by that whole hearted song in such a style. . . .

From enthusiastic cheering there followed a breathless silence as the father of Canada addressed the audience.

J. Pennington Macpherson, *Life of The Right Hon. Sir John A. Macdonald*, vol. 2 (1891), pp. 397-400

Senator John M. Godfrey recounts a story told to him by his father, the late Honourable Mr Justice John Godfrey.

In 1891 [John Godfrey] was President of the University of Toronto Conservative Club. As such he occupied a seat on the platform at the last meeting Sir John A. Macdonald addressed in Toronto before the election of 1891. There was an overflow crowd outside and my father, as the youngest and most athletic on the platform, was given the job of clearing the way for Sir John A. to leave the hall . . . and find a suitable place for Sir John A. to speak for a few minutes to the crowd outside. My father saw the house next door which had a balcony on the second floor which he thought would be a suitable place. With Sir John A. in tow he knocked at the door and a lady answered. My father introduced Sir John A. to the lady and asked if he could use her balcony. She replied, 'Certainly as long as you think you can trust the old gentleman with me.' Sir John A. thereupon gave his last speech in Toronto from the balcony of a house which turned out later to be one of Toronto's better known brothels. Needless to say, this incident did not improve my father's standing in the Conservative party.

Another story involving the same meeting was told to me by the Hon. J.M. MacDonnell, MP. According to Mr MacDonnell, Sir John A. was intercepted on the way out by an elderly gentleman who told him how much he enjoyed his speech and told him that he had a terrible confession to make. He had not voted for Sir John A. in the last election but would vote for him in the next, and he hoped Sir

John A. would forgive him. Sir John A. replied that certainly he
would forgive him—the problem was, would God?

Senator John M. Godfrey

Over and over he made it clear that this campaign was his last.

On many occasions in this campaign, he spoke of himself as soon to
disappear from the stage, and at London he said all he desired to see
was the country once more in a prosperous condition, and on the
road to become great among nations. When this had been attained,
he felt he could sing his *'Nunc dimittis'*.

E.B. Biggar, Anecdotal Life of Sir John Macdonald (1891), p. 171

The campaign, though stubbornly contested, was not the desperate
battle of 1886-7. Various circumstances contributed thereto. To
begin with, it did not seem to me [Joseph Pope] that there was in the
latter years that absolute unity of sentiment and of action among
the Opposition which marked the earlier conflict. . . .

But if the prospects of the Government were somewhat more
favourable in 1891 than in 1887 as far as I personally was concerned,
I shall always look back on Sir John's last election campaign as the
most arduous experience of my life. We left Ottawa for Toronto on
the 15th of February. . . . After a short stay in Western Ontario, Sir
John left for Kingston where his presence was urgently required
both in his own and surrounding constituencies. His strength
proved unequal to the task, and after a few days he was obliged to
take to his bed. To me this period was one of undiluted anxiety. To
begin with I was alone, and the task was too much for one man. Sir
John stayed with Dr Williamson, his brother-in-law, a widower
who lived in a desolate-looking house with the minimum of comforts of any kind, painfully lacking the evidence of a woman's
touch, and was besieged by politicians who thought only of their
immediate interests, intent only on extracting from him the last
measure of service. 'Joe', said Sir John to me one afternoon as he lay
half dozing in his cheerless room, 'if you would know the depth of
meanness of human nature, you have got to be a Prime Minister
running a general election!'

Maurice Pope, ed., Public Servant: The Memoirs of Sir Joseph
Pope (1960), pp. 76-8

*His life had come almost full circle when on 24 February 1891 John
A., exhausted and ill with a cold, gave a speech in Napanee, the
town he had gone to as a neophyte law student.*

When the old man stepped from the train he was greeted with
strains from a bag-pipe, blown by a Highlander in full costume. Sir

John was greatly pleased by this happy reference to the time when he was younger and was a piper in the St Andrew's Society, Kingston. He left much to be implied when he said: 'I am not quite as young as I used to be.' . . . The Opera Hall would not hold half the crowd, so an overflow meeting had to be held in the Town Hall. As the demand was imperative, he had to make two speeches instead of one. Although they refused to accept any excuse in the excitement of expectation, yet, as soon as he stood before them, his audience felt that the beginning of the end had come, and clamour gave place to sympathy and regret. During his speech, the old man leaned on his staff, weakened by the strenuous exertions he had made all through the campaign, yet showing the reason of his success. He gave the impression not of the haughty indifference of one resting on the dignity of his high station, but the calm confidence of one who rested his claim on the simple fact that he was a man wishing the sympathies of his fellow men. His whole appearance indicated an exhausted frame that was only supported by the extreme vitality of his spirit; yet some were ungenerous enough to misconstrue his weakness and vilify his name. At the close of his address, Mr Elliott, Collector of Customs, approached Sir John and intimated that he had done enough for one day. Seven years had passed since the two had stood face to face, and as Sir John in his uniform kindness of heart pressed Mr Elliott's hand warmly, he said, 'It is the last time, Elliott!'

E.B. Biggar, *Anecdotal Life of Sir John Macdonald* (1891), pp. 275-7

FINAL DAYS

It was somehow fitting as well as touching to see the aged father and his only son, so often separated in the past, reunited in Parliament.

Parliament met on the 19th of April [1891], and Sir John had the gratification of sitting down in the legislative hall with his son, who had been elected by a large majority for Winnipeg. The occasion, to his political friends at least, was a moving one. Only a year before Hugh John Macdonald's name had been brought up in the House in connection with the Ryckert timber limit scandal. Sir John in a few words, in uttering which it was evident he was labouring under emotion, said he knew his son had faults, but from his knowledge of him from youth up, he believed that dishonesty was not one of those faults. After the case was gone into, Mr Mills arose from the Opposition benches and said that after a careful examination he believed that nothing had been done by Mr Macdonald that reflected upon his honour. At this vindication of his son's character the Premier was deeply moved. He did not speak, but with tears in his eyes bowed towards Mr Mills.

A newspaper correspondent described the Premier's appearance in the House with his son: 'Just as the hands of the clock pointed to the half hour after twelve, a burst of applause from the Conservative benches greeted the veteran Premier as he entered arm in arm with his son. The old chief never looked better. He was dressed in a frock coat with light trousers, with the traditional red neck-tie and a "stovepipe" hat. His eye was clear, his step elastic, and everything betokened that he was in good condition for the hard work of the session. After the Premier had exchanged greetings with his followers, who pressed forward to grasp his hand, father and son together took the oath and together affixed their autographs to the parchment, the son signing on the line below Sir John.

E.B. Biggar, Anecdotal Life of Sir John Macdonald (1891), pp. 278-9

The astonishing loyalty that so many felt towards John A. was perhaps exemplified by his favourite cab driver, Patrick Buckley.

For thirty-eight years he had driven Sir John, and from the time of Confederation the Premier seldom rode with anyone else. When Sir John was defeated and resumed his old profession at Toronto, Buckley went there too. When Sir John saw him driving along one day he hailed him, and went over to his cab to shake hands. During all the time Sir John was out of power this faithful old man insisted on driving him about, and refused to accept a cent for the service—a circumstance that could not be attributed to mere policy, as there seemed little likelihood that Sir John ever would be Premier again. It could not have been Buckley's good looks nor the pompous appearance of his vehicle that had won the favour of Sir John, for in former days his old sorrel horse and lumbering, faded, saggy-doored cab were the reverse of attractive, while the wizened, wrinkled face —over which a short sandy grizzly beard bristled out in all directions, and matched well with a pair of shaggy eyebrows, from beneath which a funny pair of big eyes twinkled—was more curious than handsome. A curious little cap he used to wear made his head look smaller than it really was. But Sir John in this odd figure read the one trait he required in a man for this service, and that was faithfulness.

On whatever business Sir John required him, Buckley was always there, and on time; and no paltry consideration of an extra fare would induce him to risk the disappointment of Sir John. He might be in front of the Parliament Building knowing that he had a clear hour before Sir John would be likely to come out, but though his cab was a public one he would not move for any offers. One day Lady Macdonald came out of the Parliament Building and observed to Buckley that, as it would be twenty minutes before Sir John would be out, she would take a spin down to a place in Wellington street. 'No, my lady,' said Buckley, humbly but firmly. When he objected and she still pressed him, 'I can't leave this spot till I get the word from Sir John.'

Sir Frederic de Winton wanting urgently to communicate with the Governor General one day, made the same request with all the authority of his high office, but Buckley declined in a more blunt manner still, adding, as he jerked his thumb over his shoulder, 'There's plinty av cabs down there at the sthand.'

Buckley used to think that no living man dressed with the same taste as Sir John, and what increased his affection for his chieftain was that the Premier would never allow the old man to carry his parcels from the cab. When he would insist on doing it, Sir John would say, 'No, no, Buckley, I am just as young a man as you are,' and would run up the steps with his own books. Buckley would often contrast this with the autocratic way with which some of the junior departmental clerks would order him to carry a parcel up to the office, while tripping up empty handed themselves; and then carrying the contrast on to every other member of Parliament, would sum up with, 'He's the most whunderful man in the worruld!'

One morning Buckley greeted the Premier with 'I'm glad to see ye lookin' so well this morning, Sir John; and may it be a long time before I see anybody else in yer shoes.' 'You won't, Buckley,' replied Sir John, 'as long as I've got them on!'

When the Premier was in the throes of his last illness, Buckley was on hand to render his humble service day and night, and as the tears rolled down his cheeks, he said to an *Empire* reporter: 'I have driven Sir John for thirty-eight years, winter and summer, and now they tell me he must die. I have never known him to be out of temper; never known him to say a cross word, no matter how rough the road might be or how careless I might drive. Do you remember his grey suit of clothes? One time I called for him and he had on another suit. As he was going to meet some important people I said to him (for I knew him so well I could take liberties with him), I said, "Sir John, why didn't you put on your grey suit? You look much better in it." "Is that so, Buckley?" said he, and he went and changed his clothes. . . . Dear, dear, they say there is no hope. My, my, his like will never be seen in Canada again.'

Ibid., pp. 241-4

Perhaps Sir John had a premonition that the end was near when, on his last day in the House, he settled his account with the parliamentary hairdresser, Napoléon Audette.

. . . while Audette was shaving him, the Premier said, addressing one of the attendants, 'Boy, hand me that picture.' This was a photograph of the celebrated engraving of the members of 'The special Court assembled under the authority of the Seigniorial Act of the Provincial Parliament, 1854, on its opening on the 4th day of September, 1855.' Sir John gazed on the faces of the judges for several minutes, put the picture down, and sighed. A few seconds after he took it up again, recalling to mind the old days of Morin, Day, Duval, Bowen, Augers, Caron, Loranger, Mackay, Beaudry, Dunkin, Badgley, Short, Meredith, Smith, Lafontaine, Drummond, Cherrier, and others who formed the Court at that period. He looked intently over the faces again, and, putting it down, muttered, 'All gone, all gone.' He then took out some silver, remarking, 'Now, Audette, I think I owed you for a visit to Earnscliffe,' and, settling the account, presented the attendants with his remaining change. This was his last visit to that portion of the Parliament buildings. Audette gathered up the hair he had cut from the Premier's head, remarking afterwards, 'I would not part with it for a mine. I fear poor Sir John felt he was not long for this world. He looked so much at that picture of the old faces.'

Ibid., pp. 282-3

He was always kind to his personal staff, as Joseph Pope tells.

A few weeks before his last illness he sent for me. 'I am going up to Toronto on Monday,' he said. 'I want you to come with me. See about the arrangements as usual.' A few minutes later he rang. 'By the way,' he said, as I entered, 'I don't think Mr Beard' (his assistant secretary) 'has ever had a trip anywhere with me.' I replied that he had not. 'Well,' said Sir John, 'If you don't mind, I think I'll take him up to Toronto with me. It will give the young man a change.'

This consideration extended even to his servants, among whom was his faithful attendant Chilton. When Sir John left Ottawa for the country in 1885, he instructed Chilton, who lived in town, to bring his wife out to Earnscliffe to take charge of the place. Shortly after reaching Rivière de Loup the need of a messenger became apparent. I pointed this out to Sir John, who observed, 'I think I'll send for Ben. The sea air will do the old man good' (he was twenty years younger than Sir John). So he instructed me to write Chilton to come down. After the letter had been addressed a thought struck him, and he added with his own hand a postscript to the effect that, as Mrs Chilton would be alone at Earnscliffe, she was to invite her married son and his wife to take their father's place during his absence. These incidents may be trivial, some may regard them as out of place, but it seems to me they afford more clearly than a ream of State papers an insight into the character of Sir John Macdonald.

> Joseph Pope, *Memoirs of the Right Honourable Sir John Alexander Macdonald*, vol. 2 (1894), p. 284

On 12 May 1891 Sir John suffered the first of a series of strokes.

On Tuesday, the 12th of May, I went over to his private rooms in the House of Commons as usual. About a quarter to four he came in, and went into the inner room, called me, and said that he was to meet his Excellency the Governor General and Sir John Thompson at four o'clock. I noticed at the time that there was something wrong with his speech. I had had no experience of paralysis, but I felt sure this was a premonition of something serious. I came back to tell him Sir John Thompson would be there very soon. He said, 'He must come at once, because he must speak to the Governor for me, as I cannot talk. There is something the matter with my speech.'

When the interview was over, his Excellency and Sir John Thompson spoke to me privately on the subject, and both expressed their greatest concern, Lord Stanley saying he felt sure there was cause for alarm, as he had seen similar symptoms in the case of one who died of paralysis. After they left Sir John came into the outer office and spoke to me. For the first time in my life I noticed a trace of nervousness in his manner. 'I am afraid of paralysis,' he said; 'both my parents died of it, and,' he added slowly, 'I seem to feel it creeping over me.' I at once called a cab, and there being some delay, he and I walked down the Parliament grounds to meet it. He was then better, and got into the cab without difficulty. I begged him to let me drive home with him, but he would not permit it, saying, 'There is no necessity.' He added, 'You must be careful not to mention this to Lady Macdonald.' There was a ball at Government House that evening, on my way to which I called at Earnscliffe, and found Sir John in bed reading. His speech was almost restored again, and he had seen the doctor in the mean time. This attack passed off, and on Saturday, the 16th, he gave a dinner, at which he looked wretched, but on Monday morning he seemed better, and all through the week was more like his old self. On Saturday, the 23rd of May, he gave another dinner. On the morning of that day he asked me to prepare a list for a dinner on the 30th, which, alas! he was destined never to eat. On looking over it, he said, 'Thursday is a holiday, is it not?' I answered that it was. 'Well,' said he, 'I think we might give a dinner on Thursday as well as on Saturday. However, let that stand until Monday.'

Joseph Pope, *Memoirs of The Right Honourable Sir John Alexander Macdonald*, vol. 2 (1894), pp. 258-9

At the end, John A. was too tired to deal with Israel Tarte, his principal Quebec organizer, who exposed the Langevin-McGreevy affair.

At the time of Macdonald's death the political outlook for that party was far from rosy. In addition to the usual disintegrating forces at work, the Opposition confidently looked forward to obtaining power, within a short period, by what were known as the Tarte-McGreevy charges of corruption brought by the late Joseph Israel Tarte against Sir Hector Langevin, then Minister of Public Works. . . .

One day during the Chief's last illness, Mr Tarte called at Earnscliffe and told me that he particularly wished a few minutes of private conversation with Sir John; that he had a matter of great urgency and importance to communicate to him. Mr Tarte, whom I knew very well as an old-time Conservative, went on to hint that a settlement of the Langevin-McGreevy affair was not beyond the bounds of possibility. He did not at the time know how near Sir John was to his end, nor indeed did any of us. At his pressing request I went upstairs and repeated the substance of this conversation to the sick man, who simply said, turning his face to the wall as he spoke, 'It is too late now', and would not see him.

Maurice Pope, ed., *Public Servant: The Memoirs of Sir Joseph Pope* (1960), p. 80

He rallied slightly, only to suffer the fatal stroke on 29 May. He lingered until 6 June.

A week later it was a different story. While in bed recovering from a cold and a slight stroke, Macdonald was overtaken on Friday, May 29th, by a devastating stroke that in seconds had paralyzed his right side and bereft him of speech. Up at the House of Commons a lively debate was going on. Langevin suddenly received a message from the doctor, Sir James Grant. 'I have just seen Sir John,' it read, 'haemorrhage into the brain. Condition quite hopeless. As you are next to the Chief, I thought well to send you this private note.' Langevin stared at it. He crossed the floor to tell Laurier, and in a voice so low and tremulous he could hardly be heard, announced it to a now silent House. The House at once adjourned. Langevin didn't move. He had worked with Macdonald for thirty-three years. He had served him loyally, and stood by him through thick and thin. Now he sat at his desk beside Macdonald's, the tears streaming down his face.

Macdonald died peacefully on Saturday, 6 June 1891.

P.B. Waite, *Macdonald: His Life and World* (1975), p. 213

LAURIER'S EULOGY

Wilfrid Laurier delivered a eulogy in the House of Commons on 8 June.

I fully appreciate the intensity of the grief which fills the souls of all those who were the friends and followers of Sir John Macdonald, at the loss of the great leader whose whole life has been so closely identified with their party; a party upon which he has thrown such brilliancy and lustre. We on this side of the House who were his opponents, who did not believe in his policy, nor in his methods of government; we take our full share of their grief—for the loss which they deplore to-day is far and away beyond and above the ordinary compass of party range. It is in every respect a great national loss, for he who is no more was, in many respects, Canada's most il-lustrious son, and in every sense Canada's foremost citizen and statesman. At the period of life to which Sir John Macdonald had arrived, death, whenever it comes, cannot be said to come unexpected.

Some few months ago, during the turmoil of the late election, when the country was made aware that on a certain day the physical strength of the veteran Premier had not been equal to his courage, and that his intense labour for the time being had prostrated his singularly wiry frame, everybody, with the exception, perhaps, of his buoyant self, was painfully anxious lest perhaps the angel of death had touched him with his wing. When, a few days ago in the heat of an angry discussion the news spread in this House, that of a sudden his condition had become alarming, the surging waves of angry discussion were at once hushed, and every one, friend and foe, realized that this time for a certainty the angel of death had appeared and had crossed the threshold of his home. Thus we were not taken by surprise, and although we were prepared for the sad event, yet it is almost impossible to convince the unwilling mind, that it is true, that Sir John Macdonald is no more, that the chair which we now see vacant shall remain forever vacant; that the face so familiar in this Parliament for the last forty years shall be heard no more, whether in solemn debate or in pleasant and mirthful tones. In fact, the place of Sir John Macdonald in this country was so large and so absorbing, that it is almost impossible to conceive that the political life of this country, the fate of this country, can continue without him. His loss overwhelms us.

For my part, I say with all truth, his loss overwhelms me, and it also overwhelms this Parliament, as if indeed one of the institutions of the land had given way. Sir John Macdonald now belongs to the ages, and it can be said with certainty, that the career which has just been closed is one of the most remarkable careers of this century. It would be premature at this time to attempt to fix or anticipate what will be the final judgement of history upon him; but there were in his career and in his life, features so prominent and so conspicuous that already they shine with a glow which time cannot alter, which even now appear before the eye such as they will appear to the end in history. I think it can be asserted that for the supreme art of governing men, Sir John Macdonald was gifted as few men in any land or in any age were gifted; gifted with the most high of all qualities, qualities which would have made him famous wherever exercised and which would have shone all the more conspicuously the larger the theatre. The fact that he could congregate together elements the most heterogeneous and blend them into one compact party, and to the end of his life keep them steadily under his hand, is perhaps altogether unprecedented. The fact that during all those years he retained unimpaired not only the confidence, but the devotion—the ardent devotion and affection of his party, is evidence that besides those higher qualities of statesmanship to which we were the daily witnesses, he was also endowed with those inner, subtle, undefinable graces of soul which win and keep the hearts of men. As to his statesmanship, it is written in the history of Canada. It may be said without any exaggeration whatever, that the life of Sir John Mac-

donald, from the date he entered Parliament, is the history of
Canada, for he was connected and associated with all the events, all
the facts which brought Canada from the position Canada then
occupied—the position of two small provinces, having nothing in
common but a common allegiance, united by a bond of paper, and
united by nothing else—to the present state of development which
Canada has reached.

Although my political views compel me to say that, in my judgement, his actions were not always the best that could have been
taken in the interest of Canada, although my conscience compels
me to say that of late he had imputed to his opponents motives as to
which I must say in my heart he has misconceived, yet I am only too
glad here to sink these differences, and to remember only the great
services he has performed for our country—to remember that his
actions always displayed great originality of views, unbounded
fertility of resources, a high level of intellectual conceptions, and,
above all, a far-reaching vision beyond the event of the day, and still
higher, permeating the whole, a broad patriotism—a devotion to
Canada's welfare, Canada's advancement, and Canada's glory. The
life of a statesman is always an arduous one, and very often it is an
ungrateful one. More often than otherwise his actions do not mature until he is in his grave. Not so, however, in the case of Sir John
Macdonald. His career has been a singularly fortunate one. His
reverses were few and of short duration. He was fond of power, and,
in my judgement, if I may say so, that may be the turning point of
the judgement of history. He was fond of power, and he never made
any secret of it. Many times we have heard him avow it on the floor
of this Parliament, and his ambition in this respect was gratified as,
perhaps, no other man's ambition ever was.

In my judgement, even the career of William Pitt can hardly
compare with that of Sir John Macdonald in this respect; for although William Pitt, moving in a higher sphere, had to deal with
problems greater than our problems, yet I doubt if in the intricate
management of a party William Pitt had to contend with difficulties
equal to those that Sir John Macdonald had to contend with. In his
death, too, he seems to have been singularly happy. Twenty years
ago I was told by one who at that time was a close personal and
political friend of Sir John Macdonald, that in the intimacy of his
domestic circle he was fond of repeating that his end would be as the
end of Lord Chatham—that he would be carried away from the floor
of the Parliament to die. How true that vision into the future was we
now know, for we saw him to the last, with enfeebled health and
declining strength, struggling on the floor of Parliament until the

hand of fate pinned him to his bed to die. And thus to die with his armour on was probably his ambition. . . .

James J. Talman, *Basic Documents in Canadian History* (1959), pp. 119-22

THE FUNERAL

On the day of his funeral, the writer was standing on Parliament Hill, when, as the imposing ceremonials were in preparation, a white-haired man, bent with years and tremblingly leaning on a staff, approached and stood near him. Falling into conversation on the subject of the day, the writer asked, 'Did you know him?' 'Know him?' repeated the aged man in astonishment, as he turned upon the questioner. 'Know him? For thirty years I've *known no other name.*'

E.B. Biggar, *Anecdotal Life of Sir John Macdonald* (1891), pp. 235-6

At one o'clock on Wednesday, the most imposing funeral pageant ever witnessed in Canada formed in front of the Parliament Build- ings, and proceeded to St Alban's Church. In the procession were the Governor General and staff, Lieutenant Governors of the provinces, Judges of the Supreme court, Commander in Chief of the Militia, members of the Privy Council, Senators and members of the House of Commons, officers of the Militia, mayors of cities, depu- tations from various corporations, and various societies in bodies. The official robes and dresses of the dignitaries of State, the bright uniforms of the soldiers who marched with arms reversed, the contrast presented to the uniforms by the mourning emblems, the solemn faces of the crowds, the bands of music, — from the throats of whose polished instruments the strains of grief so piercingly expressed in the 'Dead March in Saul' lift the dead echoes of the stifling air, — make a combination of sight and sound to move the most unemotional spectator. . . .

The procession moves on to the church through streets draped in mourning and crowded with mournful spectators; and after the service for the dead in St Alban's the procession is reformed to proceed back through the city to the Canadian Pacific Railway Station, whence the body would be conveyed to Kingston. For days the air was heavy and sultry, and no rain had fallen for a long time, but while the procession was reforming, banks of black clouds rolled down upon the city, and as the funeral car slowly passed the Parliament Buildings, the forked lightnings played above the tower, and, with the echoing crash of thunder, torrents of rain came down, drenching the processionists. It was the first thunderstorm of the season at the Capital.

The heavily draped funeral train—the first funeral train that ever went over this line—was met at every station by crowds who came to pay some floral or other tribute, as it proceeded to Kingston, where the body of her beloved citizen was received by the people and placed in state in the City Hall, with every mark of grief and affection. Another long and imposing procession followed the remains the next day through the draped streets of the city of his youth to the picturesque cemetery of Cataraqui, and here, by the side of his mother and father and the members of his family who had passed on before, the great Canadian was laid to rest. On the granite shaft which had been erected by him to commemorate the dead of his family the single word 'Macdonald' was cut in plain Gothic letters, and on his own casket only the plain name 'John Alexander Macdonald' was engraved.

Ibid., pp. 291-3

ACKNOWLEDGEMENTS

PIERRE BERTON, *The National Dream*, used by permission of the author.

J.M. CARELESS, 'George Brown and the Mother of Confederation' from *Canadian Historical Review, Historical Papers* (1960) and *Careless at Work: Selected Canadian Historical Studies* by J.M. Careless (forthcoming). Used by permission.

D.G. CREIGHTON, 'George Brown, Sir John Macdonald, and the "Workingman" ', *Canadian Historical Review*, vol. 24 (1943), used by permission. Reprinted by permission of Macmillan of Canada, A Division of Canada Publishing Corporation: *John A. Macdonald: The Old Chieftain* and *John A. Macdonald: Young Politician*.

HARRY GUTKIN, *Journey Into Our Heritage* (1980). Used by permission.

SANDRA GWYN, *The Private Capital*, by Sandra Gwyn. Used by permission of the Canadian Publishers, McClelland and Stewart, Toronto.

A.R.M. LOWER, 'Sir John A. Macdonald' from *Dalhousie Review*, vol. 19 (1939-40). Used by permission.

LENA NEWMAN, *The John A. Macdonald Album* © 1974 Lena Newman, Tundra Books, Montreal.

MAURICE POPE, *Public Servant*. Used by permission of Oxford University Press Canada.

LOUISE REYNOLDS, *Agnes: The Biography of Lady Macdonald* (1979). Used by permission of Samuel Stevens.

JEFFREY SIMPSON. Quotations from *Spoils of Power* by Jeffrey Simpson are reprinted with permission of Harper & Collins Publishers Ltd., and are Copyright © 1988 by JCS Publications Inc.

OSCAR DOUGLAS SKELTON, *The Life and Times of Sir Alexander Tilloch Galt*. Used by permission of Oxford University Press Canada.

PHOTOGRAPH CREDITS

BIBLIOGRAPHY

Adam, G. Mercer. *Canada's Patriot Statesmen*. London: McDermid, 1891.

Angus, Margaret. *The Old Stones of Kingston*. Toronto: University of Toronto Press, 1966.

Bailey, A.G., *et al. Confederation Readings*. Toronto: University of Toronto Press, 1967.

Beck, J. Murray, ed. *Joseph Howe, Voice of Nova Scotia*. Toronto: McClelland and Stewart, 1964.

_____. *Joseph Howe, Anti-Confederate*. Ottawa: Canadian Historical Association, 1965.

Berton, Pierre. *The National Dream*. Toronto: McClelland and Stewart, 1970.

_____. *The Last Spike*. Toronto: McClelland and Stewart, 1971.

Biggar, E.B. *An Anecdotal Life of Sir John A. Macdonald*. Montreal: John Lovell and Son, 1891.

Bosc, Marc., ed. *The Broadview Book of Canadian Parliamentary Anecdotes*. Peterborough, Ont.: Broadview Press, 1988.

Boyd, John. *Sir George Etienne Cartier, Bart*. Toronto: Macmillan Co. of Canada Ltd. at St-Martin's House, 1915.

Brown, R. Craig. *The Illustrated History of Canada*. Toronto: Lester and Orpen Dennys, 1987.

Buckingham, William, and George W. Ross. *The Hon. Alexander Mackenzie: His Life and Times*. Toronto: Rose Publishing, 1892.

Canadian Illustrated News (Montreal, various dates and issues).

Careless, J.M.S. *Brown of the Globe*. 2 vols. Toronto: Macmillan, 1963.

_____. *The Union of the Canadas, 1841-57*. Toronto: McClelland and Stewart, 1967.

_____. *The Pre-Confederation Premiers: Ontario Government Leaders, 1841-67*. Toronto, University of Toronto Press, 1986.

Cartwright, Richard. *Reminiscences.* Toronto: Briggs, 1912.

Chadwick, E.M. *Ontario Families.* Toronto: Rolph Smith, 1895.

Collard, E.A. *Canadian Yesterdays.* Toronto: Longmans, Green, 1955.

————. *The Story of Dominion Square.* Toronto: Longmans, 1971.

Collins, J.E. *The Life and Times of Sir John A. Macdonald.* Toronto: Rose Publishing, 1883.

Cornell, P.G. *The Great Coalition.* Ottawa: Canadian Historical Association, 1966.

Creighton, D.G. 'George Brown, Sir John Macdonald and the "Working man" ', *Canadian Historical Review* 24 (1943).

————. *John A. Macdonald: The Young Politician.* Toronto: Macmillan, 1952.

————. *John A. Macdonald: The Old Chieftain.* Toronto: Macmillan, 1955.

de Kiewiet, C.W., and F.H. Underhill, eds. *Dufferin-Carnarvon Correspondence, 1874-8.* Toronto: Champlain Society, vol. 33, n.d.

Dent, John Charles, *The Last Forty Years: The Union off 1841 to Confederation.* Abridged and with an introduction by Donald Swainson. Toronto: McClelland and Stewart, 1972.

Donaldson, Gordon. *Eighteen Men: The Prime Ministers of Canada.* Toronto: Doubleday, 1985.

Gibbon, J.M. *Steel of Empire: The Romantic History of the Canadian Pacific, the Northwest Passage of Today.* Toronto: McClelland and Stewart, 1935.

Grip (Toronto, various issues).

Gutkin, Harry. *Journey Into Our Heritage: The Story of the Jewish People in the Canadian West.* Toronto: Lester and Orpen Dennys, 1980.

Gwyn, Sandra. *The Private Capital.* Toronto: McClelland and Stewart, 1984.

Hofter, Ruth. 'The Riel Rebellion and Manifest Destiny', *Dalhousie Review* 45, no. 1 (Spring 1965).

Johnston, J.K., ed. *The Letters of Sir John A. Macdonald, 1836-57.* 2 vols. Ottawa: Public Archives of Canada, 1968.

————, ed. *Affectionately Yours.* Toronto: Macmillan, 1969.

————. 'John A. Macdonald, the non-politician'. In *Canadian Historical Association Papers.* Ottawa: Canadian Historical Association, 1971.

_____. 'John A. Macdonald and the Kingston Business Community'. In Gerald Tulchinsky, ed. *To Preserve and Defend, Essays on Kingston in the Nineteenth Century.* Montreal: McGill-Queen's University Press, 1976.

Kerr, D.G.G. *Historical Atlas of Canada.* Toronto: Nelson, 1966.

Li, Peter S. *The Chinese in Canada.* Toronto: Oxford University Press, 1988.

MacDermot, T.W.L. 'The Political Ideas of John A. Macdonald', *Canadian Historical Review* 14, no. 3 (September 1933).

McGinnis, Edgar. *Canada: A Political and Social History.* Toronto: Holt, Rinehart and Winston, 1969.

Mackenzie, Alexander. *The Life and Speeches of Hon. George Brown.* Toronto: Globe Printing Co., 1882.

McLennan, C. Prescott, 'Reminiscences of Parliamentary Leaders'. *Dalhousie Review* 26, no. 1 (Spring 1946).

McLeod, J.T., ed. *The Oxford Book of Canadian Political Anecdotes.* Toronto: Oxford University Press, 1988.

Macpherson, J. Pennington. *Life of the Right Honourable Sir John A. Macdonald.* Saint John, NB: Earle Publishing Co., 1891.

McSherry, James. 'The Medicine of History', *Queen's Quarterly* 95, no. 3 (Autumn, 1988).

Mail (Toronto, various issues).

Masters, D.C. *Reciprocity, 1846-1911.* Ottawa: Canadian Historical Association, 1965.

Morton, W.L. *The Kingdom of Canada.* Toronto: McClelland and Stewart, 1963.

_____. *The West and Confederation.* Ottawa: Canadian Historical Association, 1965.

Native Studies Review, vols. 1-4 (1984-88). Saskatoon: Native Studies Department, University of Saskatchewan.

Newman, Lena. *The John A. Macdonald Album.* Montreal: Tundra Books, 1974.

Parkin, George Robert. *Sir John A. Macdonald.* Toronto: Morang, 1908.

Pope, Joseph. *Memoirs of the Right Honourable Sir John Alexander Macdonald,* 2 vols. Ottawa: J. Durie and Son, 1894.

_____. *The Day of Sir John A. Macdonald.* Glasgow: Brook, 1915.

_____. *Correspondence of Sir John A. Macdonald.* Toronto: Oxford University Press, 1921.

Pope, Maurice, ed. *Public Servant: The Memoirs of Sir Joseph Pope.* Toronto: Oxford University Press, 1960.

Preece, Rod. 'The Political Wisdom of Sir John A. Macdonald', *Canadian Journal of Political Science* 17, no. 3 (September 1984).

Preston, W.T.R. *My Generation of Politics and Politicians.* Toronto: Rose Publishing, 1927.

Purich, Donald, *The Metis.* Toronto: James Lorimer, 1988.

Reynolds, Louise. *Agnes: The Biography of Lady Macdonald.* Toronto: Samuel Stevens, 1979.

Riendeau, Roger. E. *An Enduring Heritage: Black Contributions to Early Ontario.* Toronto: Dundurn Press, 1984.

Robertson, R.W.W. *Sir John A. Builds a Nation.* Toronto: Burns and MacEachern, 1970.

Roy, James A. *Kingston—The King's Town.* Toronto: McClelland and Stewart, 1952.

Schull, Joseph. *The Nation Makers.* Toronto: Macmillan, 1967.

_____ . *Ontario Since 1867.* Toronto: McClelland and Stewart, 1975.

Shortt, Adam, and A.G. Doughty. *Canada and Its Provinces.* Toronto: Edinburgh University Press, 1917.

Simpson, Jeffrey. *Spoils of Power: The Politics of Patronage.* Toronto: Collins, 1988.

Skelton, O.D. *The Life and Times of Sir Alexander Tilloch Galt.* Toronto: Oxford University Press, 1917.

Slattery, T.P. *The Assassination of D'Arcy McGee.* New York: Doubleday, 1968.

Stacey, C.P. 'Lord Monck and the Canadian Heritage', *Dalhousie Review* 14 (1984-85).

Stanley, G.F.G. *Louis Riel, Patriot or Rebel.* Ottawa: Canadian Historical Association, 1956.

Stewart, Gordon. 'Macdonald's greatest triumph', *Canadian Historical Review* 63 (1982).

Stewart, J. Douglas, and Ian E. Wilson. *Heritage Kingston.* Kingston: Queen's University, 1973.

Swainson, Donald. *John A. Macdonald, the Man and the Politician.* Toronto: Oxford University Press, 1971.

_____ . *First Prime Minister, Macdonald of Kingston.* Toronto: Nelson, 1979.

Sweeney, Alastair, *George Etienne Cartier: A Biography.* McClelland and Stewart, 1976.

Thomas, W.K. 'Canadian Political Oratory in the Nineteenth Century: 1 & 2', *Dalhousie Review* 39 (Spring 1959).

Thomson, Dale C. *The Life and Times of Alexander Mackenzie: Clear Grit.* Toronto: Macmillan, 1960.

Times (London; various issues).

Waite, P.G. *The Charlottetown Conference.* Ottawa: Canadian Historical Association, 1963.

————. 'Sir John A. Macdonald: The Man', *Dalhousie Review* 47, no. 2 (Summer 1967).

————. *Canada 1874-1896.* Toronto: McClelland and Stewart, 1971.

Wallace, W. Stewart, ed. *The Dictionary of Canadian Biography.* Toronto: Macmillan, 1926.

Ward, Norman. 'Electoral corruption and controverted elections', *Canadian Journal of Economics and Political Science* 15 (1949).

————. 'The formative years of the House of Commons, 1867-91', *Canadian Journal of Economics and Political Science,* vol. 18 (1952).

————. 'Prayer in the Commons', *Dalhousie Review* 32, no. 2 (Summer 1952).

Whitelaw, W.M. *The Quebec Conference.* Ottawa: Canadian Historical Association, 1966.

Willison, John S. *Sir Wilfred Laurier and the Liberal Party: A Political History.* 2 vols. Toronto: Morang, 1903.

————. *Reminiscences: Political and Personal.* Toronto: McClelland, 1919.

————. *Sir Wilfred Laurier.* Toronto: Oxford, 1926.

INDEX OF NAMES

INDEX OF AUTHORS

75325